a reappraisal
of economic
development

a reappraisal of economic development

Perspectives for Cooperative Research

**Andrew H. Whiteford
editor**

 Routledge
Taylor & Francis Group

LONDON AND NEW YORK

First published 1967 by Transaction Publishers

Published 2017 by Routledge
4 Park Square, Milton Park, Abingdon, Oxon OX14 4RN
605 Third Avenue, New York, NY 10017

Routledge is an imprint of the Taylor & Francis Group, an informa business

Notice:
Product or corporate names may be trademarks or registered trademarks, and are used only for identification and explanation without intent to infringe.

Library of Congress Catalog Number: 2008035632

Library of Congress Cataloging-in-Publication Data

Midwest Research Conference on Educational Research and a Reappraisal of Economic Development (1964 : Chicago, Ill.)
A reappraisal of economic development : perspectives for cooperative research / [edited by] Andrew H. Whiteford.
p. cm.
Includes bibliographical references and index.
"Sponsored by the Library of International Relations, Chicago, and Rosary College."
Includes bibliographical references.
ISBN 978-0-202-36267-0 (alk. paper)
1. Developing countries--Economic conditions--Congresses. 2. Economic development--Congresses. 3. Newly independent states--Politics and government--Congresses. I. Whiteford, Andrew Hunter. II. Library of International Relations. III. Rosary College (River Forest, Ill.) IV. Title.

HC59.7.M5 2008
338.9--dc22

2008035632

ISBN 13: 978-0-202-36267-0 (pbk)

The Third Biennial Midwest Research Conference on Underdeveloped Areas / 1964
Sponsored by The Library of International Relations, Chicago and Rosary College in
cooperation with The United. States Office of Education.

ADVISORY COMMITTEE
Philip M. Mauser
Department of Sociology
University of Chicago

Leonard Binder
Department of Political Science
University of Chicago

Wesley R. Fishel
Department: of Political Science
Michigan State University

Bert F. Hoselitz
Research Center on Economic
Development and Cultural Change
University of Chicago

Sister Thomasine
Department of Economics
Rosary College

George I. Blanksten
Department of Political Science
Northwestern University

Norton S. Ginsberg
Department of Geography
University of Chicago

George J. Stolnin
Department of Economics
Indiana University

Andrew H.Whiteford
Department of Anthropology
Beloit College

Secretary
Eloise ReQua, Director
Library of International Relations

Conference Participants

C, Arnold Anderson	University of Chicago	Comparative Education Center and Department of Sociology
Robert Armstrong	Lake Forest College	Department of Economics
John Augelli	University of Kansas	Department of Geography
Jack Baranson	Indiana University	International Development Research Center
Leonard Binder	University of Chicago	Department of Political Science
George 1, BHanksien	Northwestern University	Department of Political Science
Karl de Schweinitz, Jr.	Northwestern University	Department of Economics
A. A. Fatouras	Indiana University	School of LEW
Wesley R. Fishel	Michigan State University	Department of Political Science
Norton S. Ginsburg	University of Chicago	Department of Geography
Philip Haring	Knox College	Department of Political Science
Philip M. Hauser	University of Chicago	Department of Sociology
James B. Hendry	Michigan State University	Department of Economics
H. Murray Herlihy	Lake Forest College	Department of Economics
Robert T. Holt	University of Minnesota	Department of Politcal Science
Bert F. Hoselitz	University of Chicago	Department of Economics
Scott D. Johnston	Hamline University	Departraent of Political Science
Frank H. H. King	University of Kansas	Department of Economics
Mordechai Kreinin	Michigan State University	Department of Economics
W. Arthur Lewis	Princeton University	Economies and International Affairs
Marvin Miracle	University of Wisconsin	Department of Agricultural Economics
Theodore Morgan	University of Wisconsin	Department of Economics

Manning Nash	University of Chicago	Department of Anthropology
Raymond L. Randall	Indiana University	Department of Government
Hugh Schwartz	University of Kansas	Department of Economies
Hal Serrie	Beloit College	Department of Anthropology
George Stolniiz	Indiana University	Department of Economics
Sisier Thomasine	Rosary College	Department of Economics
Charles F. Warren	University of Illinois, Chicago	Department of Sociology and Anthropology
Edward Werner	University of Wisconsin	School of Commerce
Andrew H. Whiteford	Beloit College	Department of Anthropology
T. David Williams	Northwestern University	School of Education and Department of Economics
Daniel Wit	Northern Illinois University	Department of Political Science

U.S. Office of Education Peter S. Mousolke, Acting 'Regional Representative (OC)
Library of International Relations   Eloise ReQua, Director
Librarv of International Relations   Jane Statham, Associate Director

Contents

Foreword: George I. Blanksten, Conference Chairman   xi

Preface: Andrew H. Whiteford   xv

I.   Unemployment in Developing Areas: 1
       George I. Blanksten, Chairman

       Opening Address: W. Arthur Lewis   1

       General Discussion   15

II.   Underdeveloped Countries in the World   37
       Economy: Leonard Binder, Chairman

       Introductory Statement: Karl de Schweinitz   38

       Discussants: Andrew H. Whiteford   42

                  Raymond L. Randall   45

       General Discussion   47

III.   The International Politics and Diplomacy   73
       of Development: George I. Blanksten, Chairman

       Introductory Statement: Robert T. Holt   73

       Discussants: A. A. Fatouros   84

                  Mordechai Kreinin   86

       General Discussion   88

IV.   Economic Growth in Newly Settled Areas as   113
       Contrasted with Old Settled Areas:
       James B. Hendry, Chairman

       Introductory Statement: Theodore Morgan   113

       Discussants: Jack Baranson   124

                  Scott D. Johnston   126

       General Discussion   128

V. Cultural Change in Development: 147
        Frank H. H. King, Chairman

    Introductory Statement: Manning Nash   147
    Discussant: Daniel Wit   151
    General Discussion   155

VI. Perspectives for Cooperative Research: 187
        Philip S. Haring, Chairman

    Introductory Statement: C. Arnold Anderson   187
    Discussants: T. David Williams   196
                  Norton S. Ginsburg   205
    Genaral Discussion   208

APPENDICES   211
    Conference Program   214
    Biographical Notes   ??
    Selected Bibliographical References on Economic   ??
    Development   223

Analytical Table of Contents

I.   Unemployment in Developing Areas   1

    The Rural Sector   15
    Economic Development and Social Tension   16
    Modern and Traditional Sectors: Japan   18
    Wage Differentials and Mechanization   20
    Africa: Mining and Education   24
    Alternatives to Capital-intensive Mechanization   25
    Differential Growth Rates   28
    Export Development   30
    Education, Employment, and Expectations   32
    Labor Unions   34

II.   Underdeveloped Countries in the World Economy   37

    Institution Building and Economic Development   49
    The Effectiveness of Theory   51
    Incentives and Job Prestige   61
    Interdisciplinary Research   63

III.   The International Politics and Diplomacy of Development   73

    Political Science, Theory, and Practical Democracy   88
    Economic Nationalism: Monuments and Development   91
    The Diplomacy of Development   98
    Foreign Aid and International Development   101
    International Economic Cooperation   106

IV.   Economic Growth in Newly Settled Areas as   113
        Contrasted with Old Settled Areas

    Savings vs. Investment   128
    The Frontier and Development   131
    Social Structure and Economic Growth   133

Theory Formation   135
Transformation and Trade   138
The Concept of Technological Breakthrough   142
Religion and Economic Development   143
Foreign Factor Economy   144

V.   Cultural Change in Development   147

Time and Signs of Change   155
Stage Theory   157
Ontological Uncertainty   158
The Case of Modernizing Oligarchies   159
Polarization and Change   169
Identifying Societal Segments   178
Cross-disciplinary Influence   182
Conclusion   185

VI. Perspectives for Cooperative Research   187

Foreword

The central business of the Third Biennial Midwest Research. Conference on Underdeveloped Areas, as is made clear by its theme, "A Reappraisal of the Process of Economic Development." involved a species of theoretical stocktaking. Many of the social sciences have now been concerned for more than a decade with problems of the underdeveloped areas. After these years of intensive effort in theory-building and empirical research, what have we learned and what are we *now* able to say about the developing areas? In short, what do the social sciences have to show for a decade of systematic attention devoted to this category of research problems?

As the following pages indicate, the verdict of the Third Conference is that the answer to this question, must be mixed. On the one hand, substantial progress can be reported in some areas, and social scientists may feel that, on the basis of some types of research results, the decade has been well spent. On the other hand, fundamental lacunae remain, pointing to still unresolved problems which, even at this late date, lie ahead of the social scientist in the underdeveloped areas.

On the positive side, the Conference makes it plain that, important strides have been taken in matters of Identification and definition. The process of economic development has now been substantially isolated and operationally defined, and it is not necessary today, as it was a decade ago, to assign concerted effort to the examination of the properties of that process, This indicates, I think, that that effort of an earlier time was well directed, and that today the social sciences are, to an appreciable extent, profiting from the results of that work.

Again, enough progress has been made in the 1950's and the early 1960's to permit us to cope today with new problems and different concepts than occupied the attention of the social sciences a decade or so ago. The Third Conference devoted its attention to such questions as unemployment in the developing areas and international issues such, as the role of underdeveloped countries in a world economy, the international politics of development, and the comparative study of newly and old settled areas. As recently as the First Biennial Midwest Research Conference on Underdeveloped Areas, it would not have been possible to cope with such problems.

Yet, impressive as these strides may be, we should not overlook the problems we have not yet solved and the issues still before us. One of these has to do with the interrelationships among various forms of change in the underdeveloped areas, On one of the forms of change, economic development, much has been done, A substantial amount of research has also been devoted, to the processes of social and cultural change, and in the last few years political scientists have begun to grapple with the problems of political development. The varying degrees of progress made in the study of these change processes reflect, among other things, the differential in. research results produced within the relevant social science disciplines. Work has hardly begun in interrelating the various forms of change in the developing areas. Significant statements of the relationships among economic development, social change, cultural change, and political development remain to be formulated. Such work merits a high place among research priorities, as was indeed pointed out at the Third Conference in the closing session on perspectives for cooperative research.

Then, too, the disturbing question of whether the current interest in development in underdeveloped areas represents a revival of evolutionary theory in the social sciences is still with us. Although some work has been done on this question,[1] much remains to be explored. Is economic development inevitable in the underdeveloped areas? Is there a fixed sequence of identifiable steps or stages in development? Is the developmental process unilinear? Evolutionary thinking is implicit in a remarkably *large* proportion of what has been said about change in the developing areas. A high priority should also be assigned to making these propositions as explicit as possible and subjecting them to rigorous testing and evaluation,

Stocktaking is perhaps inevitably awkward. The Third Conference, in causing us to look back on a decade of activity, impresses us with the major problems awaiting attack at least as much as with the not inconsiderable research payoffs achieved thus far.

George I. Blanksten

Note

1. See, for example, Herbert R. Barringer, George I. Blanksten, and Raymond W, Mack (eds.), *Social Change in Developing Areas: A Reinterpretation of Evolutionary Theory* (Cambridge: Schenkman Publishing Co., 1965).

Preface

Interdisciplinary research in the social sciences is one of the most effective techniques developed to deal with the complex study of nations, societies, communities, and people: their fascinating and puzzling joinings and separations, their growths and their declines, their progress and their apathies, their plans and their expectations. Interdisciplinary research has brought a multifaceted approach to the examination of millefaceted phenomena.

The increased interest of social scientists in their sister disciplines has not been stimulated solely by intellectual exploration into the problems which they share and the particular insights which each provides. Much of the interest sterns from the groping and searching concern of field workers who find themselves investigating problems and systems which cannot be understood adequately in terms of a single kind of analysis, be it political, social, cultural, historical, or psychological. Field work thrusts upon them the realization that their professional areas of concern overlap and converge upon aspects of life which traditionally (or academically) lie in the domains of other disciplines.[1]

In attempting to understand the "emerging" societies of the world, economists are constantly reminded that such phenomena as the growth of markets and the distribution and development of a labor force are clearly related to political policy, and the political scientists are constantly reminded that governmental decision alone, is not sufficient to bring about the development of regional markets or effective land reforms.

With the new concern of economists with problems of underdeveloped countries it becomes increasingly difficult to say where economics ends and sociology, social psychology, anthropology and political science begin. The importance for economic development of the political and cultural framework is apparent; development economists find themselves writing about such matters as the relationship between literacy and "development-raindedness" or "technology-mindedness," the impact of village organization on economic motivation, relationship of childhood training to personality traits and creativity, and the like. What then is meant by "social aspects" of economic development, as distinct from purely economic aspects?[2]

Away from textbooks and deep in the problems of a developing country, both economists and political scientists often find themselves dealing with vast territories of villages and tribes which they once regarded as the exclusive concern of geographers and anthropologists—or missionaries. And they recognize that these rural-peasant-tribal sectors cannot be ignored. The complex and necessary relationship between these sectors of the country and the urban society in which the government is centered, and from which it deals with the outside world, must be resolved before the nation can move toward either political stability or economic development. And it must be studied and analyzed before the social sciences can achieve any ordering of the elements involved and the processes at work. Even this one problem—it is really many—is too broad to be encompassed by any single disciplinary approach. Every particle of knowledge any of us possesses must be brought into common focus even to begin upon an understanding.

But not everyone who accepts the value of interdisciplinary research has the opportunity to participate in such a program; and almost no program is fully interdisciplinary. The best substitute for the actual experience of working in field collaboration with members of other disciplines is to meet with such colleagues in free and open discussion—to pick their brains and allow them to criticize each other's interpretations. Simply living on the same campus does not always serve the purpose; the daily duties have an overwhelming tendency to interfere with such discussions. Many times the colleagues one would like to consult, those who have dealt with problems, topics, or approaches of special interest, are far away or engaged. Getting together is more difficult than it should be, and some catalyst is necessary to facilitate meetings and exchanges.

It is here that such conferences as those sponsored by the Library of International Relations serve an important and appreciated function. From throughout the Middle West—and often beyond—the conferences bring together people from several disciplines who have worked in various developing areas of the world for three days of discussion (and argument). The group is small enough to enable everyone to talk with everyone else, but it is large enough to provide diversity of experience, of training, and of convictions. The program is simple; the emphasis is upon the discussions during which examples or ideas may be presented to support or to criticize the argument, new proposals or topics may be introduced for comment, or the introductory speaker may be grilled—or roasted. The only major consideration of the program is to allow all participants an opportunity to talk; this they do throughout the conference, throughout the meals, and often far into the night.

Discussion is not only desirable, it is necessary. Professional journals carry space for reader response to articles which appeared several months previously and their book reviews often reflect at least one reader's disagreement with an author. This is far from being a discussion, however. Some journals publish symposia and books appear with the papers presented at conferences. But those who did not attend almost never know what reactions the papers inspired in the members of the audience. Most conferences and practically all professional meetings are so dedicated to formal programs that discussion is confined to the groups which gather later in the local "lounge." Any paper serves only a small part of its purpose if there is no opportunity to discuss it.

Those of us who have had the good fortune to participate in the conferences of the Library of International Relations know what insights, what stimulation, what a variety of questions and interpretations can emerge from an untrammeled discussion following a short but provocative paper. It is in the belief that our colleagues, and perhaps others, will find considerable interest in the agreements and disagreements of these discussions that we agreed to have them published That the discussion sometimes ran far afield from the original topic is obvious, and this was inevitable where interest was high and the topic had many facets. The chairmen of the sessions encouraged exploration of any subject in which the members of the conference indicated interest by waving or shouting for his attention. Only the clock finally closed the sessions,

In editing the discussions, I have tried to bring together all the comments on a particular topic; during the arguments, they were not always in this sequence. The introductory papers have been edited by their authors and I have not tampered with them. Only those few comments which elicited no response or which appeared to be unrelated to the progress of the discussion were deleted, but I have retained many side-comments or irrelevant remarks in order to preserve the informal quality of the meetings. In each session various issues and topics were introduced. I have attempted to separate them and have given each a subtitle which I hope will be of help to the reader.

All participants had the opportunity to edit their own contributions, but they have not seen what I have done with them. For any distortions I may have introduced, or for any unacceptable statements or words I may have put in my colleagues' mouths, I hope they will forgive me. It was a good and stimulating conference and I am certain they will join me in expressing again our appreciation to Eloise ReQua and the Library of International Relations for inviting us.

Andrew Hunter Whiteford

Notes

1. We "knew," of course, about the relationships between our fields and others before leaving graduate school, but often it is only in the confrontations of research that we truly learn that data from these related fields are absolutely necessary for a full understanding of our own.
2. Benjamin Higgins, "An Economist's View," in *Social Aspects of Economic Development in Latin America* (Paris: UNESCO, 1963), vol. 2, p. 145.

Session I

Unemployment in Developing Areas

Chairman BLANKSTEN: As Chairman, my primary responsibility is to open this first session of the Conference.

I am very honored and pleased to be able to present Mr. W. Arthur Lewis. He is, as you all know, a pioneering writer in the field of economic development, one of the first to start a train of largely productive thinking in the economic growth field.

I have always admired him as a man who, when it seems wise to do so, does not hesitate to change his mind and to admit that, he does so.

Mr. W. Arthur Lewis will talk tonight on the problem of unemployment in the developing areas.

Mr. LEWIS: Underdeveloped countries did relatively well in the 1950's, with respect to the growth of output. According to the United Nations,[1] real output grew over the decade at an annual rate of 4.1 per cent in Africa, 4.2 in the Far East, 5.2 in West Asia, and 4.6 in Latin America. All these rates exceed what most experts would have prophesied in 1950. The subject of this paper is the curious phenomenon that unemployment seems to be growing as fast as output. I refer not to disguised unemployment on family farms, but to actual unemployment among people who work for wages. The phenomenon, if true, is curious because, after much discussion of this possibility in the early part of the nineteenth century, economists have grown to believe that unemployment must diminish in an economy growing as rapidly as at 4 per cent per annum. We have special explanations for cyclical unemployment, such as all developed economies experience regularly, and for structural unemployment in depressed industries or areas, such as Great Britain experienced in the 1920's. Both result from declining investment. Unemployment associated with rapidly increasing investment is an unfamiliar animal.

1

I.

We must begin with problems of measurement. We are dealing only with people who work for wages, and are not therefore concerned with the surplus, if any, on family farms. Unfortunately there are no reliable measures of unemployment in underdeveloped countries. None has comprehensive social insurance, from which the numbers in receipt of unemployment compensation might be derived. Many have registers, to which the unemployed are invited to add their names. For example, the registered unemployed in India[2] increased from 254,000 in 1948 to 1,754,000 in 1961. However, since in most cases registration brings neither a job nor relief pay, many unemployed do not register, and doubtless some keep their names on the register even after they have found employment; also registration is usually confined to the larger cities.

A census can provide useful information if it includes questions about employment; and some countries have also made special surveys of unemployment from time to time. However, one of the problems is then to define the labor force. For example, 48,000 persons told the census takers in Jamaica in 1960 that they wanted a job and had never had one.[3] Should they be included in the labor force, of which they would then be 7 per cent? If so, the average rate of unemployment in the census week was 21 per cent, including persons who worked for part of the week. However, a substantial proportion of those who wanted a job but had never had one were over 30 years old, and must be presumed to be able to get along without finding employment.

Experience in Western Europe in the 1950s has emphasized that the size of the labor force depends on the amount of work offering. Thus in Great Britain the number of people aged 15 to 64 increased only by 400,000 in the 1950s, but the number of working people in that age group increased by 1,400,000. Women seek work where work is available, but not otherwise. Thus in Lancashire, a cotton area, the proportion of women in the labor force is much higher than in South Wales, a mining area. If the number of persons in the labor force is flexible even in a highly developed economy like Britain, it is even more flexible in underdeveloped countries, which contain enormous reservoirs of people outside the labor market who will enter that market gladly if work becomes available. And if you cannot define the labor force, you cannot say how many persons are unemployed.

Another problem is that, alas, not all the unemployed are employable. Many young people who leave school are unable to find continuous employment. They then commence a disastrous pattern of living. A young man gets one day's work here; gets no work tomorrow; cadges a meal the next day from his aunt; finds another job for a few hours; steals some small thing while the owner is not looking; shares a meal with a friend; borrows a few cents from a patron; and so on. After one has lived this life for two or three years, one becomes unemployable, and could not do eight hours work a day for five days a week even if it were offered—for psychological no less than physical reasons. Thus governments which set up public works programs to relieve the unemployed are sometimes puzzled by the discrepancy between the numbers known to be unemployed and the number who turn up for work. The unemployables want only a few hours work per week, and cannot do more.

It is unsatisfactory to talk about unemployment without being able to define the unemployed precisely. It is also unsatisfactory to assert that unemployment has increased during the 1950s without being able to document the statement. Nevertheless one must report that this opinion is widely held. Throughout the underdeveloped world a few already large towns are exploding in size, with the number of people increasing faster than the number of jobs. Unemployment, juvenile delinquency and crime are becoming major concerns in towns where it used to be safe to go out and leave your door open. One knows cities where, in the absence of unemployment pay, burglary has become the largest Industry. One cannot offer statistics, but can only report the surprise and despair of seasoned observers who notice that in spite of rapid rates of growth of output, and high rates of capital formation, unemployment nevertheless seems to increase. Jamaica's may be an extreme case. There, as far as we can see, net investment during the Fifties averaged 18 per cent of national income, and real output increased at an annual rate of 6 per cent. Eleven per cent of the labor force emigrated, yet unemployment seems to have been as great in 1960 as in 1950.

II.

Population pressure is not a primary cause of unemployment. Countries with high population pressure learn over the centuries how to provide some work for everybody. If farming is on a small-scale basis (in contrast to wage labor), the farms get smaller and smaller, and surplus labor stays on the farms, so everybody has a claim to income, even though he may not be fully occupied. This is not possible if agriculture is operated by large-scale capitalists who hire only as many laborers as it pays to hire at the current wage, The surplus is then driven into other sectors. Social custom imposes on the middle and upper classes the obligation to burden themselves with hordes of useless servants; having many servants becomes a status symbol which extends even deep down into the lower middle and upper working classes, if population pressure is severe; it becomes almost immoral for any man of status to do for himself what a servant could do for him, or to soil his hands with manual operations. Even entrepreneurs get caught up in this spirit, if they accept the social mores, and burden their businesses with large numbers of useless clerks, messengers, and other hangers-on. Wages are low, barely adequate to keep body and soul together, not adequate for serious hard manual work, and more of the nature of charity than of payment for hard, serious labor, which is neither given nor expected. The rest of the surplus swarms into casual trades; markets are crowded with peddlers and stallholders making occasional sales; and there is a vast reservoir of casual laborers, gardeners, dock workers, construction workers, and porters. Thus everybody has some sort of job, however great the pressure of population.

Unemployment is due to the breakdown of this social system before it is fully replaced by another. When wages cease to be a form of charity, and start to rise sharply, jobs begin to be confined to those whose productivity meets the test of high wages. The economy divides into two sectors; a highly productive sector using capital and modern technology and paying high wages; and the rest of the economy. If these two sectors could be insulated from each other, there need still not be unemployment, but this insulation is not possible. If wages in the modern sector diverge sharply from earnings in the traditional sector, the latter can no longer hold, the surplus labor, and disguised unemployment is converted to open unemployment.

We have usually expected wage rates in the modern sector to be about 50 per cent above the income of subsistence farmers. This brings the modern sector as much labor as it wants, without at the same time attracting much more than it can handle. It means, however, that wage rates in the modern sector must not rise with productivity in that sector: the increase in productivity must go to profits, or taxes, or to the subsistence sector via improved terms of trade.

It seems that during the nineteenth century modern sectors expanded very considerably at constant real wage rates. Historians dispute what happened in England. Some say that real wages were constant; others say that consumption increased.[4] These two are consistent with each other, since a transfer of persons from a low-income to a high-income sector will increase consumption even though real wage rates are constant. Students of the Japanese situation also conclude that real wage rates were constant there in the crucial first 40 years after the Restoration.[5]

This seems not to be possible in developing countries in the second half of the twentieth century, some discrepancies are fantastic. The bauxite mining industry in Jamaica pays unskilled labor a wage which is five times the normal. This is typical of mining countries—say of oil in Venezuela and Trinidad, or copper in Northern Rhodesia, Manufacturing and plantation industries cannot afford such wages, but they also tend to pay substantially more than is current elsewhere. Three factors operate to have this effect, which were not so powerful in the nineteenth century. First, trade unions. Secondly, a more powerful social conscience among capitalists, which causes them to wish to share the fruits of progress with their workers, and to limit profit ratios. Thirdly, strongly nationalist governments which support the claims of workers as against foreign capitalists.

A sharp increase of wages in a profitable sector has drastic effects. First, it reduces employment opportunities in that sector, and encourages instead highly capital-intensive production. Bauxite is merely scraped off the surface and carted away. At £5 a week this would offer employment to tens of thousands. At £15 a week the Jamaican companies invested instead £80 million, employing only 3,000 people. Half of 1 per cent of the labor force produces 9 per cent of gross domestic product. Secondly, these high wages act as a magnet, which causes towns to explode. When the urban wage is only 50 per cent higher than the rural, part of which is absorbed in higher living costs, demand and supply can be in equilibrium. But when the urban wage is three times the rural, there is a great influx into the towns, seeking nonexistent jobs. Having come in to town, men do not necessarily go back, for they are held by what the town has to offer—bustle, anonymity, water out of a nearby tap, freedom from obligations to relatives and chiefs, schools, cinemas, hospitals, buses, the chance of occasional employment, even in a few cases the chance of assistance from welfare agencies. Thirdly, and most of all, the high wages in the modern sector pull up wages in all other industries and occupations, helped perhaps by other trade unions as well as by normal human envy. If your cousin in the factory or mine is getting six pounds a week for unskilled labor, you are not so willing to be a garden boy for one pound a week, and so emerges the common phenomenon of employers complaining of shortage of labor, while workers complain of shortage of work. The clerk's wife kept a servant when all this cost was ten shillings a week; but a maid demanding three pounds a week is more likely to be replaced by an electric cooker, a refrigerator, a vacuum cleaner and a washing machine. The housewives get rid of their servants, and the businesses purge themselves of useless clerks and messengers. So the employment created by the modern sector can be more than offset by the effect the modern sector has on wages throughout the economy.

Adverse effects are not confined to the traditional sector. Other industries in the modern sectors are subjected to pressure. Wages in sugar, bananas, and factory industries have chased the bauxite wages, These industries are subject to international competition. They are therefore mechanizing as fast as they can, and dismissing labor. The rise of a new export industry can destroy existing exports, and existing industries compete with imports, not by taking away their labor, but simply by raising wage costs out of line with international competition.

Another new factor in the labor market is decasualization. It is normal in an underdeveloped economy for certain sectors to live by employing casual labor, attaching to themselves many more persons than they could employ continuously: most notably the clocks, the building industry, plantation agriculture, and to a lesser extent the mines and the factories, Modern personnel theory is against casual labor. Men on the permanent staff feed better, work more effectively, have a higher morale, and cause less trouble. Unions also object to casual labor, because it is more difficult to organize. Decasualization does not increase the average level of unemployment, but it makes unemployment less supportable. If 100 men each work three days a week, they can all live. When 60 work five days a week and 40 become continuously unemployed, one faces a major social problem. High wages stimulate decasualization, since the employer seeks to get best value from those he employs; and also because high wages make him put in machines, which require him to train a staff and keep it.

In sum, high wages in modern industries cause the traditional sector to stop shielding the labor surplus and throw it openly on to the labor market; while at the same time the modern sector expands by importing machines rather than by taking on a lot more men. This is probably the largest factor in growing unemployment, but there are other factors to be probed.

III.

Another factor which differentiates the twentieth century is permanent balance-of-payments crisis. In the nineteenth century, countries developed in response to growing demand for their exports. *Ceteris paribus*, this results in a persistent tendency to run a balance-of-payments surplus. In the second half of the twentieth century, several countries are trying to develop by investing to meet home demands. Except insofar as the goods produced are substitutes for imports, this results, *ceteris paribus*, in a persistent balance-of-payments deficit, since the increase in income is bound to increase the demand for some imports, and neither a cut in other imports nor an increase in exports is guaranteed.

Our interest is in the effect of the balance-of-payrnents crisis on the prospects of industries which have to meet international competition, whether exporting industries or industries producing for home consumption in competition with imports. As we have seen, an increase in one export may destroy others by raising wages out of line with world prices; this, however, is not a necessary result; it derives only from errors of incomes policy, to which we refer later.

On the other hand, developing new industries with an eye on the home market only is bound to cause what the Latin Americans now call structural inflation. Unbalanced growth produces the persistent tendency to a balance-of-payments deficit; this makes necessary import controls and tariff protection; these raise the cost of living, and therefore wages. Exports are discouraged. Devaluation is forced. The cost of living rises more, and so on. In such economies, investment for the home market can be maintained by stricter and stricter control of Imports. Exports, however, tend to be overlooked. Such countries have *a* chronic tendency to price themselves out of the world market. The failure of export industries to expand is one of the causes of growing unemployment in Latin America and in Asia.

IV.

An important factor in Africa is the recent explosion of the primary school population. In 1950 hardly any African country south of the Sahara had more than 20 per cent of children in school. But one by one, as new nationalist leaders came into power, universal primary education was made an immediate goal, and some areas were by 1960 taking as much as 80 per cent of the seven-year-olds into school. The outpouring of these young people into the towns has become a serious cause of unemployraent.

In a community where only 20 per cent of children enter primary school, and only 10 per cent finish the course, the demand for primary school graduates is such that they command considerable salaries in white-collar jobs. If the number entering primary school is pushed up from 20 to 80 per cent of the age group within ten years, as has happened in some West African countries, the result is frustration. The children pouring out of the primary schools look to the town for clerical jobs, and are disappointed when they do not find employment. The towns fill up with discontented youths, faster than houses, jobs, water supplies, or other amenities can be provided, and urban slums and delinquents multiply while the countryside is starved of young talent.

The situation is sometimes blamed on the failure of rural schools to adapt their curricula in such a way as to orientate rural children to rural life. This, however, is only part of the problem. The primary-school leaver's expectations derive not from the curriculum but from the status which his immediate predecessors have enjoyed. In a developed economy the wage of an unskilled laborer (which is all that primary education produces) is about one-third of the average income per occupied person; but a primary-school leaver in Africa expects about twice the average income per occupied person. Obviously, if literacy became universal, it would be impossible to pay every literate person twice the average income. If the primary-school leaver is to get twice the average income, he can fit only into those parts of the economy which yield twice the average income, and the rate of absorption of primary-school leavers then depends on the rate at which these modernized sectors of the economy are expanding. He will fit into a revolutionized agriculture, with modern practices and equipment, but it is useless to expect him to fit into the three-acres-and-a-hoe farming of his father. Any good primary school will widen a child's horizon and create expectations which primitive farming cannot fulfill. So even if rural schools concentrate on rural life, their products are bound to suffer frustration unless the whole social fabric of agriculture is being modernized at the same time.

This is a temporary phenomenon. The young people will discover that the towns cannot employ them, and that work at twice the average wage is not to be had anywhere. They will lower their sights, and learn to make do with the opportunities in rural areas. But the learning will be painful, psychologically and politically, and in the meantime, the towns will be in trouble.

V.

I have mentioned at several points the excessive rate of growth of towns, as one of the phenomena of unemployment. People who should remain on the farms where they have some income, and in Africa or Latin America certainly add something to output (India and Pakistan are more doubtful cases), turn up instead in the towns, living by small opportunities for casual employment.

Current reactions to excessive urbanization make things worse. The best way to keep people in the countryside is to spend public funds on providing amenities in country towns—secondary schools, water supplies, hospitals, electric power, and so on. Instead, public expenditure tends to be concentrated in a small number of large cities, thus adding to their drawing power. For this there are many reasons. The tendency for political talent to concentrate in the larger cities, depriving the countryside and country towns of leadership and influence. Erroneous theories that only large cities can carry the overhead of industrialization. The fact that the larger cities, because they are growing fastest, seem to have the greatest needs—which is really a circular argument, since the more you concentrate public facilities there, at the expense of the rest of the country, the faster they grow, and the more they need.

European cities did not explode in the first half of the nineteenth century. Some tendency towards excessive urbanization existed, and caused concern: British poor-law authorities were trying to control it administratively at the end of the eighteenth and the beginning of the nineteenth centuries. But when Europe was beginning its industrial revolution the logistic problems of large cities had not yet been solved, so industry had to develop in many small towns instead of a few large ones. The first suburban bus service started in Paris in 1855. Twentieth-century advances in transportation, sewage disposal, water supplies, preservation of milk and meat, and house-to-house communication by telephone make it possible for even the poorest nations today to struggle with heaps of four or five million people, while much richer countries in say 1870 would have found four or five hundred thousand barely manageable.

VI.

So far I have mainly been explaining why the labor surplus is no longer held in the traditional sectors, but is instead throwing itself or being thrown into open unemployment on the labor market. The other blade of the scissors is that economic expansion now seems to be more capital-intensive and less labor-intensive than in the nineteenth century. In country after country where the rate of investment was unusually high in the 1950s, there is astonishment at how little employment so much investment has created.

The proposition under consideration can be stated as follows. Let us suppose that in the nineteenth century x per cent of national income had to be invested, net, to provide additional employment for 1 per cent of population. It appears that in the second half of the twentieth century underdeveloped nations are getting less than 1 per cent addition to employment for x per cent of national income invested. I put this forward not as a proven fact, but as part of our agenda for research.

Let us first begin by analyzing the effect of invention on the ratio of capital to labor. Suppose an economy in which capital is stored-up labor, so that an increase in wages increases the price of machines in the same proportion. Suppose further that there are two farms, one keeping the weeds down with machines, and the other keeping the weeds down at the same cost by hand. An invention may be of three kinds; it may change the relative efficiency of weeding by hand or by machine, without changing the relative cost of the machine; it may introduce a new technique which alters the ratio of machines to labor; or it may reduce the cost of making the machine, while leaving both its efficiency and the machine-labor ratio the same.

An invention which eliminated weeds easily by hand would cause the first farm to abandon its machines, and so reduce the ratio of capital to labor; an invention which improved the efficiency of machines in eliminating weeds would cause the second farm to turn to machinery, and so increase the economy-wide ratio of capital to labor. In general the trend of the past century has favored ways of making things with machines rather than other ways, so tending to increase the ratio of needed investment per unit of employment.

Next, an invention which increases the efficiency of a machine may increase, reduce or leave unchanged the ratio of machines per man. If the ratio is unchanged, fewer men and fewer machines eliminate the same quantity of weeds. Some inventions have, reduced the quantity of capital per unit of labor, for example the substitution of the tape recorder for earlier recording processes. But, the general trend has favored increasing the amount of capital per man.

On the other hand, statisticians tell us that in Britain and the United States over the past 80 years, the ratio of investment to labor in. our terms has varied very little. Capital per man measured at constant prices has enormously increased, but our interest is not in this, but in the proportion of national income invested required to employ a man, which we can identify roughly as the ratio of the number of men it takes to make a machine to the number of men it takes to use it, or the ratio of capital to the wages bill. We are told that for several decades prior to the Second World War there had been very little change in the ratio of labor income or capital income to output, or of net investment to output, both of which imply that the percentage of net investment required to employ 1 per cent more people had remained roughly the same. The explanation of this is the third type of invention, which reduces the cost of machines. This works both ways. On the one hand it encourages the displacement of labor-intensive processes, so increasing the economy-wide capital-output ratio. On the other hand it reduces the labor-cost of capital, and this has been powerful enough to offset all the other factors making for an increase in the capital-employment ratio.

The countries developing today differ from those which, started during the nineteenth century in several respects, which raise the investment-employment ratio.

First, we have already seen that for various reasons there is a persistent tendency for wages to rise sharply. This would not alter the ratio of capital to employment in a closed economy, since the price of capital and the price of labor would rise together. But it is very important in an open economy importing machinery from countries where costs are not subject to the same degree of inflation. This persistent increase in wages has caused excessive mechanization in many countries. But there are also other factors.

A second factor—minor but spectacular—is the high ratio of public to private investment in the newly developing countries. Nineteenth-century entrepreneurs were willing to start factories in barns; private schools or hospitals sprouted in the most unlikely places. But public factories, schools, hospitals or other structures are nearly always colossal, striking and expensive, built to the glory of their architects and their supporting politicians. So public capital investment provides less continuing employment than private investment of the same amount.

A third factor is that much of the capital invested in these countries is under-utilized. Capital is going into many industries where the demand is insufficient for production on an economic scale; plants are built ahead of demand, and run below capacity. Double and treble shifts are not as popular as they were a hundred years ago. Superhighways carrying a handful of vehicles are a common sight. Strict economic calculus in investing capital is not practiced as it was a hundred years ago. This is related to the greater influence of governments on investment, though it is riot confined to public investment; tariffs, subsidies, and licensing are used to protect private investments which would otherwise be made more modestly.

A fourth factor in comparisons with developed countries is that the difference in *per-capita* outputs is greater in the capital-producing industries than in other industries, Hence, insofar as the underdeveloped make their own capital goods, it takes more investment to support a unit of employment. They can import machinery, and this reduces the ratio, but the terms of trade will lie between the developed countries' ratios and theirs, so the ratio of capital to wages should still be higher in the less-developed countries. In equilibrium, therefore, an underdeveloped country would have a higher capital-wages ratio in those industries which were capitalized, but would have fewer industries capitalized than a developed economy because of the greater cost of capital,

Fifthly, the product-mix is different. Developed countries achieve 4 per cent overall growth by having 5 per cent industrial growth and 3 per cent for the rest of the economy; while underdeveloped countries get the same overall result by having 8 per cent industrial growth and 3 per cent for the rest of the economy, Since the modern industrial sector is the most, highly capitalized part of the underdeveloped economies, its high growth rate increases capital formation sharply while doing little for employment.

Finally, high capital intensity is probably a natural consequence of technological lag. Approaching these countries from the angle of the Ohlin version of the Law of Comparative Costs, economists have argued that they should avoid capital-intensive investments. The Ohlin version assumes that technologies are everywhere the same. The Ricardian version focuses instead on differences in relative efficiencies. Capital should be used where it adds most to income. This is more likely to be in those parts of the economy where capital brings much more productive technology than in those parts where efficiency depends rather on skill. When one orders industries in terms of the comparative efficiency of resources, Ricardian style, underdeveloped countries will be nearly as efficient as developed countries in industries where capital is the crucial factor, and will be least efficient in those where advanced skills are the crucial factor. So, even after the relative scarcity of capital is brought into the account, some highly capital-intensive industries will still prove to be the most productive investments.[6]

When the effects of technological change are considered, there is no a priori reason why economic development must increase rather than reduce employment. This is an old story. You will remember that Ricardo demonstrated to Mai thus that investment must increase employment. Their model has an unlimited supply of labor at a subsistence wage. Hence extra capital is met by extra labor in the same proportion; the rate of profit is constant; and unlimited expansion is possible—except for a shortage of land.

Later Ricardo thought again, and added to the third edition of his Principles a chapter on Machinery, admitting that an invention which reduced the cost of machinery could destroy more employment than it created. However, he argued, this would increase profits, savings, investment and therefore employment. Here we have the distinction between the sort of investment which merely produces more of the same—two factories in place of one—and therefore increases the use of labor, and the sort of investment which embodies new invention, which may reduce the cost or increase the effiency of capital, and so cause it to he substituted for labor.

Marx added nothing useful to the distinctions. He simply asserted flatly that the course of history would be that the amount of unemployment created by the flow of labor-saving inventions would exceed the amount of employment created by more investment of a duplicating kind, so that the number of unemployed must grow continuously. Marx was clearly wrong for developing economies in the nineteenth century. But we cannot deduce that he must be wrong for developing economies in the twentieth century. There is now such an accumulation of labor-saving processes which have not yet been introduced into underdeveloped countries that the potential for destroying employment by new investment is very considerable. It is not at all inconceivable that a stream of new investment in transport, distribution, and agriculture would create much more unemployment than a similar stream directed to industry and services would absorb. Output and investment could thus increase while employment declined.

VII.

I began by saying that unemployment is not created by population pressure, since a well-ordered society absorbs a population surplus in its traditional sectors. This is no longer true when the social mechanism breaks down. We have seen how high wages cause the traditional sector to throw the surplus onto the labor market, and cause the modern sector, by becoming highly capital intensive, to leave most of the surplus on the market. The bigger the surplus, the bigger the unemployment; so population growth, absorbable when the society is in equilibrium, causes growing unemployment when the society is in disequilibrium. Putting all these factors together, it is no surprise that unemployment is growing despite high levels of investment.

VIII.

If there are remedies for this situation, the most important would be to prevent wages in the modern sector from moving out of line with incomes in the traditional sector.

The fact that the mining industry is profitable is no justification for paying miners five times as much as other workers can earn. The higher productivity of mining is a rent element which should accrue neither to the workers nor to the capitalists, but to the owners of the natural resource, which should be the state. The proper answer to abnormal profits in a particular industry is not higher wages in that industry, but a system of royalties or taxes which draws the rent element into the public treasury, where it can finance the public services, and capital formation. In general, wages in the modern sector should be kept at about 50 per cent above the farmer's income, and excess profits should go not to the workers but to the general public.

Worker's incomes should be raised partly by aggressive measures increasing farm productivity, and partly by the steady transfer of men from agriculture to higher-paid jobs in other sectors.

This policy is anathema to unions, but several governments of new states have already adopted it—especially new states in which the government is the largest employer of wage labor, but also by some which want the profits to spend on schools or roads, and do not therefore support union demands. This is producing a crisis between union leaders and political leaders, for example in Nigeria and in Northern Rhodesia. It is also producing a new philosophy of the role of trade unions in developing countries, for example in Ghana and in India. The problem of unemployment can be solved only at this political level.

General Discussion

Chairman BLANKSTEN: We do not have any specially appointed discussants for tonight's session and *we* will therefore be able to move more directly into the general discussion.

The Rural Sector

Mr. NASH: I cannot quarrel with Mr. Lewis's analysis of the modern sector, but when he takes the other part of his dual society, I think he errs badly.

The developing countries have not been, since colonial impact, at least in Asia and Africa, in any empirical state of equilibrium. They have been accommodating to their surplus population by in fact decreasing the per capita income of everybody in it. They do have accommodation mechanisms.

Mr. LEWIS: Asia has surplus population, not Africa.

Mr. NASH: Asia, all right. Overpopulation there is a problem and what it continues to do, empirically anyway, is to subdivide tasks so that the net output is not larger but the individual shares are reduced. The modern sector exercises a pull, not only because of its wages, but also because of the declining level of living in the countryside year after year after year in places like India and Indonesia, I think Mr. Lewis has to build in the notion that these are "pathological" dual societies (urban and rural), and that they are not in any sense in a state of equilibrium.

For a long time there have been great pressures on the people in the countryside to break away and anything will pull them out.

Mr. LEWIS: All I am saying is that so long as they are on the family farm, they have some income. Now, you do something which brings them into the town, I am not worried only about the people from the farms. There is also the surplus in urban employments that gets thrown out because of higher wages; but, if you pull the people on the farms into the towns where they have no income, this becomes a social problem,

Mr. NASH: They are social problems back home anyway.

Mr. LEWIS: They are not anything like the same social problem back on the farm that they are in the town.

Mr. NASH: Well, that: depends on the country and its political organization.

Mr. LEWIS: Let us put it this way, that when they are on the farms they are a hidden social problem and when they are on your doorstep burgling your house at night in the towns, they are an open social problem.

Mr. NASH: They are in many ways a more serious social problem in the country. In Burma, for example, or in Indonesia or Vietnam, one of the sources of the recruitment of insurgents is this rural population which takes off for dacoiting under political banners and keeps the government in a state of turmoil all the time. They are real social rural problems; you do not have to bring them into the cities.

Mr. LEWIS: I would not accept Burma in your list of countries that are overpopulated, I would agree if you have in mind India and Pakistan, for example, but not Burma.

Mr. NASH: Burma has this same kind, of rural trouble. One of the reasons is that boys can leave the family farm without lowering its income and take five years off as a dacoit. as a PV Volunteer or as a Red rebel; this keeps the country in a terrible state of turmoil.

If you look for the sources of the peasant revolts in countries like Burma that, are relatively prosperous, you will find them in this "pathological" development in the countryside.

Mr. BARANSON: I think this is also true in Colombia. The problem becomes insoluble in the countryside; the greater pressures are there, and you cannot say that urbanization, despite the problems it creates, is more of an evil and more of a problem.

Mr. KREININ: I think Africa is different, and Mr. Lewis's discussion is really more applicable to Africa.

Economic Development and Social Tension

Mr. ANDERSON: Without any reservations on your economic analysis, Mr. Lewis, is the intensity of the crises these countries are facing, which you sketched out, serious? Or, to what degree are the crises intensified by the technologically reduced death rate of recent years and by the new technology, so to speak, of political arousal that has been brought into these countries that was not present in Europe a hundred years ago? To what extent does this intensify these problems beyond this strictly intrinsic growth problem?

Mr. LEWIS: This ties up with something else that was talked about before and I think it is important. I said, essentially, that in certain countries which are overpopulated, primarily some countries of Asia, not Africa and not Burma, there is a surplus of disguised unemployment which, is now coming out into the towns, for the reasons which I analyzed, and that this is a bad thing because it would be better if they (the villagers) were to stay in the areas where they are for the time being until there has been a sufficient expansion of the capacity of the modern sector to absorb them and provide them employment.

I was challenged on this by people who, if I understand them correctly, take opposite points of view and say, "No, it is a jolly good thing for these chaps to get: out and become unemployed in the towns because unemployment in the towns somehow or other is not quite as bad as unemployment in the countryside." I do not understand, really, how people can think that, because it just does not accord with my experience. One of the things it does not accord with is precisely your very last point about the political position.

It has been fashionable in some quarters to believe that economic development will bring social peace, or even world peace, but most of us know very well that economic development is a very disturbing process, and on the contrary, produces the very greatest social tensions. It is only in the later stages of development that you reach social stability. Economic development, as Marx saw it around him—and exactly the same thing exists in the developing countries today—produces very great tensions, and produced very great political arousal in Marx's day and very great political arousal in our day.

I think these countries would get along better if the population and employment surplus remained in the countryside where it could share in the income of a large family pattern. The countryside does provide a social security system, and it provides a place for these people psychologically.

When you put them into the towns where the cultural patterns are not ready to receive them, the only things waiting for them are the politicians and the agitators. I think some of these countries are much more likely to tear themselves in pieces if the surplus population comes into the towns before the towns are ready for them, than if they had stayed in the countryside.

Mr. ANDERSON: It depends on what kind of disorder you want.

Mr. HENDRY: It seems to me that, from experiences in Indonesia there are factors at work that go beyond the economic situation. I am impressed by Professor Mash's questions.

As you see people pour into Djakarta, for example, a city of 3,000,000 people that was designed for 500,000, you get a feeling that these people are not really concerned about whether or not they are casually employed or unemployed. They come because there are-many other incentives. They simply like people. They like mob scenes. They like to associate with other people. They like the power structure of Djakarta. They like to participate in the mob scenes.

There are bread-and-circus aspects to this thing that I am not sure you can measure in terms of the economics of the situation. Also, I would not. be convinced that the typical Indonesian would recognize that he was unemployed, either in a disguised version of unemployment or an overt form, of unemployment. He seems to get by at a very low marginal or submarginal subsistence standard. I think my observation is that there are many factors here at work other than the factor of the real level of wages these people earn in these urban centers,

Mr. FATOUROS: I think there is a clear implication at least from a factual description of the results of the transfer from the traditional sector to the modern sector in many of the underdeveloped societies, that the modern sector will have to provide a high amount of social welfare to the people who, on transferring from the traditional to the modern sector, lose the implicit social welfare advantages they had in the traditional sector. This makes necessary (and this necessity is political as well as economic) a level of social welfare, social security, and so on, which would not compare with the much lower social welfare level in Western societies at a corresponding stage of development. Would Mr. Lewis agree with that, as a factual statement rather than a normative one?

Mr. LEWIS: As a factual statement, yes. Going back to the point about politics, the towns are better organized than the countryside to make claims upon the government, and this is one of the reasons why it is much easier for the government when the unemployment is hidden in the countryside rather than in the towns, because the pressure that is then put on the government to do something about it is terrific and they are forced, as in Ghana, to create a Workers' Brigade or start some kind of social welfare measures.

Modern and Traditional Sectors: Japan

Mr. GINSBURG: I wonder if some of the points Professor Lewis made about the contrasts between the modern and traditional sectors do not present us with a taxonomic problem that needs resolution?

I think we probably have a reasonably consistent common sense understanding of what is meant by the modern sector of an economy, but I wonder whether we have the same conception of what a traditional sector is? My point is that the definitions of the traditional sector may vary so much as to make it very difficult to generalize concerning the relationship, say, between the two sectors. Let me illustrate with the case of Japan, which I realize is far from an underdeveloped country, but is certainly a developing one. Every year approximately 300,000 people move into Tokyo alone, from "non-Tokyo." By "non-Tokyo" I mean primarily rural Japan, but also the smaller towns, though we are not quite sure just where the migrants come from.

Now, what happens to most of these people? Most of them, incidentally, are employable. They are literate. Japan has a 99-point something literacy, in spite of the "devilish" language which makes Westerners think that all these people just possibly cannot communicate with one another. They are employable, and they are young. I do not have precise figures with me, but about half of these people go into tertiary activities, and some of them certainly are quite marginal in terms of the value of output that is associated with them. Of the remainder, only a very small proportion, in spite of their literacy, go into what we might call the modern industrial sector. The vast majority go into what we would call the traditional sector. What is this traditional sector of the economy like? I am talking, now, about industry, not commerce. It consists, as we all have read, of relatively small firms employing 25 people or less and mostly considerably less, paying wages which are considerably lower than wages in the modern sector.

Theoretically, I suppose, and I think that you suggested this, because these wage differentials are very great, there ought to be a massive flow of these employables from the traditional sector to the modern sector. There is some flow, of course, but it is not as massive, perhaps, as the Japanese would like. Now why don't they flow? They do not flow to the extent one might speculate they might because of certain built-in restraints in the Japanese culture pattern—which, of course, includes the economy.

For one thing, there is a certain "stickiness" about this traditional sector which can be defined in part in terms of the kind of "extended family" type of relationship between employer and employee which is developed there. Perhaps even more important, however, is the institutionalized set of roles played by these traditional-sector firms on the one hand and the modern-sector firms on the other, The small firms of the traditional sector, which are much more labor-intensive, I suppose we might say, than the firms in the modern sector, are tied in with the larger firms by means of contractual arrangements that are of very long standing. In other words, the small firms are linked with the larger ones in supplying certain kinds of parts and services.

We have all read about bicycles, for example, but I am not just thinking of bicycles. The huge electronics industry in Japan has taken on the
same characteristics that the bicycle industry had decades ago, and still
has. This formalization of relationship has resulted, in a relative stabi-
lization of roles between the two sectors.

Now, we are talking about Japanese society or a particular attribute
of it. It is something we do not find in the newly developing countries,
certainly not in Africa, about which I know virtually nothing and therefore can make such a gross generalization.

In Japan in the 1870s and later, there existed a society which was
predominantly rural in terms of population but which was urban in terms
of its conception of the way people ought to live. The city was something
that was known, it existed, and it was indigenous, not colonial; but there
were in the cities artist-craftsmen establishments supplying the elite,
which were organized much in the same manner that the small firm in
the traditional sector is now organized.

The traditional sector is Japanese; it is related to the modern sector
in describable ways, in ways that are understandable to the Japanese.
We do not find this kind of phenomenon, so I understand, in the African
countries or in certain of the Southeast Asian countries, for example,
where urbanization, and industrialization have been associated both with
colonialism and with the import of foreign labor: Asians or Lebanese
into East Africa, or Chinese and Indians into Southeast Asia.

Let me ask Professor Lewis whether he thinks all this is relevant to
his schema and could be used to distinguish among various types of
cases.

Mr. LEWIS: It is very relevant, and I have thought about it quite a
good deal, because the problem with which I am concerned is in marked
contrast to the Japanese situation. The conclusion I come to is that there
must be a difference in the trade union situation which makes it possible
for people to flow into Japanese small-scale industry.

Wage Differentials and Mechanization

I do not know what the present situation is. Ten years ago in Japan I
was told that it was quite common for small industrialists to be employing people and paying them half the wages that next door they were
being paid, by the big industrialists. Now, this means that we have a
situation in Japan in which, as the surplus flows into the towns, a wage
level is adopted which makes it possible to absorb these people in spite
of the fact that a much higher wage level is being paid to some other

people. It is the absence of this phenomenon that causes the trouble in the economies with which I am concerned.

If it were possible for the sugar industry in Jamaica to go on paying three pounds a week while the bauxite industry was paying fifteen, the sugar industry would not have mechanized. You spoke about the mining industry. The mining industry has enormous flexibility. Underground mining does not have this flexibility. A good deal of the mining in these countries practically all of the iron mining in West Africa and bauxite mining in the West Indies involves merely scraping the stuff off the ground, and you do not have to have bulldozers and so on to do it with.

The mining industry could employ four or five times as many people as it does.

Mr. KREININ: What, then, is the cause of the capital intensity?

Mr. LEWIS: Capital intensity is caused by the high wages.

Mr. KREININ: I do not agree with you.

Mr. BINDER: I am still intrigued by your recommendations—contrary to your viewpoint ten years ago—for the holding-down of wages in the modern sector.

In one or two places near the end of the paper you used the word "should," indicating that the increased income to these Industries was a rent factor and that this should go to the owner of the resource, which *should* be the state, or *is* the state in some cases. I am not sure which the term was.

There are a number of recommendations made, possibly including one that the state should be the owner of the resource, which is a highly questionable recommendation.

What I would like to explore is whether or not your "should" regarding the holding-down of wages in the modern sector refers to the explicit value of reducing unemployment in the economy as a whole or whether you are after other values going beyond that? If you are concerned only with the value of reducing unemployment or of limiting unemployment, the materials you have presented appear to demonstrate that unemployment has not fallen, but I am not quite sure that it has increased.

Mr. LEWIS: Oh, yes. I think, really, we ought to start at that end to see whether my impression of the places I have been to is supported, namely that open unemployment has been increasing.

Professor Harbison has just come back from Venezuela and he tells me that there they are terribly concerned and extremely puzzled. They have had a 9 per cent per annum rate of growth of the national output for a long time now and unemployment is just mounting by leaps and bounds.

He has been around the world in recent years. Our impressions are both the same, that, this is a real phenomenon and not something we are dreaming up, but perhaps we could start at that end.

Chairman BLANKSTEN: With respect to some of the distinctions that are drawn here, for example, you talked about unemployment in the modern sector and another distinction that would occur to me would be that between skilled and unskilled labor. Would not these distinctions be especially crucially important in this kind of a problem?

Mr. LEWIS: This is all unskilled unemployment one is talking about, really. Let me give a particular example.

You ask me why one should be so concerned. Let me take a man who is now extremely concerned, and he is the Prime Minister of a state which came into existence yesterday or the day before yesterday, Zambia. Northern Rhodesia has one really profitable industry, the copper mines, and Mr. Kaunda and the copper companies are on very good terms at the moment.

Fifty per cent of the profits of the copper mines goes to the government of Northern Rhodesia in the form of a corporation tax. The copper mines employ very few people. The mines, as you know, in all of these economies employ very few people but they produce a tremendous amount of wealth.

If you were in the position of Mr. Kaunda and the few people that are employed by the mines at relatively high wages (I do not know what the figure is in Northern Rhodesia but I would wager that it is at least five times what the average person in Northern Rhodesia is able to earn) came up with a demand for a 20 per cent increase in wages, what would you do? Ten years ago Mr. Kaunda, being a Nationalist, would have been backing the demand solidly, but if you were in his position, would you now be backing that movement or would you be saying, "If the copper mines are making extra profits, these belong to the economy of Northern Rhodesia and we will use this money to build roads, to develop agriculture, to build schools, hospitals and so forth?" What would you do?

Mr. BINDER: The question is unfair. You see, if the issue is what ought to be done, then it is unfair to put me in the position of Mr. Kaunda or in the position of a miner. I have to stay in my own position and ask what ought to be done. That is why I wanted to have you refer your recommendations to a particular value.

Mr. LEWIS: What do you think ought to be done in your own position?

Mr. BINDER: Well, of course, I may feel that I do not even care that the state of Zambia continue in existence. You are setting a framework for your social responsibility which is that of the state of Zambia. Within the framework of that assumption one might say, then, that in order for the state to persist it might be necessary to have some source of revenue, but there are a host of other questions. For example, if unemployment is increasing in the non-modern sector and at the same time, by this capital-intensive development, the national product is increasing at the rate of 9 per cent per annum, is it not possible, or conceivable, that if you hold wages down in the modern sector, the national product will not increase so fast?

Mr. LEWIS: In fact, it might increase faster. The trouble with these economies is that they are increasing the national product by importing machinery. The thing does not make any sense whatsoever. Jobs which could be done by people are being done by machines which are imported, so wealth is being created to send away when the same wealth could be created by labor and kept in the economy. It does not make any sense at all.

Mr. BINDER: I am not certain that your assertion as to the "same wealth" is correct. Machines are far more efficient. I remember the Harbison-Ibrahim volume on Egyptian industry and the testimony of the man-agers of Egyptian industry that the machines are much more efficient than the men.[7] The managers want the machines and they feel that they can trust the machines more than they can the men.

Mr. LEWIS: Of course the profit is greater and this is why they put them in. Let me give you a concrete example. A major political issue in Jamaica today, and for the last five years, is the loading of bananas on the ships. Bananas are loaded on ships by hand in Jamaica and they are taken to Bristol where they are unloaded by machinery at half the price it takes to load them.

Wages have gone up and up and up in the banana-loading industry because they are chasing the bauxite wages and now it has reached the point where the banana industry of Jamaica is being squeezed. It is not itself a very efficient industry, and it cannot afford to pay these high wages for loading bananas. The farmers are threatening to load the bananas themselves rather than go on paying these wages, and they have demanded the right to import machinery. The machinery will do it much more cheaply than the people, but all that would happen is that income which could be used to support some people in Jamaica will instead be used to support the makers of machinery in Birmingham. Now, what, sense does that make to the people in Jamaica?

Africa: Mining and Education

Mr. KREININ: I believe your recommendation is sound, and apropos of Mr. Binder's point, it is equivalent to restoring development which takes account of factor proportions in the economy. If an economy with surplus labor develops, taking account of relative factor endowments, it should introduce less capital-intensive industries, thereby increasing both output and employment at the same time. This however, may not be possible where mining industries are the main natural resource. By their very nature mining operations are capital-intensive and I am not sure that substitutabil-ity is possible there. That is, I am not sure that you could mine very well with less capital-intensive technique.

If this is the case, then obviously the rent factor exists and should not accrue to labor. That is, the share of labor should be the same share which would have accrued to it had development proceeded along lines that are more in accordance with factor proportions. I think your recommendation would in a sense bring that about by, so to speak, spreading the investments over the economy, and it is for this reason that I do not think even the University of Chicago people should object to it, because It essentially eliminates market imperfections.

Now, concerning the problem of unemployment in Africa, with which I have some familiarity, I would say that it is not really an increase in unemployment but a transfer from disguised to overt unemployment. What you said about the type of education that the Africans receive *is* probably true, but that is only a minor factor. It Is not only rural education that Is not oriented toward retaining them in rural life, but the elementary education which prepares people for the professions is also at fault.

I was involved in technical assistance studies in Africa and one of the proctors was very upset because in order to be a certified bricklayer in Africa, students had to pass the London examinations, which meant that they had to spend a third of their time learning how to construct fireplaces; no bricklayer in Africa will ever construct a fireplace.

This is just a side point, but I think the kind of education they receive at the elementary level does affect the "school leavers" to some extent. It may not be the major part of the problem, but it cannot be ignored.

Alternatives to Capital-Intensive Mechanization

Mr. SCHWARTZ: Professor Lewis, you spoke before about, I think you called it the fundamental change, primarily in innovation, or at least in innovation with respect to relative factor supply proportions, which at present is bringing about situations in which smaller and smaller additions to employment result from a given amount of investment. I would like to ask to what extent you think this change has been, and to what extent do you think this need be, "so fundamental," and. I have in mind three things, particularly:

First, to what extent have the countries promoted, and to what extent could the countries themselves promote, policies facilitating the adaptation of machinery that would be somewhat less capital-intensive, and somewhat less labor-saving, as I believe Japan did to some extent in the nineteenth century, the late nineteenth century?

Second, could not some international agency loans be shaped towards this purpose?

Third, to the extent that a fair amount of the new industrial expansion in these countries (certainly at this stage) has resulted from either foreign investment which has been trying to forestall the loss of a market, or exchange licensing aimed at a similar objective (and thus which is rather inevitable), could there not be more in the way of requirements that such foreign capital be permitted to enter only if certain changes are made so that some or all of it contributes to less labor-saving and more labor-using than formerly?

All three of these are possibilities. My supposition is that these things have not been done to a very great extent, but might there not be major possibilities here? What is so fundamental about the nature of innovations if you set up important financial incentives in an effort to redirect innovational developments, either re-adapting given machinery or developing new machinery? High wages in relatively labor-abundant economies need not lead to the same degree of substitution of labor as in the past, if there are additional varieties of machinery which permit the selection of alternatives other than a highly capital-intensive operation when it becomes too costly to employ a highly labor-intensive operation.

Mr. LEWIS: You do not have to create new machinery to solve this problem. The incentive is very simple, and I am amazed that what I am saying apparently is not accepted.

Let us take the bauxite industry in. the West Indies. The removal of bauxite in the West Indies is an industry that is something like 50 years old. If the bauxite industry had not had to pay the rate of wages which other industries have to *pay*, it would not; have mechanized so rapidly. The sugar industry, which has now thrown out half of its workers, is 300 years old in the West Indies. It has only mechanized at this rate because wages have gone up so rapidly. But apart from those industries, I think we really need to investigate the type of problem of which India is an example.

Compare what has happened in India over the last ten years with what has happened in Japan, for instance, or any other developing country that you can think, of In the nineteenth century. There has been an enormous investment in India, a big increase in output and so forth, and extraordinarily little impact on employment, and it is perfectly clear that if the Indians go on at the present rate they will never catch up with their labor surplus, and they will become worse and worse off.

Mr. FATOUROS: A footnote to the remarks of Mr. Schwartz, I think there have been some attempts to induce labor-intensive development, first, in the case of China where, of course, we do not know if there was any choice; then, Algeria in a recent foreign investment law gives special incentives to industries employing a certain number of workers, although this may relate to the size of the firm as much as to its labor-intensive character.

Mr. BARANSON: I think you have made a very basic point on this matter of rapidly rising wages, and its influence upon the inhibitions to development. In the first place, rapidly rising wages contribute to the burgeoning of cities, and in the second place they aggravate the balance-of-payments problem; and. as to this business of technological choice, they intensify capital-intensive choices.

I would suggest that one of the differences between Japan and India is that. Japan is a developed country in the sense that it can make a choice between a labor-intensive and a capital-intensive technology, and India has much greater difficulty in doing that. I think the reason is that Japan is more advanced industrially and socially capable of adapting various techniques. I was doing a study on Diesel engine manufacture, and in the case of Japan they could take *a* part and break it down into 21 labor-intensive processes—in the United States it is produced by two machines, two processes. India cannot do that. It does not have the engineers, it does not have the technical draftsmen, it does not have the relationship between the production plant and the bureaucracy in New Delhi.

Japan adapted labor-intensive techniques as an interim measure, because it would take a year or two to buy more mechanized equipment, whereas India has difficulty in adapting either alternative.

I have only one exception to your thesis. I think your thesis is a very fundamental one—this whole business of rapidly rising wages and the fact that it is inducing aggravations to the development process—but I would not overlook the basic nature of underdevelopment and the fact that the choice is not so open ss you would suggest about labor-intensive technology.

India cannot make the choice, even with the wage differential, and this is the important qualification I would make to your thesis, that the wage differential in itself Is not the thing that places the choice and suggests that it therefore should be; In other words, if you hold down wages, they will then have the alternative of choosing labor-intensity. I think India is a long way off from that, much different than Japan was 50 years ago or today; it is a long way off from having a developed stage of society in which they can make the kind of choices you are talking about, despite wage differentials.

Mr. LEWIS: I agree with you where this choice involves innovation, where they have to sit down and invent a way of making the part in 20 pieces instead of one. That I would agree with. There are other choices, however, that do not involve innovation, and of course, they have made these choices.

In India some of the dams are being built by huge bulldozers and other dams are being built by people carrying buckets of mud on their heads. Choices do exist. I am not disagreeing with anything you say, but some of the choices that could be made are not made when wages go up.

Mr. KREININ: There is also a choice between industries, not only within industries. For example, why should India manufacture Diesel engines? Why not textiles, or something like that?

Mr. BARANSON: This is part of the business of developing a heavy industrial capability. You either do it or you do not.

Mr. BINDER: How would you set up a program for research whereby one could prove that higher wages led to capitalization rather than the other way around?

I get the idea that the culture of the manager in some of the underdeveloped areas is such, judging again from the Middle East and some reports on the Near East, that he prefers machines to people and that if it is not going to be too much more expensive he would rather have a machine than bother with all of these people, and the political aspects, of course, are Important, too. If you do not have people, you just have machines, you do not have too many problems about managing the people. I have, therefore, *a* tendency toward hypothesizing that it is the purchase of labor-saving machinery which runs ahead of increasing wages.

Mr. LEWIS: This is true marginally, I would say, but to answer your question specifically as to how one would set up a research program, fortunately there are a number of Industries in the underdeveloped countries which are quite old and which are mechanizing, and we can find out why they are mechanizing.

The governments in some of these territories are resisting mechanization and therefore the industries have to produce data. Take, for example, the West Indies. We know year by year exactly what the situation is with regard to mechanization in the sugar industry, because government after government is fighting it. We know year by year what the situation is in the banana industry, and we know year by year what the situation is in the bauxite industry, so it is possible to do research on particular industries and find out exactly why they are mechanizing.

Now, what you say is also an incentive to mechanization, that it is nicer not to have to deal, with so many chaps, but on the other hand, if wages were not so high it would be more profitable to do it with more chaps, and if capitalists are as rapacious as all that, if It is more profitable to do with more chaps, they will do with more chaps rather than the machines.

Differential Growth Rates

Mr. MORGAN; I wonder if I might go back to the first data that Professor Lewis gave us on the growth rates in the 1950's as reported by the United Nations statistics; they are very high indeed. Four point one (4.1) was the average for Africa, with a maximum 5.2 per cent in West Asia. My impression is that the average is higher than that for high-income countries in general (with some considerable exceptions) and that even after you subtract the higher rates of population growth in low-income areas, you come out with the judgment that the gap in standard of living between low and high-income areas is no longer increasing perceptibly, Perhaps it is even shrinking.

If so, the change is remarkable. The world is reversing a trend that has been going on for centuries—three or four centuries at least. It is so remarkable that it is almost unbelievable. One is impelled to ask whether the data are accurate or whether we are being fooled. Assuming the data are accurate, I should, like to ask a supplementary question. If it is true that the trend has been suddenly changed in the 1950s, is it possible that this might have been due to the upheavals of war, to the movement of armed forces and refugees, which have brought a temporary stimulus to growth, rather than a new secular trend?

Mr. LEWIS: Well, let us take the developed countries: It is true that the growth rate of the United States and Canada and Great Britain is low, but the growth rate of Western continental Europe in the same period would be of the same order of magnitude or even higher than the figures the U.N. gives for underdeveloped continents. The French growth rate is fantastic and the Italian growth rate and the West German growth rate are fantastic, also. I think if you take Western Europe, it has been increasing at this kind of rate or faster, and it is really only Britain, America and Canada that have been below it,

I too was surprised by the high rates in the underdeveloped countries. West Asia one understands; these are the oil areas plus Israel, India is about 4 per cent, which is not bad. Pakistan, perhaps, is a little less than that, Malaya is very high. Thailand, it is reported, is doing quite well. Taking all this into consideration, I do not know of any reason to query the rate they have given for Southern Asia.

The rate I find difficult to comprehend is the African rate. The figures produced in the U.N. survey I was quoting from do not accord with earlier figures produced by the Economic Commission for Africa, but when somebody writes down a figure and says, "This is the rate of growth of the African economy between 1950 and 1960," you and. I know that there has been a lot of messing about with figures. (Laughter.)

Let us take these countries that have achieved this high rate and see what it is associated with. The big failure is in agriculture. The growth of output of agriculture is probably 2 to 3 per cent, or barely keeping up with the population growth, but on the other hand there have been enormous increases in mining output throughout the underdeveloped countries, not merely the output of oil, but iron, bauxite and all kinds of minerals, and the rate of growth of manufacturing has been extraordinarily high. Very many countries have seen a growth of manufacturing output of 8 or 9 per cent. They are starting from quite low levels of manufacturing, perhaps 10 per cent of the GNP, but it all comes into the picture, and therefore, it. is not really difficult, to accept a 4 per cent rate of growth, certainly not in Asia; and it is certainly possible for some economies of

Africa, where a 4 per cent rate of growth is not at all out of the question. Africa as a whole, it seems to me, is a little more difficult to accept on that basis.

Mr. HOLT: You presented a comparison, Dr. Lewis, with the kind of development that occurred in eighteenth- and nineteenth-century Europe, where factories grew up in barns and schools and rather out-of-the-way places; I got the impression from this comment that it might be desirable in developing countries today if there were less ostentation in the buildings and less concern for glory for the politicians and the architects. Were you also implying that conditions could be improved if there were a greater proportion of investment in the private sector?

Mr. LEWIS: Well, these fellows certainly are too prestige-minded, and this has a very high cost,

Mr. HOLT: Would not one of the solutions be to transfer some of this investment into the private sector?

Mr. LEWIS: I am merely pointing out that money goes much less far today than it used to go in the underdeveloped countries because of the difference in the channels through which it flows.

Export Development

Sister THOMASINE: Dr, Lewis, two years ago at one of these conferences I asked Professor Ellsworth what he would recommend in the way of increasing exports from Latin America.[8] He came over to me afterwards and said, "I did not answer your question. Sister, and I am not sure now that I could," I wonder now if you could answer it? If the export industry should increase in countries which, we will say, are typically or maybe at. least partially agricultural, what can they increase and to whom will they sell it?

Mr. LEWIS: Well, this is a different subject, is it not?

Sister THOMASINE: I know, but you said that they had chronic deficits, and one of the ways of reducing the chronic deficits would be to increase their exports. I just wondered if you had ever given that any thought?

Mr. LEWIS: Yes. I have given it a lot of thought. The development of Latin America in the last 15 years or so, like the development of India, has been based to a considerable extent on import substitution which has its limits because you must have imports for which to substitute,

Brazil has had a very rapid increase of industrial production based on import substitution. It has had very great opportunities for doing this.

If you have import substitution as a basis for your development, you do not run into balance-of-payments problems.

Chile is a highly developed economy. It has run through its possibilities for import substitution and cannot continue developing at a high rate now unless it can export, because the only alternative to developing through exports is developing through balanced growth, and for balanced growth you must have all of the resources required to meet a variety of growing demands. This is impossible in a country like Chile, and therefore it must expect its development to lead to higher imports which have to be met *by* higher exports.

Therefore, countries that have run through the import substitution possibility simply have to get back to looking at the export market. Now, in Chile their principal export has been copper, which has been greatly handicapped for years by an annual inflation of 20 per cent, which is a very serious handicap to any kind of export industry. The other thing that they have to do, and the thing to which the Chilean economists attach the greatest importance, is to increase the productivity of their agriculture. As you know, the structural inflation theory is that as the economy develops, there is a greater demand inside the economy for agricultural products and it is the failure of agriculture to respond, because of the absence of land reform, as they see it, that creates the major balance-of-payments problem, and so on.

The whole situation would be eased if these countries could succeed in licking the agricultural problem, just to meet the home demand, let alone the external demand.

Now, what about the longer run future? This is really outside tonight's frame of reference, but you have asked the question. As you know, in the 1950s world trade has been expanding at phenomenal rates, 6 or 7 per cent per annum, much greater than anything for the last hundred years, but the expansion of the exports of the underdeveloped countries has not been of this order of magnitude, and also world trade in primary products of the kinds that the underdeveloped countries produce has expanded only by 3.5 per cent per annum,

Some people who are concerned about the future of the underdeveloped countries, and who have been trying to calculate what the trade of the underdeveloped countries would be at a 5 per cent rate of growth of national output, have come up with very large increases in imports as being necessary; and do not see where the exports will come from. The way they look at it is that in the past the main market for the underdeveloped countries has been the developed countries and if the developed countries are only going to increase their demand by 3 per cent, where will the underdeveloped countries manage to get the foreign exchange to pay for what they need to import?

For myself, I think this is a kind of myopia, because it leaves out the possibility of the underdeveloped countries trading with each other. As the underdeveloped countries expand, one of the reasons why their import need goes up is because they need more raw materials and food products of various kinds; these they could get from each other. Even if what they want is machinery, or insofar as what they want is machinery, there is an easy answer. Because the future of India depends (given the particular set of natural resources India has and does not have) upon India's becoming a major producer of steel and machinery. So even if the developed countries were to sink under the sea, you can foresee the underdeveloped countries building up a very large trade among themselves in commodities of all kinds, both raw material commodities and. industrial commodities. This is the thing which, it seems to me, is left out in all of these calculations which tell us that the underdeveloped countries are really sunk because the developed countries have such a slow population growth, and so forth.

My general answer to you, therefore, is that if the underdeveloped countries did indeed look at their exports again (they have neglected them, they have allowed export costs to rise and rise and rise beyond what the world market will permit) those that need to would find that this was an opportunity for growth. But this is a separate and large subject.

Education, Employment, and Expectations

Mr. ANDERSON: Supposing you could design an educational system for these developing countries—waiving, now, the question of whether what, you would design would be politically acceptable—can you design an educational system which would function under the dual and to some degree contradictory conditions that A, it has to be run by ha lf-trained and half-literate teachers, and that B, it must, produce a sizable cohort of people who can match world standards for secondary school performance and entrance to universities?

If you consider that question, this idea that, there is some new content of education that is going to solve these problems will turn out to be more difficult

Mr. WILLIAMS: I have a comment to make and a ques tion to ask. They relate to this question of the relationship between the expansion of education and unemp l oyment.

First, this problem of urban unemployment seems to be one that has been with us for an enormously long time. In Africa, taking on the one hand Ghana, which has very extensive educational facilities, and on. the other hand Togoland, which has very limited educational facilities, it was in Togoland and not in Ghana that: the unemployed threw out the President, Certainly, even if one looks at the history of the Gold Coast Itself, I think one finds continually the complaints of colonial governors that the problem about having an educational system is that you get a drift of people, to the towns even though, the educational system is extremely limited and by contemporary standards an inadequate one.

My own feeling is that the reason people drift to the towns is because this is where opportunities are. If you extend educational opportunities, what happens possibly Is that you get a slightly higher level, in educational terms, of unemployed in the towns. But it is not that, the education itself creates a problem. If one attempted to establish some kind of operational hypothesis about this, and relate those areas in which this problem of urban unemployment is serious to the existence of educational facilities, I do not think you would find a very good correspondence.

The only area in which I have any personal experience. other than West Africa, is Central America; my feeling is that the problem of urban unemployment is, let us say, as serious in Guatemala City as it is in Accra, and yet. Guatemala is characterized by an educational system in which, while very many people go to the first grades, very few people go beyond the third grade, I think that the primary impact of expanding educational opportunity is not that it creates a greater degree of unemployment per se, but that it may possibly create a somewhat more highly educated level of unemployment.

To establish the view that education itself creates unemployment, or is a great stimulus to unemployment, one would have to show that people who have received an education have a rather unrealistic notion of the probabilities of receiving employment. Phillip Foster of the University of Chicago has an interesting piece discussing the expectations of Ghanaian school-leavers which shows that in fact; they had really quite sensible notions of what results they might expect,

It is, of course, true that because the opportunity exists in the city, a person might go there for a little while and even expect temporary unemployment on the off-chance of getting a good permanent job later. In this sense he is something like a graduate student who will stay around Chicago or Cambridge rather than go to Hopscotch Junior College, because he knows that once he goes there he is not going to get away.

In the same way, I think some people who have had some education will go to the city rather than go to the farm, because if they go on a farm they know they are not going to get away. In terms of the amount of education, I think it is probable that increasing the amount of education simply means that what you have is middle-school unemployed laborers, as you now have in Accra, instead of third-form unemployed school-leavers, as you had in Accra 30 years ago.

Mr. LEWIS: What I was talking about was societies in which the entry into education has shot up from 20 per cent to 80 per cent in ten years. I was not saying anything against education or pretending that education is the major cause of this unemployment. I was saying that if you have a community in which, over the. course of ten years, you increase the entry from 20 per cent. to 80 per cent, you get into trouble because the expectations of the 80 per cent are the same as the expectations of the 20 per cent and cannot be fulfilled.

But over and above this, your view of the situation in Accra and mine are not, by far, the same. When I was in Accra advising the government, the ministers were extremely bothered, about the stream of people that were coming out of the schools, and this was the reason why, at very great expense, they established something called the Builders Brigade; it was primarily to deal with what they regarded as a very serious problem. Exactly the same problem exists now in both the Eastern and Western regions of Nigeria. It is not due to education. It is due to the acceleration in such a short period of time, and it is only to be found in the countries where they have made this particular effort.

Labor Unions

Mr. NASH: I spent about a decade disinterring the hidden sociology in every economic statement. (Laughter.)

Let me see if I have the sociology of Dr. Lewis's recommendations correct. It seems to me that we have a built-in political-economic villain in the form of trade unions which not only keeps productive wages high but accounts for this phenomenon of the less productive modern industries chasing after those; your hypothesis for Japan sociologically was that the trade unions are schizophrenic; they push the worker up in the modern sector, they keep him down in the lower sector. I think that is one of your important sociological assumptions: that the trade unions in these developing countries must be in opposition to the government, whereas in Japan thev must be an arm of the government. Would you comment on this?

Mr. LEWIS: I gave three different reasons why this is happening, of which the trade unions were one. The second was the social conscience, which is stronger in the second half of this century than it was in the first half of the nineteenth century, so even in situations where there are no trade unions, the employers regard it as their duty to keep paying higher and higher wages if they can. The third situation is linked with the second, that the nationalist governments of new states have been putting pressure on foreign employers. No capitalist finding himself in Northern Rhodesia or Trinidad is going to refuse to pay high wages if he can afford to do it, whether there are trade unions or not, because the government is breathing down his neck. That is the third reason.

Mr. BINDER: You squeezed out the middle one, now.

Mr. LEWIS: No. The second is an independent fact, too. Why, in Japan, do the modern capitalists pay such high wages if they do not have to?

Mr. GINSBURG: Well, there are Japanese labor unions, and they are increasingly effective, but they are less effective than they may be in some other places largely because there are other institutions within Japanese society that regulate economic behavior. I would say also that industrialists in Japan are paying increasingly higher wages because they do require ever higher levels of skills. Literacy is not enough.

Mr. LEWIS: I really do not think that the sociologist should be surprised that in the twentieth century the social conscience of capitalists is different from what it was in the nineteenth, and they behave differently. This is happening all over the world. This is not true only in the underdeveloped countries. You mean you do not find this in the United States?

Mr. GINSBURG: I find that they are as rapacious as they ever were.

Mr. WHITEFORD: I wanted to ask a question to see whether I was coming to a logical conclusion as the result of what you said. In the modern segment of the economy, where labor apparently is well organized in unions and is asking for raises, you would recommend that the raises not be given in order that income or profits would flow back into the government and be distributed on a wider basis.

This, it seems to me, and I am not an economist, would be possible only if this were private enterprise and if the tax level was high enough to put the money back into the general treasury. Even so, you would run a very great risk of still having considerable profit so that an increasingly wider range in income would develop between those who owned the companies and the labor force which was operating on a set level of income.

I come to the conclusion, therefore, and I want to know if this is correct, that the onlv way really to balance this situation and keep the money going back into the. general economy is for the government to own the industries?

Mr. LEWIS: That is certainly a way, but do not forget the 50 per cent corporation tax and the possibilities of partnership arrangements between governments and new Industries opening up in their countries and so forth, of which there is a great deal,

The thing we are talking about now Is the attitude of governments in underdeveloped countries to their trade unions, which is one of political crisis, especially In Africa, but. not exclusively in Africa. In Africa government after government put into power by the trade unions turns round and kicks the. trade unions in the teeth. It is a real problem, and there is no simple, easy solution to It.

Chairman BLANKSTEN: I once attended a meeting in which we had such a spirited and heated discussion that we ran far overtime in the session until finally somebody said, "Let's forget about what we are here for, and let's get back on schedule." (Laughter.)

We should have adjourned about a quarter of an hour ago. I am not going to try to summarize the discussion tonight. I think we have done a good job this evening of opening up a number of avenues which I hope we will be able to pursue during the next day-and-a-half of our sessions.

Notes

1. United Nations. Department of Economic and Social Affairs. *World Economic Survey*, 1963 (New York, 1964), p. 19.
2. Unied Nations, Statistical Office. *Statistical Year Book, 1962* (New York, 1963), p. 58.
3. Jamaica. Department of Statistics. *Census of Jamaica*, 1960, vol. II, part H.
4. For a recent survey, see the articles by E. J. Hobsbawm and R. M. Hartwell in the *Economic History Review*, April 1964.
5. Kazushi Ohkawa, *The Growth Rate of the Japanese Economy since 1878* (Tokyo: Kinokuniya Bookstore Co., Ltd., 1957).
6. For an arithmetical example, see my paper, "A Review of Economic Development," American Economic Review, May 1965.
6. For an arithmetical example, see my paper, "A Review of Economic Development," American Economic Review, May 1965.
7. Frederick Harris Harbison and I, A. Ibrahim, *Human Resources for Egyptian Enterprises* (a project of the International Relations Section, Princeton University; New York: McGraw-Hill, 1958).
8. Ref. to Prof. P, T. Ellsworth, Dept. of Economics, University of Wisconsin, commenting at Midwest. Research Conference on Obstacles to Economic Development in Underdeveloped Areas, Allerton House, University of Illinois, May 18-20, 1962 Proceedings not published.

Session II

Underdeveloped Countries in the World Economy

Chairman BINDER: The procedure that we are to follow in these sessions will be that we will impose upon the discussion leader to make the initial presentation, and we expect him to put forth some bright and interesting ideas that concern him and his own research in recent years, months, days, hours, and minutes, and to present any questions which he *may* have on his mind and matters of general interest to us bearing on the topic. Hopefully, these ideas would have some form to them but not close off the rest of us from plunging in with ideas of our own and perhaps capturing the ball and taking it off in different directions in terms of our own interests. It is an open-minded kind of goal that we have.

The role of the discussants, after the opening remarks of the discussion leader, is, of course, critically important in that they are to set some of the direction as well as having the wonderful opportunity of getting the first potshots at the discussion leader, and hopefully they will add increased form to our deliberations. After each of the discussants has had an opportunity to add his own ideas to those of the discussion leader, then we will have an open discussion which will involve not merely questions but also lengthier statements of your own on the matters that have been brought before us.

Now, Professor Karl de Schweinitz, the discussion leader, studied at Dartmouth where he got his Bachelor's degree in International Relations and later took a doctorate at Yale in Economics. He is a Professor of Economics at Northwestern University at the present time, and he has just returned from Japan where he has spent a year doing research on economic development and political change since 1868. He is the author of the book, *Industrialization in Democracy*, which was published by the Free Press in 1964.

The two discussants are Professor Raymond Randall and Professor Andrew Whiteford. Dr. Randall is a member of the Department of Government at the University of Indiana, and his interest is in the decline of rationalism in Indonesia. He has spent some time in Indonesia in the public administration project which is being run under the auspices of the Department of Government of Indiana University.

Professor Whiteford is the head of the Department of Anthropology at Beloit College. He is associated with the Logan Museum. He has just had a wonderful year in Spain, which research experience has just been added to his previous research experience in Latin America, Colombia and Mexico, where he has done extensive studies on urban affairs, particularly the delineation of social class.

Mr. de SCHWEINITZ: Thank you.

There is and always will be a tension between mac-rocosmic and microcosmic approaches to knowledge, between those who have a bird's-eye view of detail and those who have a worm's-eye view of system. While the one often seems to do violence to the empirical and institutional data of the real world, the other sometimes seems to be engaged interminably in collecting unfocused facts and information. Happily, the two approaches are indispensable for one another and so will continue in sibling rivalry, whatever one might, say about either one.

I do not make these observations as a preface to an exegesis on research methodology for underdeveloped countries. Rather they are intended to prepare the way for a confession of my preference for the macrocosraic approach. The remarks that follow, therefore, should be compensated for this bias.

My bias, no doubt, is appropriate, for the subject of this morning's discussion. "Underdeveloped Countries in the World Economy" is nothing if not a broad topic. Indeed I suspect that it is a kind of academic come-on designed to trap the wary professor. After all, who will admit he doesn't have something to say about it?

Let me start by paying my respects to economics. In recent years it has been belabored, both inside and outside the ranks, for failing to solve the enigma of development. The realization that the non-Western world has not responded to economic parameters in the same manner as the Western world in its initial industrialization has somehow been disillusioning; the tools of economic analysis no longer seem quite so powerful as they did when confined to their indigenous habitat.

Yet without economics it would have been impossible to map the terrain of the underdeveloped countries. The innovations of the 1930's, especially in the realm of macroeconomics, have subsequently borne fruit in the measures of income and product by which we now can establish rough approximations of stages or degrees of development. It goes without saying that we never can have enough data of this sort. It is essential for knowing how we stand, whether we have moved forward or backward, and for estimating the magnitude of the tasks before us.

Moreover, economic models at least form a skeletal framework to which one may attach the institutional flesh, sinew, and muscle essential for its motion, Analysis of saving, investment, and technological change, for example, highlights the role of the entrepreneur in development. If he has, in point of fact, not been sufficiently active in the underdeveloped countries, or has not labored in an environment conducive to growth projects, economics can hardly be held responsible.

But contemplating the growing number of underdeveloped countries in the world economy, I am struck, if I may now be provocative, by the large gap between economics and the other disciplines. It would, of course, be far from the truth to say that the tasks of economics have been, completed, but there is certainly a kernel of truth in the notion that responsibility for explaining how the mechanics of development, so copiously described by economists, are to be set in motion now rests with the sister disciplines. Let me acknowledge immediately that: this statement is unfair.

I once heard Kenneth Boulding berating a group of political scientists for not having solved the problem of war, when economists had solved the problem of unemployment. There is not much doubt but that problems of inducement and motivation are a good deal more difficult to explain than analyses of mechanisms. Nonetheless, this does not deny that the most important areas of research in the underdeveloped countries lie outside economics.

Judging by the interest evoked among students of underdeveloped countries by the recent works of David McClelland and Everett Hagen, I gather that the views I have expressed here about, the limits of economics are widely shared. *The Achieving Society*[1] and *On the Theory of Social Change*[2] provide a convenient point of departure for my remarks about research needs outside of economics. For while I applaud the imagination, verve, and industry with which McClelland and Hagen have explored the murky realm of the individual psyche, I am far from being, convinced that we all ought to become psychologists or psychoanalysts. I suspect, indeed, that their work is informed by a search for first-causes which can no more be tracked down than the fountain of youth. Further, their preoccupation with the why of development tends to divert attention from the how.

Falling back now on my methodological bias, it seems to me that the most fruitful area for research lies in the organizational, macrocosmic dimension, specifically in the area of politics. I have the impression that in the underdeveloped countries there is no lack of willingness to work, no fear of making money, perhaps even no scarcity of entrepreneurs.

The problem is the absence of an institutional context capable of focusing the potential energy and drives of individuals and groups on the production of the goods and services which generate sustained growth. Moreover, the stimuli for economic development are ubiquitous to the point of being overbearing. They no doubt are not so effective as they once were in transmitting the forces for autonomous industrialization.

The late Professor Nurkse has made us all aware of how the changing structure of demand in the advanced economies has tended to reduce the rate at which the markets for the primary products of the underdeveloped economies grow, thus threatening them with a perennial balance-of-payments problem. Nor are these countries likely to attract private capital or a skilled professional, technical, and administrative migrant population. Yet, the demonstration effect broadcasts the glories of material well-being to all and to at least a few a burning desire to develop the potential of their country's resource endowments.

The drive for independence itself in the formerly colonial world is a manifestation of the stimuli for development. However mistaken they may be in their expectations, the leaders of the new countries in Asia and Africa believe that independence places destiny in their hands and that they can consciously achieve what so many of the old nations in the Western world did unconsciously through the private market economy.

But why do I single out politics as the most important sector on the research front in underdeveloped countries? Because, as suggested above, the responsibility for surmounting the obstacles to development now seems to fall on government. Whether these obstacles are sociological, economic, or political, the systematic use of the collective and legitimate power of society is needed to clear them away.

I should quickly observe that I do not necessarily have in mind a Leviathan that dragoons and coerces the civil community into growing and modernizing, as, say, in Russia or China. But suppose that the difficulty in an underdeveloped country is the vast gulf between the elite and the masses which inhibits mobility and perpetuates a social order that ascribes roles and depreciates achievement criteria. Surely it is in the political realm that the initiative must be taken for modernizing these social conditions. And certainly there is plenty of evidence, as, say, in Latin America, that when a feudal elite retains a monopoly of political, power there is little progress in establishing the pre-conditions of development.

Or how is the underdeveloped country to cope with rural and urban idleness? Whether one attacks it from the demand or the supply side, i.e., providing jobs for the existing unemployed or training them for useful skills, government, as a minimum, must determine the investment priorities likely to bring about the desired result.

And most ineluctable of all, how is an underdeveloped country going to tackle any of these problems if it does not contain a widely held consensus which confers legitimacy on government and thus gives it leeway to deal with them in a systematic and rational manner, In countries that are not yet nations and bereft of the communion of national origins so useful in muting debilitating conflict, the first order of business must be the manufacturing of consensus. And this as often as not leads to domestic policies and foreign adventures which are not consistent with the needs of the country for economic development, at least in the short run. At a time when new countries are proliferating so rapidly in the wake of receding empires, this surely is the pre-eminent problem.

It seems to me that by now we have accumulated a tremendous amount of material which throws light on the relationship between politics and economic development. We have, in the first place, the historical experience of the Western world where industrialization took place in political systems stabilized within nation-states. Secondly, there is the brilliant performance of Japan where the leaders of the Meiji Restoration achieved an extraordinary tour de force in adapting traditional institutions to the formation of a modern state while shedding those customs and traditions which interfered with the economic mobilization of the society. Thirdly, the centrally administered economies in Russia, China, Yugoslavia, and Eastern Europe provide varied case studies of the consequences for modernization of an explicit commitment to the use of the coercive powers of the state to create an institutional environment conducive to growth. The non-incremental, Utopian deployment of political power in these societies can reveal a good deal about the limits of collective action. Fourthly, in the underdeveloped countries today, unhappily, there is no lack of examples of states which must devote a large part of their energy and resources to establishing the legitimacy of their political power. In the Congo, Indonesia, and South Vietnam one observes various approaches to this end, none of which can be said to confer growth benefits on the societies.

Out of this experience it ought to be possible to generate political theories of varying degrees of generality which could guide us in evaluating the prospects for the underdeveloped countries of the world. Indeed, if I were Commissar of Research, I would want, for the time being, to place more emphasis on theorizing than on collecting new data in case studies. I would urge Gabriel Almond to try again. I would also urge the country specialists to acquire new countries in new settings, i.e., Africanists to become Asianists and vice versa, in the hope that this broadening of interest and experience would stimulate the capacity for generalization.

Finally, I would want my political scientists to be insistent on the primacy of politics in their search for the how of development and riot be diverted by multifactor explanations giving equal weight to all factors. That may make good history, but does not always make good analysis. My instructions, then, are for the theorists to mobilize the role of political power and authority in explaining development, as David McClelland mobilized the "need for achievement" and Everett Hagen the "withdrawal of status respect."

Mr. WHITEFORD: In introducing opposing points of view at this particular point in our calendar, we could predict that Dr. de Schweinitz' emphasis upon the role of government would be emphatically opposed by many people—Barry Goldwater for example. We can, I think, all accept with sympathy Dr. de Schweinitz' desire to see political stability, and we can recognize this as a necessity for economic development. Certainly the situations in Southeast Asia, Latin America and Africa point up the very great importance of this factor. We can also agree, I think, with his recommendation or his stipulation that such e government not. be a dictatorship or some other kind of coercive force. This is a particular bias in our own case as we are committed to the fundamentals of democracy. Third, I think we can accept his basic assumption that the government must, as he says, contain a widely held consensus which confers legitimacy to deal with these problems.

Certainly on these three factors we can be in basic agreement, or at least I find myself in agreement with him. He also wants to concentrate research on the problems of how economic development and political stability can be attained and, at least temporarily, put in a secondary-seat research which is focused on the *why*. At the same time he proposes a de-emphasis upon what he calls multifactor explanations.

This is the point at which I, with my own particular anthropological bias, would raise questions and perhaps objections. Dr. de Schweinitz says that he has been provocative here and in some respects I get provoked,, which is exactly what I think should happen, because it appears to me that, in some regards, he has expressed desires for various things which may not fit together; at least there is going to be difficulty in attaining all of these things simultaneously, or even in rather rapid succession, without their interfering with each other, It appears to be assumed that the forces of government already have access to viable, dependable programs for the attainment of economic development; the only further need is for research to provide guidance in instrumenting them. It is suggested that we (the government) now know what should be done but not how to do it.

Professor Lewis has given us examples from the Barbados in regard to the unemployment situation. Here unemployment, became one of the major issues in the election; the party which had made unemployment an issue won the election and after putting its plans into effect discovered that it was dealing with something it really had not understood before it came to power. This is certainly one example of the kind of situation which can arise where a governmental organization decides that it has in mind a valuable program without knowing something about its actual roots. Perhaps our own farm program would equally suggest such a shortcoming. I am sure there is an unending number of situations that could be dredged up to give some valid suspicion to the assumption that the government really knew what it was trying to do or that what it was trying to do was actually in the best interests of the country.

The second assumption about which I would like to raise some question is that the government should or would dedicate itself primarily to economic development. The question immediately arises: "whose economic development?" Is there such a thing as general national, economic development, or in every kind of economic development are there certain sectors or segments of the population which become more economically developed than others? Who is in the driver's seat and who is going to derive the greatest amount of benefit from any particular economic development program which is put into operation?

There have been situations which raise questions in regard to this assumption of Professor de Schweinitz. For instance, in Latin America various governments have been forced into programs of land reform which are in the interest of national economic development, but which actually tend to reduce gross productivity. The governments, nevertheless, find themselves in a situation where the programs are *politically* necessary even if they do not attain the economic ends which it was hoped they might,

Part of this, of course, is involved in the attainment of the consensus that Dr. de Schweinitz desires, but the consensus which is attained might actually be pointed toward or be utilized for the development of other goals than the immediate economic goal which was the objective of the land reform program. He might well serve to prevent violent political revolution at the price, of reduced agricultural production.

The point has already been made several times, and could be documented almost unendingly, that all the people in a given nation or in a given society are not equally concerned with, nor equally convinced that, the improvement of gross national product is an immediately valuable end in itself. In other words, the ends which the government is trying to attain have to be made sensible to a considerable portion of the population for any sort of a consensus to be developed. This is difficult.

The third point is Dr. de Schweinitz' assumption that we now possess adequate information regarding *why* and can concentrate on the *how*, and also his rejection, or at least temporary rejection, of multifactor explanations. I realize that multifactor explanations always give the impression at the outset of complicating the issue, but it also seems to me that one of the reasons they give this appearance is that the issues actually are complicated. Any attempt we make to eliminate multifactoral explanations tends to oversimplify the problems with the danger of distorting them out of their reality. My multifactoral anthropological orientation insists that it is only from multifactoral exploration and investigation that the eventual solutions will come.

If there are going to be real solutions, we are going to have to take into consideration a very great number of the forces which are operating in any society, In order to develop the stability from which economic development may come we must know why the peasant feels he wants to own a piece of land before we. can convince him that, there is perhaps a better solution to his problems than simply possessing his own private plot. The same thing applies to the sentiments, and I am talking about feelings—the visceral reactions—of the *hacendado* who objects to giving up his land, or to the Indian who prefers his old ways of life to new forms under a government program.

What I am saying here raises the matter of the psyche that Mr. de Schweinitz mentioned because, after you get under the programs, after you get under the structure, the sentiments of the people involved are really of fundamental importance. We can only understand what motivates people, or why they reject or accept particular programs which government may propose, by a thorough exploration of the cultural context within which these people operate. This is my anthropological bias right out in the open.

The only alternative to some kind of extensive multifactor exploration, it seems to me, is some kind of authoritarian regime. This is no more desirable to Mr. de Schweinitz than it is to the rest of us, but it necessitates some sort of authoritarian regime which assumes that it knows what is best—on the basis of research or on the basis of some other factors—and decides to ignore the feelings of the ignorant populace, This way a program can be put into operation very rapidly, and a great number of changes can be introduced—perhaps successfully, We are well aware, as anthropologists, that, within the relatively short period of a generation, a great many sentiments can be changed also, but whether or not this is actually the "best" means of attaining the sort of ends with which we are concerned, is one of the issues raised by Professor de Schweinitz, Perhaps I have overinterpreted him; if I have, so much the better.

Mr. RANDALL: I am one of these people who is going to back into this from the microcosmic standpoint. My experience in the field of development administration comes from a very specific experience in Indonesia and a very enlightening and constructive experience immediately following that in the Philippines. Prior to that I was only incidentally exposed to this area in the form of public administration, but public administration as it is practiced by the federal government.

I am going to, if I may, give you some information that is more illustrative of the thesis presented here this morning than anything else. In terms of the decline of rationalism as I saw it in Indonesia, it was very much a puzzle to me as an amateur economist. It seems to me, however, that the Indonesians tend to approach, since 1952 at least, since the fall, of the Wilopo cabinet, everything in terms of the context of emotional nationalism. The only things that are really efficient, in Indonesia are the printing presses, and they approach the problem of economic planning, for example, from a very immature standpoint. It reminds me of the lady who went into the publisher and said, "What is the length of the average novel?" The publisher said, "Fifty thousand words," and she said, "Goody, goody, I'm done,"

The Indonesians constructed their eight-year plan on much the same premise. They got their independence on August 17, 1945, so they constructed their eight-year plan in terms of eight parts, seventeen volumes, 1,945 paragraphs. Now, this is a very puzzling kind of thing. We were assigned the job of training individuals in the civil service of the Indonesian government to try to develop a rational administrative base for the Indonesian government,

One of the things we ran into quickly was the emphasis upon ascriptive criteria as against achievement criteria for selecting people to come to the United States. We tried, as best we could to break this down, to try to get a broader base of selection for these people, on the thesis that a participant training program should communicate both hope and promise to those people who were not selected as well *as* to those who were selected, that both groups should understand the basis for either action in terms of the standards as they were derived for the selection of these people. This the Indonesians simply would not go along with. They were using the development of high talent manpower in Indonesia as a means of building personal empires, in my opinion, rather than in terms of building the country.

Now, in terms of a strategy that goes beyond what we know now in the field of development economics and development administration, I am much impressed, as I follow it, with Harbison's thesis on human capital formation, Harbison has a three-fold strategy, if I read him correctly. His strategy for the short run, or up to three or four years, is that of in-service training, of getting the expatriate institutions to do a good job of training individuals within their organization and trying to get a seeding effect from this training back into the community at large.

We estimated in Indonesia, for example, that the high-talent manpower need for the country in terms of executives and entrepreneurs was in the neighborhood of 30,000 people, something on that order of magnitude. Using the Harbison formula for a tactical supportive group, this would then give us something of the order of magnitude of 100,000 technicians.

This in itself prescribes a major effort in one of the areas mentioned in the paper this morning and that is that, of institution-building: institution-building in the form of universities to provide the foundation for future training, and institution-building in the form of training institutions that are capable of carrying on. this job. Just recently, an institution-building consortium has been established which will tackle this problem. This consists of Pittsburgh, Syracuse, and Indiana, and the direction for this institution-building consortium will come out of Pittsburgh. I think it holds a great deal of promise in terms of a new research approach and a new perspective on the problem of development administration and development economics.

General Discussion

Mr. de SCHWEINITZ: I would like to make a few comments about Professor Whiteford's comments on my opening remarks.

On the issue of whether government knows best, I do not take any position on this. I simply observe that, in the world today relative to the world of the nineteenth century government does seem to be playing a much more important role and apparently this is because the conditions confronting the underdeveloped economies are such that one does not get autonomous growth generated in the private sectors. I do not mean to suggest that in consequence of these conditions you have to have central planning. There are any number of policy measures that can be devised to generate development, but it seems to me that it is hare to deny that in the underdeveloped world today, government plays a role which it did not play in the nineteenth century.

Now, as far as the multifactor analysis is concerned, as an economist I am somewhat interested in economizing effort, and I think, if we are trying to develop the predictive capacity of the social sciences, we have to look at the relevant variables and select some that we think are more important. Just as in the nineteenth century I have some sympathy with a historical approach to economic development, so in this century I have some sympathy to some kind of political determinism because it seems to be the role of government, and the uses of political power are so much more important now than they were in a day when it was more reasonable to wait upon the private sector of the economy to generate development.

Chairman BINDER: We have before us a number of issues to which I will try to call your attention, I see some of the problems that have been raised in this way:

The problems of development which we want to see in the light of world economy, it has beer, suggested, might better be seen in the light of world political developments.

The international political scene was riot so much delineated but it was suggested as a possible source of some of the difficulties of development. Indeed, the approach to economic development was seen in this context with obstacles which suggest that there is perhaps some reality to looking at the political over against the economic rather than seeing these as two facets of the same thing. In other words, the question that has been raised here in the reification of the disciplinary and analytical differences between the political and the economic which I think was spoken to by Mr. White-ford in his own phraseology.

The central problem, though, if I understood it correctly, is that of an institutional framework by which development may proceed. The question which follows immediately from this is whether or not the international community, international agencies, the United Nations, or something like that, or simply the framework of international politics can supply an institutional framework which the underdeveloped countries themselves cannot supply.

The centrality of the role of government has been questioned and it has been suggested *by* one of our discussants that we must consider economic development as one possible value over against other values and that we must bear in mind the redistributive character of economic development, that some parts of the economy will be benefited over against others.

Unspoken explicitly but nevertheless implicit in our discussion has been the problem of trade between the underdeveloped countries themselves that was raised by Professor Lewis, the relations between the underdeveloped countries and the larger economic complexes, such as the European Common Market, and the possible success or failure of regional trading arrangements in Latin America or in the Arab world under the auspices of the Arab League.

The problem of whether heavy industry should precede light industry as a policy was touched on, politics, of course, having its bearing on this. Unspoken but quite implicit, I think, in the discussion has been the contrasting roles of private investors, of public, of other governments and international agencies—the three areas of responsibility, perhaps.

Finally, there is the problem of understanding how the world economy has changed. Professor Lewis has mentioned the sharp increase in foreign trade. I do not know how to read statistics, but it seems to me that there has been some sort of a boom in the price of raw materials—perhaps I shall be corrected on that by some knowledgeable people—in recent years and there has been apparently a great spread of technology and capacity for manufacturing into many countries, so that there is possibly some increased competition between the older manufacturing countries and some of the newer ones, requiring shifts in the orientation of the economies in the developed countries,

These, I think, are the problems that are before us.

Institution Building and Economic Development

Mr. NASH: One thing about social science is that it is the kind of enterprise in which you cannot keep a rousing hypothesis down. They keep cropping up.

I think in 15 years of work—and I think that is a real number—in the underdeveloped countries we have at least stopped talking about them as though they were a single species of poverty. In some underdeveloped areas the government is not even capable of carrying out the minimal requirements for the administration of peace and order, and to expect that kind of apparatus to undertake anything in the way of economic development, I think, is silly.

In some places the government is consensual, legitimate, but not dedicated to development, so the first thing I contemplate is to leave the disciplines aside, scan the real world again and see what kind of poor countries there are out there.

As to recommendations about government, it depends upon what kind of governments and where. If you have a theory as to what governments are viable enough to carry out projects in addition to governing, that would be of some use.

There is another thing I would like to comment on, There is still some echo or prerequisite thinking of framework, of institution building, and I think that is retrograde. Most of the cultural and. social change that goes along with economic development is coterminous in the product of development. There is the kind of thinking that says, "Let's change the society's culture and then we will develop." I do not think that has ever happened historically. Every country has developed its modern institutions in the act of modernizing, and you cannot build them first and then set them in motion. I think those two links ought to break at least one side of the box.

Mr. HARING: I want to question Mr. Nash on his comment that you do not build institutions and then set them in motion. Certainly there are such things as economic systems which governments legislate into being. True, governments may not consciously legislate them into being, and I would say historically they have practically never done so, fully consciously, knowing all that is going to happen or foreseeing it, Governments may often legislate economic systems into being by implication rather than specifically,

A *laissez-faire* government—if there is such an animal, the term is no good—but a government that thinks of itself as a *laissez-faire* government is simply delegating to others various areas of responsibility. Such delegation, even if it is unconscious, even if it is implicit, is nevertheless real because responsibility is made to lie with the community as *a* whole and the community as a whole is headed up in the government, which is a sort of a shorthand definition of government.

It seems to me, therefore, that the government, always, inherently, in any situation, at any time and place, is the primary piece of the puzzle. But this does not mean that governors understand this to be so, I am looking back, now, with the benefit of hindsight.

More specifically, with respect to this building of institutions, the public school system in the United States was not built, I take it, with the notion of modernizing the country to prepare for later stages of the Industrial Revolution. I am sure that was not in mind. There were other specific objects in mind that we know about, rather romantic notions of democracy and community and the common man, equalitarianism, and this sort of thing, which all got into it.

This is all history, but nevertheless, is not the net effect of this to have built institutions that made possible the later stages of industrial development? If I am right, then it seems to me what we do is look back to find out not merely what was consciously in people's minds, but what actually took place whether they knew it or not (insofar as we think we can know it) and then apply the lessons. So it seems to me that we do not have a terribly difficult, problem with respect to the relationship of economics to politics,

Mr. NASH: I did not mean to imply that political activities were not consequential. When I referred to building an institution, I meant that people do not sit. down and design and in the real social world build the institution they design. They are always in inadvertent consequences of a purpose of action, to lift a line from another intelligent, sociologist. Governments are in some countries extremely consequential, and I think, if we traced it out to the real world again, we would find that in most places, India excluded, the consequential acts of government have been anti-developmental rather than pro-developmental.

Regardless of the intention, the institutions they have built have resulted in the clustering of industry around capital cities and a whole brokerage system, licensing and money problems. The source of change, the things that stimulate and affect governments themselves, are the sources of stimulative effect of whole populations. The government is not a separate kind of animal anywhere that is moving to its own drum beats, so we have to get wider social causes than just what they write in five-year plans, because nobody acts on them, very much.

Mr. HOLT: I certainly would agree with Professor Nash if he is holding up a straw man of a country concerned with development deciding that it has to have a full-blown educational system "and this institutional development and that institutional development before it can get under way with the business of economic growth. On the other hand, if you are looking at the analysis of historical cases of development, it seems to me that you can observe certain developments in Tokugawa, Japan, which were institutionally prerequisite to the kind of changes that occurred at the time of the Meiji Restoration. We could do the same thing for England, in the seventeenth and early part, of the eighteenth century.

I think part of our theory has to recognize that. there are certain kinds of policies and certain, kinds of developments that require a certain base and that the lines of development are in some ways sequential-lines. If you are going to try to get to C. which is development, and you are at A, somehow you have to go to B, and if you attempt to go directly from A to C, you will probably be met with continual frustration.

In this sense, not in the sense of deliberately building institutions, some concern with requisites or prerequisites would seem to me to be realistic.

The Effectiveness of Theory

Mr. BLANKSTEN: I have three things I want to say in reaction to Professor de Schweinitz' paper. The first has to do with what has been called here the reification of interdisciplinary differences, and it strikes me that in *a* large sense he has done this. The Question that seems to me to be central when we gather together people of different disciplines focusing on a common problem is—What, is it we should be doing together?—and it seems to me that what Professor de Schweinitz has given us here in the relationship among disciplines, especially between economics and political science, is a kind of a division of labor in which one discipline says to the other, "You provide the stimulus and I'll watch the response." (Laughter.)

I am not sure that this is the best way we can work together on *an* interdisciplinary basis, even though, looking back, over some of my own work in this field, I suppose I have to admit I have been somewhat guilty of this. I like to assume that economic development is taking place and I have looked for the political implications or the political response. My first question would look, toward some more fruitful mechanism for interdisciplinary research here.

The second general point I want to make had to do with the kind of research that Professor de Schweinitz is urging on political scientists. I think that there is a kind of fallacy in the notion that the role of government is central in economic development, therefore it is up to the political scientist to do the research on what it. is that government should do to give the economist something else to watch happen. Do you really believe that the most important research contribution that political scientists can make is the production of data for policy recommendations which will enable governments to institute programs for the stimulation of economic change?

My third point, and with respect to this I feel more like a devil's advocate than in what I have said so far, has to do with the relative, priorities between further theoretical work on the one hand and the gathering of data on the other. We have now for many years been saying what Professor de Schweinitz says when he urges that we place more emphasis on theorizing than on collecting new data in case studies. I agree with that, but it seems to me I have been agreeing with it for at least 15 years. When I read back and try to count the number of conferences I have been involved in and the number of times those of *us* interested in underdeveloped areas have undertaken some project—it seems to me that it must be at. least the last 15 years—that we have all sat down together and said, "Look: we need more theory." As I say, I agree, but how long do we stay in this same box?

I notice that Professor de Schweinitz, in making this suggestion, says "for the time being." Looking at the title of this Conference, one of the things I understand we are going to try to do is reappraise some of the work in economic development. After something like 15 years of talking this way and thinking this way, is this kind of relationship between theory and data collection still the same, or do we move anywhere; and are there new ways of formulating this relationship; and are there new kinds of things we might do in each of these areas?

These are my three simple questions.

Sister THOMASINE: The innumerable theories and some of the policies that have been proposed over the last 15 years can and should be reassessed, especially in the case of priority, and I think Professor Lewis's reassessment is fruitful in the economic field. We do now know things we were just guessing at then. As yet we do not know too much, but we do know a few things that we were just guessing at in 1945 and 1947. That, is one part of the awakening of the economist, it seems to me, as regards economic development.

Currently, however, economists have become extremely aware of the non-economic factoral approach. The institutional question that has just: been raised seems to me to point to this other aspect, namely, that institutions can prove to be obstacles in the way of economic development. Institutions, and I am thinking of the one to which I belong, need a good nudge once in a while, and yet certainly institutions have to be preserved.

Mr. ANDERSON: I would assume that within the limits of the state of the art, the economist can lay down a list of some of the kinds of policies that need to be adopted by a government. For example, "Wage rates shall not be more than X percentage above such-and-such." From the political scientist I would like to hear some considered judgments on certain issues, distinguishing two things. One is the question that has been raised this morning and that always comes up, namely, what is the effect on economic development of having the entrepreneurs preponderantly civil servants?

Then there is an entirely different kind of question that relates to the bearing upon economic development of the degree or kind of political arousal of population, of the ways in which the interests of the sectors of the public are articulated in relation to government policy or are not, and so on. These are fairly specific issues which I may be stating in rather amateurish words, but I think the political scientists here ought, to tell us about them,

Mr. HARING: With respect to this matter of civil servants, I would like to ask the economist: what do you think of the Russian experience? Did anything suffer, aside from the damaging trial and error, which is always involved, but did anything suffer from the main actors being on the government payroll?

Mr. LEWIS: I very much want to follow up what Professor Anderson said because in advising quite a number of these countries, I have come to the conclusion that by comparison with the politics of economic development, the economics of economic development is really trivial; I say that remembering what John Stuart Mill said about economics.

The really serious problems unsolved are the political problems and unless we solve the political problems we cannot hope to see the kind of economic devel-opment we would like to see. Now, I keep wondering: what do the political scientists have to contribute, or what are they contributing in this field? One of the things one takes for granted is that these countries need to establish a decent civil service. The governments do not take it for granted because the party and the civil service are in many of these countries locked in struggle. But one must look further than this.

As I look around at these new countries, I see very many that have fallen into the hands of rogues. An enormous proportion of the governments of new countries consist of rogues who are feathering their own nests. Now, political scientists have been studying for two or three thousand years what is necessary in a society to prevent rogues from getting into political power, and they ought really to be able to contribute and help to create institutions—I do not know whether I can get *away* with saying this—institutions. frames of mind, or something which will be helpful to these countries, but I have yet to hear a political scientist in Ghana, Nigeria, Bolivia, Burma, or .anywhere say something useful about how to create a viable political society.

The economists keep on saying what they think is right to create economic development, but what do political scientists have to say to Ghana, or Kenya or any of these places?

Mr. ANDERSON: In fact, don't most political scientists today defend the rogues?

Mr. LEWIS: Yes, they do. They tell us what wonderful guys they are. (Laughter.)

Mr. HOLT: I think you can defend the rogues, and you can defend the rogues in terms of the experience of economic development in countries in the nineteenth century, I object to economists and others saying, "Many of these problems of development are political problems. We would like to hear the political scientists tell us about them." Typically, they define the question too narrowly; they want the political scientist to tell them how to control the rogues. They do not ask the question: what is the appropriate role of the government for political development and what kind of people do you have to have in crucial governmental roles?

Mr. LEWIS: I would like to look at the situation in India. India has tremendous economic problems and it has even more tremendous political problems. Economists have done a tremendous amount of work on the Indian economy and have said a lot of useful things to the Indian government, many of which India has put into effect with the consequence that we are told India had a per capita fall in national income consistently from 1900 to 1950, but has had a 1 1/2 to 2 per cent rise in per capita national income consistently since 1950. Economists make mistakes, but they clearly have something to say to India. Much more important than the Indians' economic problem is the Indians' political problem—the possibility of survival in India of something political that is worth preserving—but I have yet to hear a single note from a political scientist of any use to the Indians in solving this important problem.

I feel sad about this. I would like to hear this note, because I think it is much more important than anything we economists have to say. India is just an example. The same is true of all these new African states that are coming forward. They can send to the United Nations and ask for assistance and they can get some sound economic advice. If they send to the United Nations and ask for a political advisor he will tell them something about creating a civil service system, but that is a minor matter in the larger context of the political problem.

Mr. KING: I wonder whether it is fair to expect a political scientist, or anybody else, to go to a country and do anything more than "tinker" with the civil service?

Supposing the only legitimate answer to Mr. Sukarno would be to say, "Step down." This is surely a solution open only to the Central Intelligence Agency if it is indeed open to them. To get rid of the rogue, they have to identify him, and this has caused trouble before.

This leads me to a generalization. When you ask whether the people in underdeveloped countries are or are not ready for democracy, you are asking the wrong question. It is not whether the people are ready or not for democracy; it is whether the leading group or elite is willing to accept it. If the elite, as in this country, decides that they would not back Mr. Washington for king, then Mr. Washington would be president. I seem to have aroused something,

Mr. LEWIS: You can say that about Sukarno but you cannot say that about Nyerere. It is not the most desirable thing in Indonesia that Mr.

Sukarno remain, but anybody who knows Mr. Nyerere knows that it is the most important thing for Tanganyika that Mr. Nyerere should remain. Mr. Nyerere is in serious political trouble. He needs political advice. The Russians are willing to give it to him and the Chinese are willing to give it to him. What do we have to offer?

Sister THOMASINE: Could it be that people trained in the Anglo-American tradition in politics have a certain reticence about giving advice?

Mr. WARREN: My own training is not in economics or in political science. Often, as I listen to the discussion, I wonder why I am here, but I see, that underlying the topic of this morning's discussion, and underlying the topic of the Conference, is a desire—and no one discusses this—a desire on the part of some one, or the members of some group, to induce change in someone else or in some other group.

In all of the discussions we have treated countries as units, and have discussed how these units, by some means or another, should be changed in the same way that personality is viewed as the unit by the psychologist; and in changing the individual you must consequently, in some manner, change the personality.

Mr. de Schweinitz' point of view, then, of approaching culture change or social change or economic change through government is perfectly plausible, because this is the expedient approach. This is the way to connect one of our units or one of our countries to another country, or one country to another country, because this is the only line of communication that is possible.

You cannot connect one government to another government and hope, then, that the second government will respond in some way as a result of its connection. You can attempt to bypass the government, and we tried this, too, in Radio Free Europe, for instance, hoping to induce change in the people by going around the government, but in most cases all of our efforts to induce change in the so-called underdeveloped countries in the world must be through their governments, or else it seems to be illegitimate in some manner or another.

We have other tactics of inducing change but up to now government seems to be the most appropriate way of doing this, so until we find some other way of hooking our unit or our country to these other countries, or to the people of these other countries, and inducing change, then the governmental approach, or the approach through the political scientists, seems to me to be the most expedient approach.

Mr. MORGAN: It struck me what a fine example of humility we from different disciplines have been successively giving in arguing that some other discipline than our own holds the key to the problems of the underdeveloped countries. One after the other of us has done this, and probably often rightly.

In this connection: economists argue plausibly that rogues in economics have often been quite useful socially—despite themselves. There have, been exceptions to the rule, of course. But there is a good deal to be said for it. It is in contrast, much harder to find support for the social usefulness of rogues and scoundrels in other lines of activity, notably government.

Several of us here are refugees, In a sense, from Indonesia. Experience there brings the issue to mind. The government there does count in economic life, and its pursuit of political advantage has had disastrous economic repercussions,

We have the notion that patriotism, or nationalism, is the last refuge of a scoundrel. It is more clearly the first resort of the scoundrel in politics, frequently with baleful effects on economic affairs. Perhaps the specialists here in political science can suggest, to us how the burden of nationalist policies can be made lighter. How can we substitute rationality for nationalism?

Mr. ANDERSON: Last night, we were given an economist's dictum which I will vulgarize as follows: strong, autonomous labor unions stultify development—economic development.

Now, is a political scientist willing to give us a similar dictum which I will vulgarize: a universal suffrage electoral system will preclude the possibility of sound governmental policy for economic development. Why don't the political scientists come out and tell us something here? You are talking about international politics.

Mr. NASH: I am not a political scientist, but I want to take on part of the burden that Mr. Lewis laid at the doorstep of those beleaguered gentlemen.

One of the major questions being asked is, how do you form a polity—a civic consensual polity—that can get on with the job of economic development. I have been reflecting on it offhand and I think most of the polities that have gotten on with economic development have had a shared and bloody experience. To get consensus, and to get a feeling of being members of a nation who would take a discount in real income for the benefit of the nation you need patriotism, which probably comes from some shared bloody experience—literally bloody.

I think of the differences between Mexico and Guatemala. At any time during the 30 years the Mexicans were running around from 1910 to 1940 shooting up each other in the countryside, the prospects for economic development looked very, very slim. When they finally got consolidated as a pretty dictatorial one-party system, they did pull the country into one of the fastest growth rates in the world, and I contrast that with my experience in Asia, In Burma the country got its independence surprisingly, Aung San outfaced them in England and there was no battle, no bloody national feeling, no shared climactic situation; only a symbolic leader who got them independence with an aura as a result of which he could not do anything but celebrate that one act. He was a ritual leader who continually celebrated the act of independence. He did not do as much harm as the new celebrant in that job, but it did not make much of a nation cut of Burma.

His main contribution was to impress political scientists like. Hugh Tinker, who wrote articles about serene statesmen, while the Irrawaddy was silting up, rice was going down, and U Nu was building sand pagodas, To Westerners he looked as though he had Buddhism and serenity and nice things to say, but he did not do much for his country except build sand pagodas.

If I were a political scientist, I would say, "Well, what you need is a shared experience which will confer on those who live through it the kind of nationhood and brotherhood which they unfortunately did not have by language or any of their other experiences," That, advice, of course, is useless, but that is the way the historical experience looks to me,

Mr. BARANSON: I want to comment on that. It struck me before that this business of timing is a very important thing. Think about the feasibility of city planning in our own country 50 years ago under a Tammany Hall regime in New York City. It is no use trying to apply a medicine that is devised for an inhospitable situation. This is comparable to taking modern medical techniques and going into the hinterland of Haiti where voodoo and magic are practiced.

Much of the talk today ran something like this: "I have a nice kit of practitioner's tricks and all you have to do is reorganize the society for me and I can go to work on it." There is one other comment I would like to make. Today's discussions reminded me of Isaiah Berlin writing about Leo Tolstoi in *The Hedgehog and the Fox*. Berlin commented that whenever Tolstoi talked about God, it was like putting two bears in a cage, I think the political scientist and the economist today are somewhat like the two bears, although I am. not. sure which one is Tolstoi and which one is God (Laughter.)

About two years ago, at a conference in Cambridge, Hans Morgenthau and Albert Hirschman played Tolstoi and God. They were reviewing Latin America. Morgenthau suggested that the problem was essentially political. Hirschman said that the economists, however, were the ones who were providing some answers. There they were arguing over whose problem it ought to be, and today it is interesting because there is a little more modesty. Each is trying to push it off on the other. But it really is not a question of who should own the problem but one of joint effort toward determining who should solve it.

One last point: I think part of the difficulty brought out today was that many people are looking for totalistic answers based on theoretical precepts involving a certain time sequence, social, predisposition, or a set of values. As for implementing the theory they say, "I leave that to another discipline. Someone else can figure out a way to work out the details. I have done my share in providing the broad theoretical framework."

I think this is putting us all in a narrow box. It seems to me the political scientist has provided us with ways for analyzing social pathologies rather than with prescriptive solutions. There are a lot of things in medicine today that we do not understand—cancer and other pathologies—but the medical sciences are not committed, to a cradle-to-grave solution for all pathologies inhibiting growth.

There is a whole range of development pathologies, and I think there are opportunities for tackling these problems piecemeal. I think the problem in this sense is a little more manageable, if the totalistic approach is *a* little more toned down, both from the standpoint of the political scientist and the economist.

Mr. SCHWARTZ: I would like to dissent respectfully from the arguments of the economists, and suggest that in addition to the fact that some of the other disciplines may not have provided us with sufficiently good tools for analyzing development, there is another problem and that is one that the economists are responsible for, namely, a certain lack of follow-through. By this I mean the following: it seems to me that sometimes much is left undone with respect to expediting a more optimal allocation of resources. The consequence is that there is either a reduced income for a given period of time or there is not the rapid rise which might have taken place. As a result, the already existing political and social pressures are accentuated and aggravated.

I have in mind particularly the situation in Argentina. It became very popular a few years back to say that the causes of the country's economic problems were, in fact, political, and these days you hear some rather good economists saying that the basic problem is sociological, but I would like to point out the following: In the 1959-1962 period there were a number of economic decisions with respect to which it is now clear (though in many cases it was quite clear even then) that what was being done constituted an inefficient allocation of resources, and threatened to seriously limit the potential increase in Gross National Product in comparison with what might have been achieved had different decisions been made. Secondly, to take a point which I think Professor Lewis has developed elsewhere, whatever the potential increase in GNP, it might not take place rapidly enough, given certain underlying political difficulties, to enable the government to remain in power. This, of course, is something else again.

In 1959-1960 some Argentine officials recognized a number of the problems, and pointed out that the policies being pursued were going to cause a severe balance-of-payments problem. But their warnings were largely ignored, and not followed up by other officials.

A recent report of the Economic Commission for Latin America states that in some of the basic equipment industries which developed, costs are only 10 to 15 per cent higher than world levels, while in others, costs are 80 per cent and more over world cost levels. Thus, whatever the basic political constraints, you are going to get better results if you focus more on the allocation of resources,

Frondizi concentrated on development of the oil industry but did not make sufficient allowance for the fact that large amounts of natural gas output would probably accompany the oil production. This is what happened, and much natural gas escaped. One economist had pointed to this possibility, and continued doing so during the course of the rapid increase in petroleum output, but he did not receive much support from the appropriate authorities—or other economists.

What I am saying is that you came to a situation in March of 1962 in which the working class had experienced a considerable redistribution of income. This redistribution of income might have been at a higher level of average per capita income if there had been a more efficient allocation of resources—quite consistent with the kinds of political decisions which the country wanted to make. Then the March election results might well have been different and the subsequent crisis might never have arisen.

What I am trying to say, in other words, is that if enough good economists look after the details of the plans they draw up, and point out where there are poor allocations of resources, there could be more satisfactory results; but if they do not stay with it, then you are not going to get the kind of economic development that is possible (even with the constraints) and you are going to aggravate the political and social pressures; I think the economists have fallen short of what might have been expected in this respect.

Incentives and Job Prestige

Mr. MIRACLE: I think I detect from this discussion an underlying assumption that economics has done pretty well over this interval we are appraising and we do know the economist's answers. Professor Lewis was talking about this a little while ago; I wonder if "he would agree that, the proper study of an economist is *response to economic incentive*? If so, I suggest that we know very little yet.

We have lots of hypotheses that some people are trying to attack one way or another but we do not really know very much and we cannot tell the political scientist, the sociologist, the government planner or others very much about how farmers in Africa will respond—particularly to price changes of economic incentive, It may be that there is a lot more to it than economics. Maybe you would want to argue that, it is not strictly an economic question, but it is an example of the need for theory or for measurement, or both.

Getting back to the original paper, I am a little bit disturbed that, as a spokesman for the economists here, the leading paper suggested that political scientists should start with more theory. It seems to me very often that in economics, at least, measurement, empirical work, case studies and all sorts of things have been the source material from which good hypotheses and good theories develop, and I wonder if this could happen in political science as well as in some other disciplines?

Mr. LEWIS: The area in which the economist's understanding of development is least, not merely of development in underdeveloped countries, but equally of development in developed countries, is what causes people to invest, Why are. investors aggressive in Germany and not aggressive in Great Britain? Or rather, let us ask, why are they aggressive in developed countries in general and not aggressive in underdeveloped countries? This is an area where one would like to see a tremendous amount of work and where no doubt the psychologists and the sociologists will make their contributions, but even this problem is not as grave a problem as we think it is.

When I look, for instance, at the African economy I do not see any shortage of people wanting to invest. I see the same things that I see when I look at the history of Europe. I see lots of little people seizing opportunities and becoming big people in the process, a man starting out by doing a little trading and then going into the trucking business, for example, and. becoming a big man in the process. All I see is that African entrepreneurs, who are numerous and aggressive, do not have at the moment the capacity to run large-scale enterprises. They cannot run a big mine employing 3,000 people.

This is not a major problem. This is something which can be learned. Some of what is necessary can even be taught by a business school. The man who will eventually come to own a large mine, working his way up from nothing, can not be taught In a business school. But large mines will employ accountants, a personnel manager and other kinds of people who are necessary to run large organizations, and who can be taught in business schools, so even in underdeveloped countries I do not think the problem of entrepreneurship is such a difficult problem as we make it out to be.

Mr. KREININ: I think that the problem of incentives is not only related to investment behavior but also to the behavior of individuals. I have interviewed quite a few Africans and people who extend technical assistance to African countries. They consistently indicated Africans do not like to do manual work, In terms of social status in Africa, doing something with one's hands—perhaps somebody *may* want to correct me on this—is the worst thing that can happen to a person. Almost every African who goes abroad six months to study a technical subject such as chicken-feeding wants to sit behind a desk.

I have come across a couple of practical nurses who refused to do any manual work while being trained abroad. When they were asked why they said, "Well, when we go back we are not going to work." "What are you going to do?" The only thing they could say was, "We are going to replace the Belgians. The Belgians didn't work. Why should we?"

So you come up against the social status scheme about which perhaps the sociologists can tell us something.

With reference to the civil service, much prestige is attached to being a Minister or a high official such as a permanent Secretary or Undersecretary of a ministry. I was amazed to see the number of medical doctors in Africa who occupy positions of responsibility in government when there is a fantastic doctor shortage *in* their countries. Apparently, although I am not sure of this, there is more prestige attached to being a government official than to being a successful entrepreneur. It is certainly superior to being an engineer. And an engineer, of course, would not dirty his hands.

I think, therefore, that a question that might be addressed to the psychologists and the sociologists is what to do about this scheme of social values that is interfering with the development no less than the political problem.

Mr. ANDERSON: I am always a little astonished that a group like this of white-collar men raises such questions. I think we have sufficient evidence to demonstrate that if *a* country, by whatever process, gets an appropriate wage structure related to the relative supply and demand of different, kinds of skills, people will respond with amazing alacrity. The problem in many of the new countries is that the governments are absolutely determined that there shall be no flexible wage structure, and of course, the government personnel set the wage structure, putting their kind of "jobs on top, so you get this result.

Sister THOMASINE: I would like to make a comment about the relationship between education and the attitude toward work. This applies also to our discussion about Japan and India.

Irrespective of the mystery of why some people like to work and some do not, we know there are a number of reasons for both, nevertheless the Japanese educational system certainly has fostered a healthy respect for the engineer and the technician that I do not think the Indian system has done.

Interdisciplinary Research

Mr. BLANKSTEN: Mr. Chairman, I have been sitting here as a defensive, sensitive, self-conscious, embarrassed political scientist listening to everybody complaining about political scientists and telling us the things that they would like to see political scientists do for them. I suppose I should confess that in listening to this I have made kind of a list for myself of the things all of you people say you want political scientists to do for you. I look at this list and I am bewildered.

You want us to figure out what difference it makes if civil servants are entrepreneurs, how to control rogues in politics, how to get India out of its political jam, how to analyze pathologies. Then we were told we ought to be doing philosophy for you people and we ought to be doing history for you, and all of this reminds me somewhat of a session in which I participated many years ago when a group of political scientists invited people from other disciplines in to give us talks on what they would like to see political science do for them. I remember at that time a talk, by an anthropologist who had been doing work among the Indians in the American Southwest. He was really bitter about the way the political scientists had let him down in his project with the American Indians, because he said that what *we* should have clone was to tell the anthropologists how to find which part of the United States Government contained the Bureau of Indian Affairs, so that they could go and contact the government on certain, problems. I remember feeling at that time, "Gee, if I had only known!" If we only had realized that what he wanted was the United. States Government Directory, or something like that, we could have, helped him.

It just seems to me that this simply highlights what I think is an error in this exercise of delineating the differences among what disciplines ought to be doing. It seems to me that the great positive way to approach interdisciplinary questions is not to divide up all the questions and work at divisions of labor and so on, but rather, to define the common thing we are trying to resolve together. What is the common problem we can all add, something to? I guess the burden of my sermon here is that. I do not think we are doing this. It does seen to me that the great need in this kind of a session is the identification of the kind of things on which we can fruitfully work together rather than on those we can split up and push out of the way.

Mr. KREININ: Couching the problem in a somewhat different framework might better identify the Issues with which we are confronted. I learned two things lust now: first, that perhaps the focus in the field of economic development should revert from emphasis on capital-output ratios to relative-factor endowments.

Second, there is perhaps some optimum of disturbance to equilibrium. Economic development is not essentially a stable thing. The emphasis on stability that prevailed in this morning's discussion is misleading because, after all, economic development is an unstable situation. You want to disturb the equilibrium. Equilibrium will lead you nowhere,

We have been shown that not every disturbance is optimal and it may often be excessive. The idea that the underdeveloped countries can jump over the industrial revolution and borrow techniques which are 200 years too advanced for them is a misleading notion. Perhaps they do have to go through some agonizing experience just as the developed countries did. There is, therefore, some kind of an optimum disturbance, an optimum stimulus that needs to be given to the economy for it to develop in a reasonably smooth way. All this was limited to economics. I suspect that in terms of the interdisciplinary approach we are examining today there is an optimum stimulus in fields other than economics.

Perhaps in the field of politics the optimum stimulus is zero, namely, the domestic political situation should be stable to provide a stable framework, With respect to sociological-psychological effects, what is the optimum stimulus? We speak of the demonstration, effect. Well, some demonstration effect is good; too much, of it is bad. Some of it would stimulate people's desires to develop, so to speak. Too much of it might lead to balance-of-payments difficulties. Here you have again the question of what, is optimal in the particular field.

Perhaps, then, we should ask ourselves, what is the optimum stimulus in various disciplines and tie them together. We should not emphasize stability; instead we should emphasize disequilibrium, but the question is how much disequilibrium.

It is in that context that I think an Interdisciplinary approach, might be very useful. We have learned from economics that there exists this kind of an optimum stimulus, but what about other fields? What about sociology? What about psychology? What about political science? This is a question I would like to pose.

Mr. FATOUROS: Historically the task of government, and not alone the task of the political scientist, has not been how to get the rogues out of government, but how to control them when in government. I think the word used by Mr. Blanksten, "control," was very-appropriate. The problem is how to control and canalize the actions of people who, for reasons of their own, which may or may not be morally or perhaps esthetically satisfying, want, to have political power and want to do certain things with that power. The question is how to canalize their actions somehow, perhaps by creating various counter-balancing forces and the like, so as to make it possible to achieve a certain desirable result.

A second point is that I seem to detect—I surely hope I am absolutely wrong in this—a kind of arrogance in the air in the way in which we look at problems and decide that since we have solved the technical problem (the technical economic problem or perhaps the technical political science or public administration problem), after we have separated it from every other problem, and after we have looked at it in the exclusive economic context or in the exclusive political context, we can say, "Well, the solution would have been that, but, of course, there is a whole background to it with which we are not dealing at this particular moment." I think that we should not adopt this kind of attitude, especially today, in the United States, where we are facing certain critical problems which are neither exclusively economic nor exclusively political, but are both at the same time. People are starting slowly to realize that the war on poverty and the civil rights problem cannot be dealt with either on an exclusively economic level or on an exclusively political one. Economic development is closely related to the effective participation of all members of a community in the community's political and economic, processes. As long as the dominant political structure in any region deprives people of political representation, the "war on poverty" cannot be won, and as long as the economic realities are ignored, the civil rights struggle is ineffective. Similar, though not identical, considerations obtain in the international context. We should focus, then, on the unity of the problems rather than on their partial aspects.

Perhaps sociologists might be able to look at problems from above, though I am afraid that, they, too, would look from a specific sociological viewpoint. And there is obviously a psychological problem as well as a moral one. It is possible, if we look at a problem, to say always, "Well, we can solve this if only we limit it to our own terms of reference"; of course, there is a metaphysical problem behind the whole question. If the philosophers would give us an answer, then we might have our solution.

To summarize: we are oversimplifying the situation when we look at each partial solution and are happy with it, instead of trying to see how we can put all the partial solutions together in order to arrive at some solution which is obviously imperfect, certainly imperfect, perhaps very often a failure, but still is a general, all-inclusive solution.

Mr. WIT: As a political scientist, I have been groping for some meaningful response to the query: "What can a political scientist provide?" I think the last speaker has suggested an element, which is that: problems are societal, not just political.

In addition to *that,* it seems to me that, when one asks the question we are faced with two types of problems. One is that we have been operating on the assumption that consensus is essential, and simultaneously, we have been talking about the fact that many of these societies lack consensus and are not nations. This suggests, then, that for many of these countries, about the only thing the political scientist could provide would be essentially a dictatorial system, a philosopher-king who would somehow or other come out with all of the types of solution—in terms of adequate policy, that could effectively implement the economic solutions which we have been told are simple, I think also of Ivor Jennings and some of his impressive efforts to provide rational political answers in countries like India, Pakistan, and Ceylon, and of the inadequacy of these answers.

I do not think, then, that it is a fair question to ask of the political scientist that he come up with "the" solution. We have certainly all recognized the diversity of the problems. We—the political scientists —cannot say, therefore, that there is a given philosopher-king who should handle the polity, or create a polity, in a specific way. All we can do is to analyze the ways in which the polities arise and some of the aberrations one finds. We do not even know the norm of "good governments" because customarily we work in terms of an Anglo-American norm and this, as Sir Ivor has demonstrated effectively, is not really applicable. Therefore, I do think, and I agree with Professor Blanksten, that we have to talk in terms of how we can mesh the efforts of different disciplines rather than how one discipline can "solve" what is not soluble within its own jurisdiction.

Mr. BARANSON: One aspect we should consider in the day or so we have left is whether we are basically concerned with practitioner's knowledge. There are many economists who have no taste for the problems of this world. They are more concerned with theory for its own sake, and I think this applies also to certain political scientists.

I think it is a fair and responsible challenge to political scientists to pose practitioners' questions, where you have to diagnose and prescribe. In "diagnosing" Sukarno, I would first like to know to whom we attach the diagnostician? Is it to the CIA? Is *it* to the opposition party? Is it to U Thant? If the question is one of political power and social change, where do vou begin?

Recently at Indiana University we were approached by AID on staffing a development advisory group in Brazil. AID was very frank, Harvard was already overextended in Latin America and elsewhere. The Yale Growth Center wasn't interested in a practical advisory group in Brazil. They don't want to muck around in politics and. a real situation like that. For economists there are practitioner sets of knowledge that deal with the problem of growth and development and they sorely need the advice and assistance of political scientists,

In Brazil we will not be able to move one step unless we have an economist who knows enough about: the political reality of the kind of advice he gives and knows where to begin, and how to tackle the economic problems in a meaningful and effective way.

I do not think that the state of the art In the applied sciences is that underdeveloped and I am certain that, there are in fact bits and pieces of theory and practice that apply to the problems of this world,

Mr. HENDRY: I would like to identify myself with the claque of humble economists who have been foisting their problems on the other disciplines, I would like to address myself to Mr. Blanksten's apparent: aim of establishing an interdisciplinary approach, which is a kind of general equilibrium approach, under which somehow we can now all pull together and come up with, a general model for handling development problems.

My own feeling is that this would not be a very fruitful direction in which to head, I would prefer, instead, more of the kind of thing Mr. Baranson lies been suggesting. Identifying from an economist's standpoint what kinds of things are inhibiting the development he would normally like to see, and then asking the political scientist or the sociologist or the anthropologist, "What is your advice on this particular point? Why, for example, is the civil service not following through on this particular policy?" This is where the communication between the disciplines is rather poor, and where the economist constantly finds himself unable to give an answer out of his own experience and out of his own training.

Mr. KING: The Singapore government has a political science training course, and George Thompson, the director, is trying to teach this sort of political philosophy. He is trying to instill a concept of government that is consistent, let us say, both with democratic processes and with economic development, The Singapore government is committed to the democratic process, but you must still take in all the civil servants as they come to you. You train them, you argue with them; they move out and you bring them in again next year, and you can say the same thing over again.

You can urge the dedicated, "If you want to solve the problems of democracy in Malaysia, go to Nanyang University and spend your career there, giving up any possibility of progress in your own profession, and argue with these people." Some day you will see these students in positions of responsibility reacting to at least some of your ideas. Some of my University of Hong Kong students are now in relatively responsible positions in Malaysia. They may be messing up things, but I feel I have had a role in the way they are messing them up.

One other point. I am worried about this idea that economists have solved the simple problem of knowing how fast economies grow. From the technical statistical viewpoint, my experience suggests that this is not true.

Mr. WIT: This goes to the heart of the matter, in one way. A couple of days ago I also spent a few hours with Mr. Thompson talking about what he is doing, and I could not for the life of me find out exactly what, it was he was transmitting other than, apparently, the attitudes of the ruling party of Singapore, and in general imposing upon the civil servants of Singapore the notion that they have to stop looking toward Europe and have to start thinking of themselves as Asians. So, he is making a gesture toward nation building and he is acting as a conveyor belt for some of the attitudes of the dominant political party, all of which are rejected by the opposition party. He is therefore in the position of being accused in Singapore at the moment of being either *a* British agent or at least an agent of the political party in authority. But he is not really providing political "solutions" to Singapore's problems,

Mr. FATOUROS: That is politics, not political science, is it not?

Mr. WIT: He is running a political center and his mission, you see, is the mission of providing advice, political advice. He has latched on to a vehicle. Really, this is all we have been saying all along; there is no all-encompassing "scientific" political ad vice that one can provide for development in these diverse types of situations. It must be adjusted to the local scene.

Mr. LEWIS: We must not object, because political advice is "political."

Mr. WIT: We have been asked for scientific solutions, and what I am saying is, as I have said before, that the political scientist, does not provide scientific solutions.

Mr. KING: No. no, no. You were not asked for scientific solutions. if you are asked for solutions, give them a philosophy as to how to run things. This is what Thompson is doing.

Mr. WIT: He is taking the official philosophy and—

Mr. KING: Because he agrees with it.

Chairman BINDER: Order, gentlemen, order. At this time I would like to ask Mr. de Schweinitz to make a few remarks.

Mr. de SCHWEINITZ: Well, I consider it a singular achievement that the political scientists here have no disaffiliated yet and we can look forward to seeing them at this afternoon's session.

I must say that I was elated with what the economists have said here. I like what Mr. Hendry said. I ani not impressed with Mr. Blanksten's notion that what we should be doing here is looking around for an area where we. can work together fruitfully. If I understand it, what we ere trying to do here is to establish some priorities in research. Early in the session Manning Nash talked about the prerequisites of economic development, being passe, because they give the impression that you first establish them arid then the economy takes off into economic growth; he points out that economic growth and cultural change are taking place all the time. With that I quite agree.

We live in a general equilibrium world where everything affects everything, but it seems to me that this does not help us much in the matter of priorities of research. What one has to do is to plug into the system somewhere and you have to decide what particular problems are most important. I would insist, along with Professor Lewis, that politics is certainly a most important area, but I also would insist that politics is not the same thing as giving advice. It may include this, but. it is a good deal more than that, I think of politics as an attempt to explain phenomenon, and whether or not out of the explanation or out of the political theories you develop you derive advice is another question. Perhaps we can look forward to this afternoon and Mr. Holt's clearing up, once and for all, all these questions that have been raised and thrown in the direction of the political scientists.

Chairman BINDER: I do hope that everyone will maintain the present level of excitement, enthusiasm, embarrassment, humility and tenseness that has come out of this morning's session, because I have a feeling that the session this afternoon will be very much a continuation of the. kind of discussion we have, been having this morning.

I hope that this afternoon we may get over our differences and find some areas of agreement. I am bound, however—if you will forgive me—I am bound as a political scientist, rather than as Chairman of the morning session, to make a few remarks. I have restrained myself up to this point and I have been embarrassed, tense, angry, humiliated, and everything else, along with the rest of the political scientists, and in more ways than one.

I will try very hard to avoid making a speech. I have not had too long to think about these things, anyway, but I do want to make just a few remarks that respond if I had two hours in which to respond to many of the terribly irritating things that have been said this morning,

Now, for one thing, there has been no clear distinction made between the role of the statesman and the role of the scholar. This is not a new problem in political science. It is not something that has come up just in the last 15 years in which we have been concerned with economic development in underdeveloped areas. This is a problem that has been with civilized society from the time it has been recorded, and I think it, is naive to think that the problems that have been at issue here are things that have just turned up day before yesterday. If these are questions that, have been contained in the great writings of all time and if they have been contained in the works of the great political philosophers, it is a matter for us today to be very much concerned with those things even as were our forebears.

American political science is not 50 years old. It is part and parcel of this great long development, and some of us do have better memories. However, this does not resolve the problem. It has come down to us as our heritage of the development of philosophy as well as political philosophy over centuries, millenia in fact, and I do not believe we have a solution to the problem that, is posed just by this issue of the role of the statesman as against the role of the scholar, because they are not merely different roles but they are different philosophical approaches, which I might present to you in the form of the opposition of the notion of purpose in politics and the notion of process.

Now, behind the notion of purpose is the idea that we can control the way in which political things work themselves out. Behind the notion of process, as far as I am concerned, is a sense that we cannot control these things because human beings are not given to that kind of control, but we can perhaps examine and analyze a process. I do not know whether economic and political development is something that we can design in our minds and fulfill by a purposeful policy or whether it is something we can examine as it occurred in the past and hope for in the future.

Nothing that has been said here gives me confidence that we can apply the notions of purpose as opposed to the notions of process. There are political scientists of both kinds in the world and I think there are economists of both kinds in the world. Now, if you believe that this is all given to us in terms of some a priori notion of what we would like to have, and if we therefore designate a policy and presume that anything can be accomplished by an effective government then, of course, you approach it from the point of view of purpose and you say to the political scientist, "Why in heaven's name have you not told us how to accomplish this purpose?"

If there are political scientists who do not believe we can control all these things, but who do believe in the radical heterogeneity of the human being as opposed to all other kinds of things under the sun, then we do take the point of view that we can examine processes and it is for that reason, I think, that the subject of this morning's session was accurately stated to be the underdeveloped countries in the world economy, and it was for that reason that I did indeed ask about some of the changes that have occurred in this world economy.

Development in these underdeveloped countries is, at least in part, dependent upon what happens in the world economy, and what happens in the world economy is in the nature of a process within which the economies of underdeveloped countries find themselves. They cannot control it; they can only react to it. It is not given to a Sukarno or to a Nkrumah to control the pattern of change of the world economy, nor is there any organisation, the United Nations or anything else like that, that stands above the world economy which can tell us how that world economy is to be controlled, it is a non-controlled process, and I think that this is a decent and dignified kind of thing for social scientists to examine.

Notes

1.   David Clarence McClelland, *The Achieving Society* (Princeton, N.J.: Van Nostrand, 1961).
2.   Everett Einar Hagen, *On the Theory of Social Change How Economic Growth Begins* (A study from the Center for International Studies, Massachusetts Institute of Technology; Homewood, Ill.: Dorsey Press 1962).

Session III

The International Politics and Diplomacy of Development

Chairman BLANKSTEN: I have a fairly clear signal that a more exact title for this afternoon's session would probably be "The Political Scientist Strikes Back."

The discussion leader this afternoon is Robert T. Holt, political scientist from the University of Minnesota. Professor Holt has been involved in problems of political development and change in underdeveloped areas. He has been doing, from my standpoint, some of the most interesting work in this area and as he left this morning's session in a somewhat angry frame of mind, I told him I hoped he would stay in that frame of mind until this afternoon. He said to me, "Don't worry—I'm always in this frame of mind," so I am sure we can depend on that.

The first of our two discussants is Mordechai Kreinin of Michigan State University. He is an economist whose chief research interest has been in the field of international trade. He has also done work on Israeli technical assistance to various countries in Africa, Asia and Latin America.

Our second discussant will be A. A. Fatouros of the Law School of Indiana University. He is a graduate of the National University of Athens. His chief research interests have been in legal aspects of international economic relations. He has been especially interested in the general set of interrelationships between international law and economic development. Now for the more substantive action,

Mr. HOLT: When Professor de Schweinitz finished his brief ten-minute talk this morning, I sat back rather smugly in *my* chair. Last, night, you remember, at the close of his paper. Professor Lewis was looking to the political scientist for answers to many questions and Professor de

Schweinitz this morning talked about the major problems of development being not economic problems but political problems. For a minute or two I imagined that I would be running with the ball behind the powerful interference of de Schweinitz and Lewis and I thought things would go pretty smoothly, After about 15 minutes of discussion this morning, however, I began to realize that this perception was a little bit false. There was a hole in the line, all right, but it was really a mouse trap and some 280-pound linemen were ready to jump on me as soon as I picked up the ball and began to run.

When I agreed to talk, on the problems of diplomacy, I said that I wanted to emphasize some of the theoretical and conceptual problems of approaching this topic rather than talking in any specific empirical detail about one or two given cases. After the discussion this morning I would like to reorient myself even further away from the direct problems of diplomacy of development and see if I can address myself to that problem along with some of the problems and some of the questions that were asked of the political scientist primarily by the economists earlier in these sessions.

There are a couple of introductory remarks, however, that I would like to make because I am sure they will in some way explain why the economist and perhaps other scholars interested in problems of development have been somewhat disappointed in the answers they have received to questions that they perceive are part of the legitimate domain of political science. The first point I would like to bring out, and perhaps there are many of you in this room who are not aware of this fact, is that of all the academic disciplines in the United States, political science is the one in which there is the least consensus about the nature of the discipline and the problems of the discipline. In the study on graduate education in the United States that Berelson did several years ago this comes out very clearly.[1] The amount of dissension, the lack of agreement, and the lack of consensus in political science set this discipline apart in a rather marked way from the other academic disciplines in the social sciences as well as in the natural sciences and the humanities. This means that when you ask a question of political scientists, you are likely not to get one answer but you are likely to get a dozen answers and you probably will find more controversy among political scientists of different persuasions answering the same question than you would find among the people that have asked the political scientists this question.

Now, this has had some rather remarkable effects upon the kinds of work that political scientists have done on problems of development. Because we are operating within very different theoretical frameworks within the discipline itself, because there are different people taking some very different approaches, the work that we have done has not been very additive. We tend to have a scholar over here within his frame of reference who has done a little bit and, another scholar over there with his frame of reference who has done a little bit, but the work of the two does not fit together. When one begins to address oneself to some of the tough problems, for example, of the practitioner who is interested in what kind of advice to give to a foreign government of a developing country, one finds that the body of knowledge in political science is not an integrated body of knowledge. No clear answer emerges; indeed, many time's conflicting answers are forthcoming,

The second point I would like to make about political science and its concern with problems of development is that the political problems specifically related to economic development have not received much attention. If one, for example, looks over the four or five volumes that have been published by the Princeton University Press for the Social Science Research Council Committee on Comparative Politics and examines the footnotes, one will find that something less than one-half of 1 per cent of the references are to problems of economic development.

Most of the scholars who have been concerned with problems of development have been concerned with the way in which a democratic polity is built and emerges in developing countries. If one asks them questions that are oriented specifically to the political implications of economic development problems, one does not get a response based on much research. There is only a very small fraction of the time and effort and energy and Interest, of a political scientist that can be geared into the work of the economist. Now, I am personally very critical of this but, nevertheless, I think this is a relatively fair assessment of the state of the discipline.

The third point I would like to make has to do with the role of the scholar, really the various roles of the scholar. In my own mind I like to make a pretty clear distinction between the scholar who is interested essentially in the scientific tasks of description, explanation, and prediction, and the scholar who is more a social engineer, who is interested in practical advice for the practical problems of the governments that are confronted with horrendous problems of development.

Now, in my own experience, the kind of personality, the kind of training and the kind of interests that an individual has to have differ for these two roles. My own concern is with the scientific problems. I am interested in trying to explain and predict patterns of development, and I feel that it takes another kind of political scientist, with other kinds of skills, to take this theoretical knowledge and transform it into the kind of knowledge which is necessary if one is going to give practical advice to developing countries.

There is a fourth general comment I would like to make in reference to Professor Lewis's paper. It was one of the first systematic treatments of the problem of unemployment in the modern or industrial sector of a developing economy. In his paper, Professor Lewis referred to certain problems of domestic capital formation, certain problems of international trade deficits and the balance of payments. It is possible for him. within the theoretical framework of economics to present a pioneering paper on a specific topic, and yet it is very clear, that this paper would link with another paper that would be done on problems of domestic capital formation, or a third paper that would be done on problems of international trade and development. This is possible because of the logical theoretical structure in economics that enables a scholar to Identify a discrete problem like unemployment, in a developing country and focus upon that problem without having to worry a great deal about the way his work will fit into the work of other economists relating to developing areas. There may be disagreements, of course, but the arguments are essentially carried on within the context of the same conceptual and theoretical framework.

I do not think, that political scientists (or anthropologists or sociologists, for that matter) have the kind of conceptual frameworks that allow them to identify discrete researchable problems, to do work on them, and to have the results of work on various problems linked together in a mutually acceptable theoretical framework.

While I am a great admirer of the degree of sophistication and integration of economic theory, I think that it has been bought at a price. Economic theory tends to be very isolated from the theories in the other social sciences. One of the reasons is that the economist, in order to increase the sophistication and integrity of his theories, has made assumptions about certain sociological, political, and psychological factors, and these assumptions constitute parameters of his theory. While these assumptions may aid the development of economic theory, they tend to hinder the establishment of firm theoretical relationships between economics and other social sciences,

I was impressed with Professor Nash's comment last night when he said he had spent a decade revealing the hidden, sociological assumptions that underlie a large number of economic propositions. One can identify these assumptions and even demonstrate that they are wrong, but this is at best *only a* small beginning to establishing some kind of common ground where economics and the other social sciences can meet. Until such a common meeting ground is established, the economist with his much more deductively powerful theories will ask the political scientist specific questions that he cannot answer.

The absence of a theoretical consensus in political science, the relative lack of concern with problems of economic development, and the different interests and qualifications of the scientist and the social engineer, combined with a proclivity on the part of many or the best political scientists to concentrate on scientific concerns, are three reasons why the political scientist finds it difficult to deal with many of the problems of development that are thrown at him in other fields. Perhaps an understanding of these characteristics of the field will help relieve the frustration that many have expressed in this conference over their failure to get the kinds of responses they feel they deserve from political science.

The first two characteristics also help to explain why I would agree to discuss the topic of diplomacy and development with you only if I could deal conceptually and theoretically with the problem. The absence of a theoretical consensus and the lack of concern with problems of economic development make it impossible to deal with the problem within a widely accepted theoretical framework, and I must start by sketching out the framework within which I operate.

I start out working with a variation of a Parsonian framework which employs a set of assumptions concerning the functional imperatives (or requisites, as I prefer to call them) of any social system, I will mention these only briefly because I am sure that most of you are familiar with Professor Parsons' work. Professor Parsons and some of his associates have postulated that there are four functional requisites that any social system must meet if it is to continue to operate.

The first one of these that he identifies is the functional requisite of adaptation. Every social system has to adapt to its non-human environment, and from Parsons' point of view and from my point of view it is this functional requisite that is concerned primarily with what in the social sciences would be labelled as economic.

A second requisite of any social system is the requisite of goal attainment. There is a set of social system goals and there must be the kind of structural organization within a social system that guarantees that at least a minimal level of these system goals will be achieved.

A third functional requisite is the requisite of pattern maintenance. I differ in my interpretation here rather considerably with Parsons, and I look at pattern maintenance as being primarily concerned with the needs of the social system to conform to the values and prescriptions that are prescribed by the cultural system. (Note that I make a very rigid distinction between a social system on the one hand and a cultural system on the other hand and treat the two as environmental, one to the other.)

The fourth functional requisite that Parsons deals with is the requisite of integration. In effect, I argue here that in order for the functional requisites of any social system to be satisfied it is necessary to have a minimal degree of role differentiation among roles that are in fact

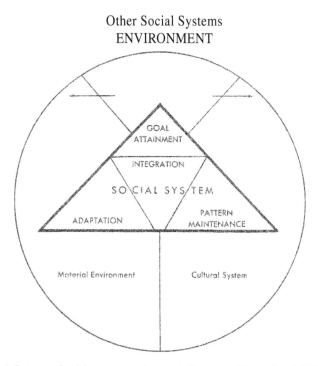

Fig. 1.—Adjustment of social system to environment. [Compare with paradigm in Talcott Parsons and N. J. Smelser, *Economy and Society* (New York: Free Press of Glencoe, 1956), p. 19.]

interdependent. One of the functional requisites of the system is to provide, the minimal amount of integration that is necessary to bring about coordination among these roles that are necessarily differentiated but are also independent.

Certain aspects of this formulation become clearer if presented diagramatically. In Fig. 1 the large triangle represents the social system at the societal level. Within the large triangle, small triangles represent each of the four functional requisites. Notice that each of the first three requisites I mentioned has an external boundary and is relevant, to an aspect of the environment. As already mentioned, the non-human environment is relevant to the adaptive functional requisite and the cultural environment is relevant to the pattern maintenance functional requisite. The goal attainment functional requisite is primarily concerned with relationships with other societies, but also has some relationship with both the non-human and the cultural environment. The integration requisite has no external boundary. It is concerned primarily with the integration of roles that are necessarily differentiated if the four requisites are to be satisfied.

With this kind of formulation, we can look at the problems of social development as the adjustment of the social system to three different aspects of the environment. Some of the work that has been done in anthropology, for example, the work of Julian Steward, would emphasize problems of social change and social development in terms of the adjustment of the social system to its non-human environment. In a sense, my formulation is carrying this work one step further. The crucial social structures are those that, develop in relationship to changes in three aspects of the environment, plus the needs of the system to maintain integration among roles that are necessarily differentiated if these three different kinds of environments are going to be dealt with.[2]

Because functional frameworks have often been criticized because they do not aid the analysis of social change, I might indicate the way in which I treat economic and social development. For any given state of the three aspects of the environment, there is a limited, range in the variation of concrete structures that can satisfy the four functional requisites. I refer to the patterns of concrete structures that satisfy the functional requisites in any given type of social system as the *social structuring* of that system. Social change is viewed as changes in this concrete structuring that occur in response to the changes in the environment, with the additional consideration that there are limits imposed on potential changes by the state of the system at any given time.

Now, I would like to make just a few comments about the problem of diplomacy in development. When we are dealing with relationships to other societies and the impact of the type of international system upon a developing country, we are quite clearly dealing with the goal attainment functional requisite. The crucial questions concern the kind of structural adaptations that are necessary to deal with certain kinds of relationships with other societies, and certain kinds of relationships with the international system. One of the interesting historical observations that I think one can make about the problems of development that arise out of the nature of the international system and of the kinds of contacts with other societies deals with the kinds of procedures that are involved in the satisfaction of the various functional requisites. In other words, there may be differences in the kind of structures that can satisfy certain functions, but there may also be differences in the procedures that can be followed to achieve these particular objectives. It is possible, for instance, that a democratic government and a totalitarian government might do pretty much the same sort of thing. The differences may be largely procedural differences in the way in which the requisites are satisfied.

It seems to me, from a look at the development of countries in Europe in the nineteenth and early twentieth centuries, one finds that the nature of the international system imposes some important limitations upon the kind of procedural alternatives for governments in these countries, I think it is interesting to note, for example, that in those countries which evolved democratic systems in the nineteenth and the early part of the twentieth centuries that later developed into stable democratic systems—these countries had their early development in a period in which foreign policy problems and foreign policy crises were relatively unimportant; Great Britain, the Scandinavian countries, and the United States are cases in point. By contrast, the countries, particularly in western Europe, where the development of basic democratic institutions coincide with a period of prolonged foreign crises, the democratic systems in the twentieth century have not been particularly stable, France, Germany, Spain, and Italy are good examples.

Now, I think the political scientist, can address himself to a whole set of reasons why it is exceedingly difficult, if there are major foreign policy crises, for democratic institutions to develop. One set of reasons deals with the necessity, in periods of foreign crisis, for the government to increase its role in the direction and control of the economy for the purpose of mobilizing resources that are necessary in the defense effort of the country. One of the propositions that would emerge out of my work is that in the very early stage of democratic development it is improbable to have a political system which is engaged in this kind of regulation that does not have what I refer to as a *highly resolved authority structure of policy making.* That is, you cannot, have a basic policy structure in which there is a whole host of representative veto groups that can block the development of a given policy.

In a modern, twentieth-century democracy it is possible to have representation and to have a resolved authority structure of policy making, as one can see in the case of Great Britain, but in the very beginning development of democracy, when the kind of disciplined democratic political parties that exist in Britain today have not yet evolved, this kind of combination is most improbable. Prolonged foreign policy crises lead to increased government direction of the economy, which in turn will tend to limit popular representation.

A second set of reasons concerns the problem of ethnic groups and the integration of ethnic groups into the larger community. This, of course, is a problem for democratic polities at almost any stage in their development. The problem is greatly magnified during periods of international crisis if some of the ethnic groups within a country have close ties to the foreign power with which there is conflict. Even in the United States in the period of the First World War we encountered this particular kind of problem with the German minority. It would seem to me that it is quite improbable that the kind of democratic institutions that are associated with the protection of ethnic minorities would develop in a country which was confronted with prolonged international crisis and in which ethnic minorities were associated with an antagonistic power.

I would like to leave the problems of international relations and their impact on the developing country for a moment, and pursue some other aspects of the development of democratic institutions that take me back to some of the issues raised earlier in this conference. In his paper last night Professor Lewis indicated that in order to deal with unemployment in a developing country, it may well be necessary for a strict limitation to be placed on the ratio of wages in the developed sector to wages in the non-developed sector of the economy. In a developing country, organized labor is likely to be one of the most articulate and influential interest groups in the society. If free elections are held, organized labor is going to have a voice in deciding what group will form a government. It is unlikely that organized labor over a long period of time will tolerate the kind of restrictions on wages recommended by Professor Lewis and it seems relatively probable that such restrictions cannot be imposed unless labor is denied some of the normal democratic freedoms.

Although I would like to argue this point in more detail, there is another issue that was raised in our earlier discussions that I feel more compelled to comment on. Several times during this conference the economists (and others) have indicated their dissatisfaction with the kind of answers they receive to the questions they throw at political scientists. I oftentimes object to the questions because they seem to me to emerge partially from the false assumptions about the political system which are too frequently made by the economist. The questions are too frequently of a very technical nature. For example, "How can we devise a civil service system in a developing country that, will keep the rogues and the rascals out of positions that are important in the control and regulation of the economy?" But how do we know that we want to keep the rogues and the rascals out? Even more important, how do we know we want to have civil servants in important positions of economic regulation?

Most economists do not ask these kinds of questions, often because they have answered the political questions on the basis of an economic analysis. Let me give an example of what I mean. Many economists; would concur with the remarks of both Professors Lewis and de Schweinitz that, the most important problems of economic development are political. I too would concur, but I object strenuously to the kind of reasoning that leads most economists to this conclusion. It is usually based on the proposition that a high degree of economic planning and consequent government regulation of the economy are necessary if development is to take place. This proposition, in turn, has been developed from an almost exclusive concern with technical economic considerations.

For example, a theorist of the "big push," like Professor Rosenstein-Rodan, argues that the technology of the mid-twentieth century that is available for import into the developing countries is much more capital-intensive than was the technology of the nineteenth century. He argues that the production functions associated with this technology are far less homogeneous. He emphasizes particularly the indivisibility of capital. He concludes from his analysis that resource allocation must be far more centralized today than it was in the nineteenth century if industrialization is to proceed rapidly and that a good deal of this centralized resource allocation should be in the hands of the government. It is reasonable further to conclude that the government must play a major role in resource allocation and that the major problems of economic development are political. But the kinds of questions that the economist throws the political scientist from this kind of analysis are purely technical problems, For example, "How does one organize a civil service so that it can handle these important resource allocation problems?"

Let us go back and look at the whole problem of the most desirable role of the government in planning and managing; the economy from a broader perspective. There are a number of very relevant considerations that are not typically considered by the economist because they lie outside the confines of economic theory, First, it has been clear in a number of historical cases of economic development that have been studied, that there is typically a minority group within the society that has provided a disproportions 1 percentage of entrepreneurial talent at very crucial, pre-industri-al and industrial stages of development. Take, for example, the Nonconformists in England, the "old believers" in Russia, the Jews in areas of Western Europe. I think an argument can be made that if the government takes over ownership and active control and regulation of important sectors of the economy in developing countries, representatives of those minority groups that have been absolutely crucial in industrialization experiences in the past may be squeezed out of entrepreneurial roles. If there is a high probability of this happening, it would be an argument against government management of the economy.

The second point I would like to make is that one of the problems that is involved in tiny developing society is the establishment of a set of social structures which enables the motivation of individuals to be geared to societal goals. This, of course, was what John Stuart Mill was concerned with when he talked about "The Invisible Hand." The profit motivation of the individual stimulated behavior that was manifested through the particular kinds of institutions and structures that were established and which contributed to the achievement of the goals of the total system, I think that the kinds of manipulation of wage rates that have gone on in the Soviet Union, in complete opposition to basic Marxian goals, indicate that: even in this kind of economy there is a problem of the way in which individual motivation is geared to, and is put in the service of, the goals of the system itself.

In a developing country what is the most desirable career for a young man with a high pecuniary motivation? If the government: in his country is actively involved in economic regulation, it may be to take a job in the government bureaucracy and put his favors up for sale. In other words, the fast avenue to wealth may be the sale of favorable decisions to the highest bidder. The money which is accumulated in this way is not likely to make much of a contribution to domestic capital formation. It is more likely to find its way into a foreign bank, I would argue that as there is an increase in the amount of government regulation, there is an increase in this kind of behavior which will tend to inhibit rapid economic growth.

Let me conclude by saying that the political scientist *may* well not provide the economist, with satisfactory answers to the question, for example, of how to organize the government so that it can best manage the economy, because he feels that the question is not a proper one. Until the economist can make more realistic assumptions about the non-economic aspects of behavior, I doubt whether he will be asking the political scientist the right kinds of questions. The kind of framework that I sketched out: is one that I think can lead to a fruitful analysis of the problems of developing areas and which can be an aid in the fruitful interchange between economists and political scientists. But because of the characteristics of the field of political science I mentioned in my introductory remarks, there is little likelihood that I will find much agreement among other political scientists.

Mr. FATOUROS: I find it extremely difficult to comment on Professor Holt's paper, partly because I am not sure I have been able to follow every aspect of it, but especially because it seems to me that this was a presentation of what political scientists are doing or should do, saying in a sense, "Well, that's what my profession is doing. How about yours?" I am not sure that there is really very much to comment on in that respect, especially since the discussion itself was an example of the kind of thing that can and should be done. Any complaint as to why a particular point was not discussed can be answered very legitimately by saying, "Well, I did not discuss everything, I left out some things by necessity," which is, of course, true.

I would perhaps add another set of topics for research, trying to find out what the factors are that affect integration in any society as such, and in the international society as a whole. This is a topic that can be studied both in the domestic and in the international context. In the international context, for instance—and this was touched upon very lightly—we have the problem of intergovernmental contacts *and* contacts through a variety of other semi-governmental, or possibly non-governmental, agencies—using the term "agencies" in *a* very general sense, in the sense of institutions. In addition to trade, you have cultural contacts. In fact, we can hypothesize in advance that the range of this kind of non-official contacts is much broader among the developed economies than among the underdeveloped ones. If you go, let us say. to an international-association meeting somewhere, you have a very good chance of meeting some French participants who do not represent the official policy of the government of France. There are very few chances of meeting people who do not represent the more or less official policies of the governments in the developing countries. This creates a problem of communication. I am not saying this to correct what was said before, but rather as an elaboration of a particular point.

In the domestic context, I suppose what has been called nationalism—that is, the modern kind of nationalism is certainly one of the integrating factors, one of the factors that make it possible to ask citizens to do things that may not be to their immediate interest at that particular moment.

Perhaps the whole legal or social order, both international and national, can be seen in these terms: an effective legal order exists (and I say a legal order in the sense of an order in which most of the expectations of its members are normally fulfilled) where every member of the order has an interest in the continuing existence, in the persistence, of the order. This I think applies both to individuals and to states. The moment an individual (or state) finds that it is not to his interest to continue supporting the order, you will have, in the domestic context, a revolutionary situation, and, in the international context, pretty much what the attitude of at least some of the developing countries has been. The interest I am talking about does not have to be of a particular kind only. This should be made clear. It can be an interest of a moral character, an interest in the order's existence because in the particular society certain values are shared, by all its members, it might be a purely material interest, or it may be both at the same time.

With respect to the integration of the international society, looking at it from the outside, so to speak—not from the point of view of the individual state but from the point of view of the international society as a whole—this perhaps is the main problem today: how to make It clear, or how to make it true, that the individual states, which are the active agents in that society, should act in a manner tending to strengthen the international society, again not necessarily out of moral considerations, but because it is to their interest. This was taken for granted in the nineteenth century, when all the subjects of the international society were, more or less, Western countries. It was taken for granted because they shared certain common interests as well as certain common values.

In fact, this particular point of view is something that I find is lacking in trying to look at the problems of economic development or the international society from a global point of view. I am not thinking in terms of expressions of wishes—"How nice it would be if things were nice," and so on—but of trying to develop the kind of analysis of factors and of situations which would assume, let us say, the necessity of avoidance of frictions within the world society in the same way in which we assume that necessity within the national society.

There is a further point which I could make if I were to discuss the problems of a legal, juridical, approach to the whole subject. I should say, perhaps, and I suppose it is self-evident, that I think there is a basic necessity for taking into account the legal factors in the problems of economic development. In fact, one of the problems I sometimes find in economic discussions (especially economic, perhaps, rather than political science discussions) is that certain legal attitudes and legal institutions are taken for granted. It is assumed that the Western legal institutions and the Western legal framework are not merely the best, but even to some extent the only ones, something I am afraid that lawyers, too, are very much wont to do, but which they somehow are trying to get away from.

Mr. KREININ: I was very much impressed by the attempt to provide a framework here. I think that for people in disciplines other than political science it was difficult to absorb everything on the spur of the moment. As Dr. Holt was talking, I was simply trying to relate a few things from my experience to that framework, because a framework is only as good as the content you can fill it with.

Let us suppose that the government gets involved in development because entrepreneurial ability is in short supply in the country. While some people sitting around this table will dispute this, I maintain that there is such a shortage and that it is one of the reasons why government needs to participate in development. Let us further suppose that along with the development process the nation also adopts democratic institutions. How compatible are these two aims? The government can follow a labor-intensive line of development—and I am trying to relate this to Professor Lewis's remarks last night—which would mean that, the investments are spread throughout the economy, raising the level of living of everybody by a small per cent every year.

Alternatively, the government can adopt a showpiece type of approach which would involve the concentration of investment capital in a few capital-intensive industries, benefiting directly only a small segment of the population.

What are the government chances of getting re-elected? Very few people would be impressed by an imperceptible increase in the standard of living of everybody under the first course postulated above. But showpieces appeal to many voters. Therefore you will find that often the drive toward industrialization and away from agriculture—much more than is warranted by factor endowments—is caused *by* the fact that the government has to seek votes afterwards. Examples of showpieces constructed partly in order to attract the votes are a large hotel in Enugu, which, as expected, is filled to 20 per cent of capacity, and similar hotels in Lagos and in Ibadan, as well as capital-intensive industrial complexes which employ very few people.

An interesting phenomenon in that context is the settlement projects in Africa. As you know, the Africans are seeking ways to reorganize their agriculture, and one thing they have been trying to adapt from the Israelis is the Moshav system, which is essentially a multipurpose cooperative. Containing about one hundred families, it combines both elements of cooperation and of private-investment initiative. It affords the utilization of large-scale efficient methods, and at the same time retains private initiative. It is the combination of these two features which is attractive, and the FAO considers it very applicable to Africa.

In Israel they also developed regional settlement units whereby about ten Moshavim are scattered around a rural center, and several such combinations surround a regional town. The Nigerians, the Burmese and others have been trying to copy that kind of settlement. While in Nigeria, I inquired about the purpose of such settlement schemes—which cost large sums of money. Are they really going to cure agriculture in Nigeria? The answers were usually couched in terms of the demonstration effect and the effect on the school-leavers in the country who might be attracted back to the farms. I asked further, "Aren't they going to absorb all the agricultural budget of the country, leaving no funds for extension?"

Curiously enough, all the extension service people were for the settlement project. I asked them why, and they said, "This, in a sense, is much like an industrial project. The government needs a showpiece. It is not about to allocate the money for extension because extension is considered a failure. Extension will not revolutionize agriculture. On the other hand, the settlement project can be pointed to at election time and, although in itself it is not going to cure the agricultural problems of Nigeria, it has made more money available to agriculture, including extension, because some extension is tied into the settlement project."

What I am trying to say, essentially, is that the democratic process can drive the government to engage in a highly capital-intensive development effort in industry as well as in agriculture, where it is not warranted by economic conditions.

General Discussion

Chairman BLANKSTEN: Thank you, Professor Kreinin. Let me, before we launch into a general discussion, attempt to focus what has been said here. In an attempt to respond for political science, so to speak, to some of the things that were said this morning, Professor Holt has pointed out that the omnibus nature of political science as a discipline has tended to be such that we have less of a central theoretical core than do many other social science disciplines. Therefore a uniform kind of response is more difficult to make for political science than for many other disciplines.

One kind of response that could be made, although, this would likely not be held unanimously among political scientists, is that, through some kind of systems analysis such as the functional requisite analysis that Professor Holt attempted to sketch here, we could have a central systematic way of responding to many of the questions that are put to political scientists.

We did not. get an awful lot said about the international politics and diplomacy of development, but it may not be stretching Professor Holt's point too much to say that the system of analysis which he outlined for us could also provide ways and means for thinking about that kind of problem as well.

Let me now throw the floor open to general discussion.

Political Science, Theory, and Practical Democracy

Mr. KING: I want to focus on the objection that you had to the presentation of political problems to political scientists in a set form with rigid constrictions. It seems to me that this is the way problems must be presented. I was told yesterday, for example, that in the development process we must not have primary education of a certain type, or that primary education creates problems, that, the people cannot go into town and so forth. Now, today I am told that they cannot have democracy.

These are, it seems to me, the very things these people are after. Thus we *are* presented with problems with constraints, We are not necessarily asking a political scientist to set up a political system which will permit economic development, but to set up a democratic political system or to set up some other specified kind of a political system.

We are told, for example, in Thailand, "We want economic development but we want Buddhism. Don't tell us that Buddhism does not lend itself to development. Fix it so we can have both."

Now, let us look at democracy and ask the question, "Is it incompatible with, development?" I am told that democracy, as opposed, presumably, to other systems, leads to capital-intensive projects. Now. this seems to me to be false. Dictatorships are notorious for setting up capital-intensive projects. This is a standard economic objection to such regimes. For example, there is the Merdeka Stadium in Djakarta. Granted, there is also a Merdeka Stadium in Kuala Lumpur. You have stadiums under both systems. The biggest one is in Indonesia, but then they have more people there—100,000,000 people.

Political parties and labor unions have been mentioned. Certainly some political parties lend themselves—or unions—to policies which are destructive of economic development. Others are controlled in such a way that they further and foster the process of economic development. In Thailand you cannot impose irrigation water rates on the farmers. Why? Because the government, which has no contact with the people through the democratic process, is afraid of the reaction of the farmers. In Malaya where you do have this sort of contact, you can convince the people, through their political representatives, that water rates on irrigation are essential.

I am not here arguing in favor of democracy or against it. I am simply saying that the economists are faced with this problem: "Here is a country which is not suited to economic development, which is not suited to GNP growth; please fix it so the gross national product grows." If we were not faced with this contradiction, there would not be any problem. We all operate within constraints. I may have misinterpreted Mr. Holt, but the tenor of his arguments appeared to imply that democracy is an unfair constraint to put upon the political scientist. I would maintain that such a constraint may be a difficult one. But I would also maintain that in the world today there is no conclusive evidence that democracy is peculiarly unsuited for the development process.

Mr. HOLT: First of all, I do not object to the stating of questions within very narrow constraints. What I would like to say is that one should not expect to get an answer within those constraints because I think oftentimes the question has been phrased to the political scientist without consideration of the economic variables and the political variables that might change those constraints.

The second point I would like to make briefly has to do with the reference to dictatorship and democracy, because I think this is an area in which there has to be a great deal more precision in our analysis. When I was talking about democracy, I was emphasizing its procedural characteristics. When you talked about dictatorship, you were associating a particular kind of procedure with a certain set of government functions, particularly control over resource allocation. I would say these are two different dimensions. You can have dictatorship with a very limited range of government involvement in the economy. You can have democracy with a great range of government involvement in the economy. The factor that is involved here is the wide range of government involvement in the economy, which I think tends to lead to these capital-intensive projects whether it is democratic or dictatorial.

As to the third point, about, "After all, we have to have democracy but we want you to tell us how to go about getting it," I would simply say that social systems are not that flexible. There are certain kinds of conditions under which you can say, "You cannot have economic growth of 4 or 5 per cent at the present time; there is a set of prerequisites that has to be met first and there have to be slower growth rates first. There is a set of institutions and there is a set of structural changes that have to come about; what we will try to do is to establish a non-democratic system, but the kind of non-democratic system that has the highest probability of giving rise to a democratic system after several generations."

What I would argue here on the basis of my work is that if you superimpose the mechanisms of democratic government—universal suffrage, et cetera, et cetera, et cetera—at too early a stage of economic development, you actually increase the probability of a totalitarian dictatorship and you might be much better off aiming in the direction, let us say, of the kind of authoritarianism that existed in England in the 1820s or in Japan under the Shogunate. If you introduce universal suffrage and freedom for labor unions too early, what you are probably doing is introducing the features so conducive to the manipulation of masses that are associated with the totalitarian dictatorships of the twentieth century.

Mr. KREININ: I would like to ask a question of Mr. King. What actually is the meaning of democracy in a country in which 90 per cent of the people are completely illiterate and really do not know what they are voting for?

Mr. KING: The first question is really whether some of these places should be countries, is it not? We are again faced with constraints. Have we, perhaps, given some areas their freedom too soon?

Mr. KREININ: Well, we cannot do anything about that.

Mr. KING: That is true. But to return to the question of democracy with an illiterate citizenry, I would say we have to play a game here—a game which is played in so-called successful democracies—where the leadership will play the game of democracy and yet not give in or not knuckle under to the demands of the mob, but rather lead the mob.

This can be done. Let me make it clear, however, that my idea was to say that if people demand democracy, if they want it, then, if the political scientist is to perform his role properly, he must come up with an answer within this constraint which will satisfy the people. I am not necessarily suggesting that democracy is everywhere equally applicable, but I would suggest that in most places it is. I am aware of the standard problems. Nevertheless, I maintain that it is the leadership that must play the game, the democratic game, and make it work.

Mr. NASH: In most of these countries which are underdeveloped the best they can do is sort of a weak-kneed tyranny. Totalitarianism is an industrial phenomenon.

Mr. KREININ: You mean a benevolent dictatorship? Is that what you mean?

Mr. NASH: No—just a capricious kind of tyranny. Totalitarianism—

Chairman BLANKSTEN: Perhaps what you mean is "authoritarian" rather than "totalitarian."

Economic Nationalism: Monuments and Development

Mr. NASH: What I think looms even larger in the developing countries is the idea of economic nationalism, whatever the political system. One of the things of the twentieth century—one of the developments in this century—is that governments are considered, even in free enterprise systems, the custodians of the GNP, Whatever the numbers are, it is their fault in any kind of system.

If you have economic nationalism with a thinly Westernized elite, you have obvious kinds of consequences. Some of these I have looted from Harry Johnson and some I have invented, but, given economic nationalism and the fact that the government is the custodian of the GNP, you will get symbolic behavior irrespective of the type of political system because they are going to put up something that, is a symbol of the nation, whether it is stadia or pagodas, You could think of all sorts of things.

The second thing you will get is a drive toward nationalization insofar as the government can nationalize. It will nationalize against: Western interest groups. The third thing you will get is indigenousization, a conscious attempt to put the economy in the hands of nationals and run out Chinese or Lebanese or whoever are around with entrepreneurial skills.

Fourthly, from a strictly economic point of view, you must get mal-allocation of resources and mal-placement, of industry, because you have to place them politically. Israel is a good example and provides an illustration I like. The cost of these frontier settlements you mentioned probably makes them one of the worst investments in the world. If they took that money and put it in AT&T, Israel would be a much richer place—but not a country. I think some of these mal-allocations, from an economic point of view, are part of the price, you have to pay for the process of building a nation.

Possibly the symbolic behavior may have long-range payoffs that are not: immediate. The symbolic behavior of the Mexicans in building large museums and restoring the Indian heritage and making people proud of it has. I think, had that sort of payoff. In the short run these nations are stuck with economic nationalism irrespective of political systems and some of them might have great payoffs.

Mr. ANDERSON: I would like a little more instruction on the process by which the public acquires the idea that these factories or dams or stadia are things on which the government is going to stake its prestige. I do not quite see how the effect of building these monuments filters down to the semi-1iterate or wholly illiterate peasants in Kenya. That is a puzzle to me.

Professor Nash has, I think, in part answered the related question, although I am not wholly satisfied with his answer. Why does economic nationalism seem to keep prosperity indefinitely postponed so far as the citizens are concerned and lead them to be willing to accept showy symbols while leaving their bellies empty? I do not see that economic nationalism gives any explanation for this. I think there are other factors that have not been mentioned.

Mr. GINSBURG: I do not think the masses really care about these matters. It seems to me that the significance of large public works is greatest, for a very small elite which has acquired its notions about the significance of these things from contact with the West and usually abroad. It takes a good deal of persuasion, I suspect, even in Indonesia, to convince the general populace that a great stadium is a good thing, that the enlarged airport is a great achievement; and I think this point has a bearing also on some questions that were raised about industrial managers in the Near East preferring machines rather than people.

It was said that these managers do not like all those chaps around. That's true. They do not like all "those chaps" around because they are more alien to them, that is, to the common laborer than they are to the machines, since they have gone to engineering school in France or Britain.

Chairman BLANKSTEN: Are there studies of the perception by these people of these monuments? I suppose there are not.

Mr. MIRACLE: There is at least one study that has been done in Latin America of what information gets down to the grass-roots level and what people at the grass-roots level perceive, and it is precious little in this particular study. They know the name of the local soccer hero, who is Pele, and apparently has had a Russian monument given to him; and they do not often know who the president of Brazil is—of course, some of us do not either because it has changed so frequently—they do not know what the country's leading export is, what a dollar is, and a lot of things like this.

Now, I would very much like to see some of this research done In Africa because I think it is tremendously important in development to see what the communication pattern is from the planners and their advisors, he they Americans or others, to the people who are locally involved in these situations.

But I wanted to try to answer part of the question that Professor Anderson raised. I think the important thing about the big showpieces is that they are so visible, not that people necessarily want them, but when they come to the city they can see them. Secondly. I do not think the people at the grass-roots level are sacrificing as individuals as much as we are led to believe by our notions of hungry people or empty stomachs.

There may be such sacrifice in education, but there has been much talk about two-thirds of the world being hungry, there are "freedom from hunger" campaigns, and so on, which is like the rate of growth of GNP in that it needs to be clarified and worked on. We do not have nutritional studies which demonstrate that Africa is hungry; perhaps India or some other place is, but what I am saying is, perhaps these people are not giving up so much. Perhaps as far as they are concerned this stadium is a net addition that was not there in the colonial regime, and they are happy to have it.

Chairman BLANKSTEN: Why is it assumed that people, upon being shown these things, will react positively to them?

Mr. BINDER: If there is a good game going on in the stadium, they enjoy it. After a lot of rioting in East Pakistan they built the stadium and it was a lot more fun to watch other people fight with one another in the stadium than to fight with one another outside.

Mr. GINSBURG: Some studies have been made of perception in environment, but it is not the kind of environment that has been talked about here. It is environment that is partially natural and partly man-created and which people have to deal with as resource complexes when they are planning particular kinds of development projects. For example, we have two students in East Africa who have been studying the attitudes of certain tribal groups toward water as a resource and toward the control and manipulation of water resource and toward the control and manipulation of water resources for developmental purposes. They have not yet found anything remarkable but this at least is one field of investigation in which pioneering is being done, and I think it quite important.

Mr. WERNER: I want to comment on this stadium business. I am not so sure that there is not a lot of mileage in such a proposition. I do know that, in Indonesia the Sukarno regime went to great lengths to publicize it. The majority of small children do attend primary school and in every primary school they were required to write little essays on what this meant to the country. Further, groups of people were invited, at their own expense, to come from all over the nation to Djakarta, to see it.

With respect to the foreign communities, this thing was publicized at great length and perhaps every foreigner who could possibly have any connection with it or see it was informed by a variety of means that Indonesia was a great country to be able to build this thing, and put it together. The fact that it was built with foreign aid was carefully concealed as much as possible, and instead emphasis was given to the fact that this was a symbol that they were putting the country together effectively.

I am not so sure that they did not try to really use this as a political tool to impress the population—both domestic and foreign.

Mr. MORGAN: To supplement Professor Werner's comment, I want to add that I think I would trust the extremely sensitive political antenna of a person like Sukarno, for whom I think no praise could be excessive as an effective politician in office—I mean this in a negative sense as well as positive—rather than surveys. I think Sukarno knows what he is doing politically, at least with respect to showplaces.

Mr. HOLT: With regard to keeping himself in power? If you are talking about sensitive political antenna, I assume it pertains to keeping himself in power.

Mr. MORGAN: Yes. That is what I mean.

Mr. HOLT: That is one kind of a problem. But you can also, it seems to me, address yourself here to the problems of what kind of political system is he evolving, and what is the impact upon economic development, and this is something else. Here he may not know what he is doing at all.

Mr. MORGAN: I do not think he has any interest, in economic growth at all.

Mr. KREININ: I think there are two points involved. First of all, it is rather unfortunate that we have placed so much emphasis upon the stadium. It is true that the stadium is a symbol but it is merely that. What I was trying to suggest was the frequent occurrence of developments of capital-intensive industry—the idea that every country ought to have a steel mill. I am not talking about, stadiums; rather, I would prefer to discuss steel mills, which are more than symbolic.

Number two, I tend to agree with Professor Werner that these projects do have some impact. In the settlement project case, farmers are brought from all over the region to observe the project and learn from it. Additionally, it is not very important whether it actually makes an impact on the population. What is really important is that the leaders believe it has such an impact; this is really what guides them. It may be that if after a certain number of years they are proven wrong, they might change their minds. So you have some interaction here between the degree of actual impact on the people, on the one hand, and the perception and anticipation of the leaders themselves on the other.

Generally speaking, I think there is some impact. In addition, there is another prestige factor, an external one. If a leader wants to acquire international reputation, he needs to have some kind of a capital-intensive complex to show the visiting dignitaries from other countries.

Mr. BINDER: Other developing countries?

Mr. KREININ: Other developing countries, that is right.

Mr. WARREN: I hate to add historical depth to this discussion, but if we would consult Robert Adams, for instance, at the University of Chicago, he would tell us that every civilization, beginning with Meso-potamia, has been involved with impressive visual symbols of one kind or another; the pyramids in Egypt and in Mesopotamia and in Central America, and so on. Evidently there is some connection between the level of social complexity and these symbols.

They may also have other important functions as Mr. Kreinin sug-gests, for instance, steel mills, Steel mills are very impressive visually, and to take it back again to the concept of the pyramids, they have other functions as well, which involve the supernatural and so on. Perhaps we are attributing certain developments to contact with Western culture which are really part of some other kind of phenomenon, namely, social complexity.

Mr. WERNER: Might I just add that in our own history we did some of these things, such as building the city of Washington, or at least lay-ing it out and starting it at a time when we could have put that money to other more economical uses.

Chairman BLANKSTEN: I hate to be a divisive force here, but may I mention stadia at state universities? (Laughter.)

Is there anything further to be said about monuments, stadia or steel mills?

Mr. ANDERSON: I am still bothered about something. I thought it was said that in these countries the governments stand or fall on the basis of these spectacular projects, I still have not understood how it comes about that the public who vote will make the government stand or fall on those projects rather than on something which is economically more presumably relevant. This issue I do not think has been dealt with yet.

Mr. NASH: I do not think it was asserted that they stand or fall on the monuments. The governments I have seen in the underdeveloped, countries stand or fail on the inherited charisma from the struggle for independence and these people are the Western elite, the remnants of the civil service, and a few soldiers who are the country. For example, in Burma this government gets elected, because U Nu, if he ever gets out of jail, could win any election any day. He enshrines and embodies the independence movement, and he is a devout and pious Buddhist, and he appeals to the peasants, and he will win any free election. He does not. have to do anything but be U Nu to win.

Now, one of the things about being U Nu is to build monuments. He does it. What drives him, I do not know, but these elites are all driven to build monuments, not to get votes. U Nu does not know how to run a country, it is pretty obvious, but one thing he can do is build a monument or build, a pagoda—the World Peace Pagoda, a beautiful thing.

Mr. HARING: I agree with what Manning Nash has just said. Building monuments is political language, and there is nothing you can do about it. A politician is going to talk the politician's language and this is a part of it.

Mr. HOLT: First, I do not know why we should associate a government staying in power with economic development. I think you can make a good argument for the fact that probably the way in which you encourage economic development is to rotate governments every 18 months. You are talking here about the problem of monuments and pyramids, and you are talking about it in the context of political advice. Perhaps what you might want to do is to tie in a United States foreign aid program with a restriction on building monuments even though it may contribute to the overthrow of the government in a short period of time.

What I was suggesting earlier is that you tend to decrease the probability of expenditure on monuments as you reduce the government's role in economy. That is the point I was trying to make. This would be the kind of recommendation in this regard that I think would be relevant.

Mr. WHITEFORD: I would like to follow up on this comment because what we are talking about, really, is communication. With the pyramids, with the stadia and with all these other things, what you have are communicative symbols by which the government or the party in power says to the people, "We're strong, we're powerful, we're able to do all of these impressive things." Some of them may be completely worthless so far as what they will do for the people of the country. Others maybe very valuable, but certainly the evidence seems to suggest that many of these projects, for example, the building of the steel mill at Paz del Rio in Colombia, are symbolical kinds of development. While *we* were in Colombia a couple of years ago, the newspapers had a great deal of information about land reform and potential land reform, and yet, when we talked to the people, the response was almost completely negative. They told us either that nothing was going on or that it was all government talk.

When we crossed the border into Venezuela, we were impressed by the fact that, all along the road we kept seeing laree signs, big billboards that were 15 feet high and 20 feet across, at frequent intervals which advertised the land reform program. I do not know whether there was any more land reform going on in Venezuela than there was in Colombia, but certainly the people in Venezuela had every opportunity to be more informed about it or at least impressed with it; I think the billboards were the same sort of things as stadia. These were the means of communication by which the government was saying to the people, "We're doing *this*," or "We're doing *something*." Frequently it does not have very much to do with whether it is something important, direct or economic, at all.

The Diplomacy of Development

Mr. GINSBURG: I am interested in the behavior of states in an existing world system which is not closed but is partly open, because over a quarter of the world (i.e., China) is not now involved in what we normally think of as a closed system. Nevertheless, there is a world political system that we can describe, or at least attempts have been made to describe it, and states play certain roles within it. What I would be interested in knowing is how the political scientist, if you like, can help us appraise the behavior of states that are developing or underdeveloped. This appraisal might be on a rather abstract and perhaps theoretical level—or, better, on an empirical level first and then on a theoretical one. How can we incorporate our observations into a systems analysis of the sort that can also be used for the examination of the internal political organization of these new and developing states? Most important, how should, all other things being equal, a state that wishes to develop rapidly behave in the world system if it wishes to maximize its opportunities for economic growth?

Mr. HOLT: I think your first question here is really one of the very fundamental ones. It is not a question, however, which is very much in gear with the earlier kinds of considerations of this conference, I think there are two or three observations that could be made. Let me talk about one of them. It seems to me that an argument can be made that as industrialization proceeds in the developing countries, some of the traditional structures which were very crucial in the social integration of that society tend to break down. One of the problems that the developing society is confronted with is the problem of developing new symbols of loyalty and the problem of developing new social structures to deal with the problem of integration.

I think that, one of the ways in which this can be done is through a certain kind of aggressive foreign policy in which you identify an external enemy, so to speak, and try to solidify, or resolidify, the community in which certain of these integrated mechanisms have broken down, on the basis of a new kind of orientation.

If you look over the sweep of history, you find some kind of empirical association of extreme nationalism and aggressive foreign policy with the periods of the most rapid economic growth. The United States at the time of the Spanish-American War, Germany in the twentieth century, France under Napoleon III are examples of what I am talking about.

Mr. GINSBURG: If this is an empirical observation, then I can think of enough exceptions to it that I wonder how valid it is.

Mr. HOLT: I think the way I would state this, and what I was trying to say more precisely, is that you may be increasing the probability of this kind of international behavior in a period in which relatively rapid industrialization is breaking down some of the traditional structures. Certainly there are exceptions to it, but I would think of this in terms of increasing the probability of this kind of behavior.

Mr. GINSBURG: Are you talking about states that want to develop, or poor countries?

Mr. HOLT: I am talking about states that have gone through a certain initial stage of development to the extent that many of their traditional structures have broken down. I am not talking about a state that is just thinking about doing it; I am thinking about states that have gone partially through the process of it, That is what I mean by "developing."

Mr. FATOUROS: Of course, it is true that the identification of a foreign enemy is very often a matter of self-assertion, rather than aggression. For instance, this attitude. The attitude itself is really tar less aggressive than self-asserting. There is a difference, I think, in the kind of manifestations that follow from each kind of attitude.

I would agree that in some cases there is an aggressive attitude as a component of development. That, of course, is a common and very old factor in foreign and international affairs. On the other hand, the role of the developing countries in the present state of the world society is becoming increasingly important; this happens in part for reasons which may seem at first glance without substance; for instance, simply because they have formal statehood. But this formal statehood does represent or make evident, to a considerable extent, substantive problems, such as the problems of the welfare of the people involved—the people represented by the state. It is probably possible to say that, in a great number of cases, developing countries, or their governments, react in the same manner as a developed country would react if it were in a similar situation, but, in fact, the developed countries are not in a similar situation. On the other hand, a great number of developing countries are in situations which are fairly similar to one another.

For instance, take their attitude on solving economic problems, regardless of whether they are correct or not in terms of economic theory. I am thinking especially of the problems of international trade or the problems of international economic assistance. Simply because their interests are common in this particular connection, this leads to the development of a kind of bloc, that is, a unified, common attitude toward certain problems. This is a new factor in present-day international politics which it is important to examine: how far the perception of the similarity of their problems leads to similar conclusions and therefore to similar attitudes toward the developed countries, on the one hand, and toward the Soviet Union, on the other.

We can go very much further in that direction. We can examine how far it is possible in international politics to talk today in terms of bipolarity; although I do not know if this is exactly what we have been talking about here. I think the presence of the developing countries has made a difference, to a certain extent. Their presence leads to a restructuring of the world society, Again, and this is somewhat more tentative, something that should perhaps be studied: how far is there a common perception of their interests even when they are not similar, or how far is there different perception when the problems are similar.

Sister THOMASINE: Let me carry that a step further and perhaps along a little bit more practical lines. Most of us are aware that last year at the various world trade conferences the underdeveloped countries outvoted the developed ones. There have been some very humorous remarks with respect to that situation, but perhaps that sense of identification between nations which normally would be rivals will have a positive world political result, something akin to what Mr. Lewis mentioned last night. Perhaps the underdeveloped countries will soon be more in a position to trade with one another and to uphold their part of the world economy.

Foreign Aid and International Development

Mr. BINDER: I have put together some notes regarding this problem of the international aspect of development. It seems to me that if our discussion is to be articulated with the scheme we have on the blackboard [See Figure 1], it of course has to do with the structural aspects of that environmental sector which is labeled "Other Societies," and one of the problems with which we would have to concern ourselves would be the changing structure of the international system to which the domestic system has to adapt itself—in that goal attainment triangle, I suppose. Some things may be done within the country in terms of economic activities—adaptation proper—and some things may be done in terms of political activity domestically, and some may be done in terms of economic activity outside of the country itself with the establishment of economic and trading blocs among the developing countries themselves, or in terms of more effective trade relations.

I would like to call to your attention three possible configurations of an international structure, terms that are in general use, although I suppose in this form Morton Kaplan may be more responsible for them than anyone else: these are a bipolar system, a loose bipolar system and perhaps a multipolar system. What I am really talking about is the decline in bipolarity in recent years, the result of a fragmentation of the blocs. The question that I am asking, for no one in particular to answer, because it is a question we all have to face, is this: what is the consequence for economic development of developing areas of the changing structures in the international system? It changed from what seemed to be a bipolar system to a multipolar one.

Under bipolarity itself I am not entirely sure that the competition between the two great blocs—over the extension of assistance to the developing nations—was a really necessary kind of competition. That is, I do not know whether it was vital to the United States and vital to the Soviet Union that they be the first ones in with assistance to the developing countries.

In other words, I am suggesting that I am not sure that the developing countries were necessary to the defense of the West or to the defense of the East against one another; and we might well have been able, in terms of a very narrowly construed self-interest, to turn our backs on the developing countries. But we did not. We assumed, for perhaps logically inconsistent reasons in terms of the rest of our foreign policy, that we ought to and must assist the developing countries. We decided, in other words, that bipolarity required our assistance in the developing areas.

Now, as the Western bloc loosened a little bit before the Eastern bloc had shown evidence of this loosening, I think there developed a pattern which was essentially bilateral—in some cases multilateral—of economic assistance from subordinate bloc members of the West, Britain, France, Holland, Belgium, and Italy. Bilateral, and in some few cases multilateral, assistance came from subordinate bloc members of the Western bloc to the members of the New National Internationale, if you will, or the Third World. The reasons for this seem to have something to do with the search for prestige on the part of subordinate bloc members of the West. They seem also to have something to do with the desire to loosen the Western bloc by increasing the power of subordinate bloc members through their relations with the developing areas, and perhaps to strengthen or to restrengthen such organizations as the British Commonwealth and the French Community.

These kinds of activities broaden the pattern of trade and the possibilities for development on the part of the new nations. They also give them a little bit of schooling in maneuver, in how to play off one possible donor against another possible donor. They have much more opportunity to maneuver than when they only had two, the United States and the Soviet Union, and in fact, in the earlier days of the postwar period it was only the United States that was really helping and it was merely a threat of possibly working with the Soviet Union that was used as an inducement. I think, the real schooling in maneuver happened in what we might call a middle period.

Now, I do not think that this kind of economic activity really was the effective thing in loosening the two blocs, but it was part of a tendency which developed while loosening was going on and it has increased, I think, now that we can look around and say that we do not really have a bipolar system any more. At least the two blocs, if there are only two blocs, are extremely loose and there is lots of room for maneuver on the part of the nations of the Third World among the various bloc members. For example, you can now set China against Russia in this framework of economic assistance, and I guess African nations particularly are able to do this.

At the very same time, with the explosion of a nuclear bomb by the Chinese Communists, this points up the possibility that some of these developing nations, unable to fulfill the aspirations of their citizens, may well be able to blast the rest of us to kingdom come, or at least set off an exchange of nuclear explosions that will lead to that. In viewing the Third World, therefore, we can ask what our attitude ought to be and what our attitude must be.

We can ask the question again: do we need to help these countries now that we see that the world is not going to divide up into two groups which will seek to eliminate each other? Do we have a more stable international picture which will permit us to say, "Well, we don't, have to worry about the disposition of every single people in every single country in the world?" Or do we have *a* situation where any country having control of nuclear weapons can blow all of us up so that we have to be concerned, vitally concerned, with the domestic tranquility of any little pipsqueak of a country anywhere in the world, because they might get hold of a nuclear bomb and heaven knows what will happen? Therefore, any tiny country of a million population or something like that can hold an atomic bomb against our head and say, "If you don't help me, I'll blow myself up." And the rest of us have to do something about it and offer economic assistance to try and straighten out the problem.

This has not yet come to be, but nuclear weapons are indeed a great equalizer and may return us to a situation of intense concern with the economic welfare of even the smallest and seemingly most inconsequential country. There is a possibility, 'which I think is even more likely, that nuclear warfare is pretty nearly impossible because much as we may need psychiatric aid, we are not that far gone. Therefore, once again one may argue, "Well, who cares? We have a lot of problems to worry about even with some of the larger countries."

It is not at all clear to me from this changing pattern of international relations and the changing distribution of nuclear weapons, and from the loosening of the blocs, that we ought to go on in the same way as we, have in the past. For 15 years we have been saying something about economic development and maybe now we can just forget about it. We have not solved the problem but perhaps we do not have to solve the problem any more for these countries. We certainly have to ask ourselves whether, given these new circumstances, the problem remains the same; and I do not think we have asked ourselves this question here.

A third possibility is, of course, that the struggle between East and West, between right and wrong, between good and bad, between up and down, will continue by other means and not by means of bloc formation. It may be fought out in terms of cultural and economic development. Perhaps we ought to redouble our efforts and recognize that this is a real front, and not try to shoot the moon, and not increase our nuclear stock-pile, but indeed, turn our efforts entirely away from military development, or largely away from military development to the seeking of means for winning friends in the Third World.

I think there is one last consideration I would like to put before you and that is that the remarks made by Professor de Schweinitz this morning were largely correct that it has been the political environment of this previous period of bipolarity or would-be bipolarity which led us to bring these countries into being. Someone had said, perhaps they should not be countries, This may be true, but is there now any residual moral obligation that we have, despite the changed structure of the international system, to keep these countries in being even though they came into being for reasons that had to do with the previous structure of the international system?

Mr. BARANSON: It strikes me as very interesting that this whole business of power relationships involves a gamesmanship of development. I think it. is interesting to recall that during the nineteenth and early twentieth centuries, nationalism and self-determination became pawns in big power politics, and sometimes ran away with events—Sarajevo and World War I are an example. In more recent times, Vietnam is a live pawn in the international power struggle.

The fact is that we have come up with some odd forms of development gamesmanship. For example, President Kennedy talked about "peaceful evolution" in Latin America, He wanted to see change, to get the process started but then he hoped to laboratory-control it so it would not go too far left and upset our power position vis-à-vis world communism. This is indeed a game involving pawns that have their own volition and dynamics and it becomes especially intricate with the United States viewing economic development in terms of political goals entailing controlled social change.

For the game we are trying to play, our understanding and know-how are themselves highly underdeveloped.

Mr. NASH: I think we have shifted the terms. We were earlier talking about elites trying to get through a process with their peasantry, and then we got up to the big powers who, I really think (except for the Alliance for Progress, in which I do not believe much more than do most Latin Americans), are not sincerely interested and do not sincerely act for economic development goals,

We act in Korea, Vietnam, Cuba, or whatever. We like economic development and it would be nice if it would pay off; but the main reason is political and not for the internal necessary benefit of the government being aided.

With respect to Cambodia, the Cambodians are not hungry, they are not striving for development, and yet we have given them $350,000,000 in the last ten years—there are only five million Cambodians—and their GNP stays exactly the same. This is an amazing business. It takes great skill to absorb all of that without improving your GNP. (Laughter.)

The problem of economic development and international relations, I think, has not really been joined. The big power relations to the poor, non-prosperous countries tends to be political and mainly oriented toward self-interest. I throw that out as a view of my own. Perhaps, as a footnote to what Professor Binder said, maybe the world situation has changed enough that the attention the powers give to the non-prosperous countries could really be in terms of economic development, but I think the situation from 1945 to 1960 was such that we could not seriously be interested in economic development so much as in allies or non-trouble spots.

Mr. FATOUROS: Do we have, really, to separate the two or the three so clearly? That is, is it really completely inconsistent to have at the same time, the goals of having a friend in Asia, and avoiding a trouble spot, and assisting economic development? If you could assist economic development, and in this manner avoid a trouble spot and have a good friend—I agree that this is a very big "if"—but if this were so, then this would be a set of consistent objectives for American foreign policy. The problem is, how far is it true that assisting economic development does not serve the two other purposes, and especially the one of avoiding a trouble spot? Of course, the problem is made worse, because no alternative is suggested, at least I have not heard yet of any possible alternative.

Assuming that international economic aid does not assist economic development in fact, or does not assist it in a proper way, that it does not gain friends and does not avoid trouble spots, what else can be done? The problem is that the only alternative that appears probable is a much worse trouble situation, as far as trouble is concerned—a purely negative situation, from the point of view of the Soviet Union, or the point of view of the United States. I do not see any positive gain in this for either party. In fact, I have the impression that part of the trouble between China and the Soviet Union can be stated in these terms. The

Soviet Union is saying, "We have to help them. We don't know what will happen if we don't, but we cannot avoid helping; we cannot take a different attitude toward the underdeveloped countries," and China is saying, "No, we prefer revolution," I have then the impression that one of the strongest factors in favor of economic aid as a tool of American foreign policy is really the fear of the alternatives rather than a positive and clear objective in extending foreign aid.

Mr. HARING: It seems to me that it is the frame in which this whole picture sits. The kindergarten facts of the nation-state system, are an analogue or parallel to the laissez-faire system. In place of economic men you have self-interested nations, and these are amoral nations, as they were amoral economic men in the laissez-faire system.

Secondly, economists know better than anybody why the laissez-faire system could not perpetuate itself. It broke up and went bankrupt for dozens and dozens of reasons we all recognize.

The nation-state system is in the process of going bankrupt in this same sense and we can predict, I think fairly safely, that this sort of power politics system just cannot last, it is impossible.

We all know this in our bones but we do not see *any* way out of it. When you think of laissez-faire states and so forth, one can do some pretty good guessing as to why is going to happen.

Then, regarding economic development, if you change these amoral economic man-nation-states into social creatures, there develops a concern for each other's affairs that has been forced upon them whether they like it or not. So, of course, they (and we) are going to be concerned with the economic development of the rest of the world for these reasons. The reasons become political as the nation-state system goes bankrupt. This is a long range trend, and I see it as being inevitable, although somebody may disagree.

International Economic Cooperation

Mr. MORGAN: I have three brief questions I want to ask. Quite honestly, I would be glad to have answers from anybody, and I suppose especially from political scientists, One is suggested by Professor Lewis's comment that economic problems are relatively simple—I have heard people from the International Bank say the same thing—and the real problems are of another kind; also his observation that there are lots of rascals in power, I wonder whether political scientists, or others, could develop any generalization on whether you are more likely to have rascals in power in low-income countries that are developing successfully, as compared with those that are developing more slowly or not at all? That is one question.

Second, it has been fashionable in recent years to be concerned with the possibilities of regional cooperation. The United States Government has the problem of the extent to which it should favor and encourage this concern. Generally the attitude has been favorable, And yet such efforts have fallen on dubious days, if not perhaps evil days.

I would generalize that the East Asia cooperative movements were mainly stimulated by the rise of the Common Market in Europe. They were visualized as defensive efforts against it. As the Common Market has seemed to be less malevolent and less threatening, and perhaps as political events have had their turbulent way in the East, these efforts have diminished.

The very successful East African organizations are, I think, now weaker than they were some years ago: Kenya, Tanzania, and Uganda are having their problems of getting along together. The Latin American Free Trade Association seems to be having its own problems. Can we generalize to any extent about the dynamics of cooperation among such areas?

Mr. Lewis, of course, suggested increased trade among low-income areas as *a way* out of some of their burdensome economic problems.

My third question is a practical one. At the Geneva meetings one of the main recommendations from low-income countries was that they would like to have trade preferences granted to them from high-income countries. The French have been awkward about this and have supported the notion of concessions by mother countries only to their previous colonies—five or six bilateral arrangements.

The, Germans have lately supported a more general arrangement in which *all* high-income countries should give trade concessions on imports from *all* low-income countries. My question is: which is the better policy?

Chairman BLANKSTEN: Does anyone want to respond to these questions?

Mr. KING: On this question of the dynamics of economic cooperation and with special reference to Southeast Asia and ECAFE, my experience suggests that, economists are playing it down. When I worked for the World Bank any mention of a common market for Asia or Southeast Asia was immediately met by the response, "This is premature." If you were to then ask, "Well, when does it become mature? When is the time?" the response was, "We don't know, but any thought before the right moment would be quite out of line."

In Southeast Asia there is, of course, fear of Japan dominating the market. Nevertheless and despite many professional economists arguing against a common market—showing that these countries do not trade with each other and there is no point to it—still the Manila Declaration at the ECAFE meeting went ahead to say that such a market ought to be created. Then political considerations prevented the furtherance of the limited goal of discussion of such matters. Here again you get this problem of a constructive policy versus a political-monument goal: they would rather have a Maphilindo [Maylasia-Philippine-Indonesia Alliance], they would rather have a Bandung atmosphere. Here again is a contrast with the little steps which may not be very dramatic: an extension service versus a stadium, a conference that examines steps toward a common market which may be 20 years off; versus the emotionalism, of the Bandung, or uncommitted powers, or New Emerging Forces!

I see a parallel here between the domestic and the international policies of the underdeveloped countries. I also see similar consequences: the threat of anarchy, the threat of the government giving up development internally, the threat of the developed nations getting fed up with the international scene and questioning the desirability of the whole assistance program.

I am sorry to have brought up stadiums again. Please forgive me.

Mr. SCHWARTZ: A minor note: the common market or free trade association arrangement regarded by economists to have the least chance of all—the Central American one—of which they spoke least favorably, even compared to LAFTA [Latin American Free Trade Association], has worked relatively well. It has certainly worked far better than LAFTA, probably for reasons which are basically political, not economic.

Mr. KREININ: I would underscore the point—that the enabling condition in the drive probably ought to be political. But I think the movement toward integration in underdeveloped countries was triggered by European integration, where you and I know that the benefits from integration, the economic analysis of integration, and the entire economic conditions leading to integration, are completely different. You are almost comparing incomparables.

When you come to Latin America, therefore, you should ask yourselves, even in strictly technical economic terms—let alone the political problems which probably are the determining factors—can these countries integrate? They face an overwhelming transport problem. It is cheaper to ship to the United States than to ship across the mountains to a neighboring country. They maintain extensive exchange control. What is the meaning of eliminating tariffs and quotas when you still have exchange controls and multiple-exchange rate systems?

Even the technical conditions for integration do not exist. Of course, the benefits to be derived from integration in the case of underdeveloped countries are different from those derived from the European Common Market or another industrial area; they ought to be analyzed differently.

Chairman BLANKSTEN: I would like to point out that about the only problem that has been mentioned in both sessions today, to which no one has responded, is the question of rogues and rascals in government. On the theory that it takes *a* rascal to catch one, I have asked Bob Holt to speak to that. Would you care to comment on rascality?

Mr. HOLT: As I understood your question, Professor Morgan, it was whether or not there is a greater likelihood that, you have rogues and rascals in a developing area or a rapidly developing area than you do in one that is relatively stagnant?

Mr. MORGAN: Yes. I was assuming that there would *be* more rogues and rascals in low-income areas because of low education generally arid other factors of background.

Mr. HOLT: When you talk about rogues and rascals you certainly have to identify the particular normative context in which you are identifying rogues and rascals, and this may differ very much from society to society.

It seems that when you have a relatively stable or stagnant kind of situation, you may get one kind of rogue. For example, if you have a new clique or *a* new dynasty coming into power, you may have rogues at. the beginning of this period and in their positions of power they proceed to redefine the mores of the community so that the same behavior which at one time would be defined as being that of rogues and rascals, at a later period—when they are still engaging in it—is considered to be a legitimate kind of undertaking.

When you are dealing with areas where there is rapid economic development and rapid political change, you certainly are increasing the frequency with which you are recruiting people into political roles, and you are tending to broaden the social groups from which you are recruiting people.

Often you have the phenomenon that the people who are coming in are not aware of the mores that govern the particular status which they are occupying and they act as rogues and rascals for a while until they learn these particular things.

From the point of economic development, however, I would like to make a further comment. When you are dealing with a situation in which the. state is performing a relatively active entrepreneurial role, I think there might be some economic advantages in having rogues in these particular political-economic kinds of roles.I think one of the important things to point out, however, is that there are rogues and then there are rogues.

I think it was Plunkett of Tammany Hall who talked about the difference between honest graft and dishonest graft. He said that it was perfectly all right (it was honest graft) if they told their friends that the city was going to condemn certain property and take it over for building, and they should buy it up because they would get rich within 18 months if they did. That is honest graft. When the Republican machine over in Philadelphia, however, sold the copper roof off the poorhouse, that was dishonest graft.

When we are looking at this problem it is necessary to identify a certain kind of roguish behavior that may be of economic advantage at a certain period, as contrasted with another kind of roguish behavior which really inhibits growth,

Mr. NASH; Sometimes I read political scientists, and Robert Dahl. I think, in his book[3] on how American cities are governed has some good clues for the kinds of systems under which rascality can flourish. He traces the change in American politics at city level from the machine kind of ethnic interests to the more pragmatic, unheroic politics, which characterized Boston, Philadelphia, and New York, and are beginning even in Chicago. His main theoretical apparatus is a good one.

There is a system of cumulative privilege. If one group has monopolies or quasi-monopolies on the resources, the education and the government, they can be "grafty," and as political systems evolve, one of the things which keeps them honest is not that they get moral or they get revelation, but it is a dispersion of privilege among groups who can do each other a lot of good or a lot of harm. No one group can do itself too much good or too much harm, so their interaction keeps them honest but does not lead to a change of heart,

He [Dahl] spells it out for one of our wicked old cities, New Haven, and I think the analysis can be lifted for the purpose of this discussion.

Mr. HOLT: I was not talking about a change of heart. I was talking about a change in the norm or a change in the structure.

Mr. NASH: I think the mechanism of cumulative dispersed privilege is the clue. How you get that started, I do not know.

Mr. HOLT: If you read political scientists on this, or if you read sociologists like Merton on the economic functions of the [political] machine in New York, you begin to get some sort of view of the economic contributions that are possible,

Mr. NASH: I do not believe in that kind of structural functional analysis. I just want to know why that machine was there. If it gave coal away, the latent function, I think, is childish. Just, why, in that kind of social system, do you have a machine?

If you say you have a machine and it stays there because it gives buckets of coal away, that is nice and interesting. Of course, Merton lived through the Depression.

Mr. HOLT: No, I was emphasizing here the comments about the functions it performed for big business in New York rather than the coal it gave away.

I merely said that it was useful, if you are talking about certain kinds of economic development. Whether these are functional interpretations or not, I do not care,

Mr. NASH: I have already exhibited my anti-functionalism.

Chairman BLANKSTEN: Before we adjourn this session, let me simply draw attention to what seemed to me to be some of the chief problems with which we have been concerned this afternoon.

In the first place, in discussing the system of analysis that Professor Holt put before us, we had a basis through functional requisite analysis to look at. certain kinds of questions, such as, what kinds of systemic properties set the limits within which governments can move in such directions as those related to economic development, arid the question of democracy, and the question of dictatorship, and wherein governments could operate in the developmental kind of context.

We discussed also, somewhat within that systemic context, the problem of monuments, stadia, steel mills, and so on. I have a feeling we did not get all of the mileage, theoretically, out of this problem that is probably possible.

Certain things seemed obvious: that these were quick visual symbols that, seemed to perform the function of mobilizing support or consent behind certain regimes. There was, I think, an interesting point in the communications theory regarding the functions of these monuments, and so on. Much of this, I think, can be handled in terms of the kinds of theoretical considerations which we opened up, but as I say, I have a kind of unfinished feeling about this monument and stadium problem, I think there is still more pay dirt in that which I do not think we reached.

We did, for a wonder, late in the session finally get to talk about international politics and diplomacy of development. Much of this, it seems to me, also lent itself to systemic analysis along the lines Professor Holt opened up for *us,* especially if we thought in terms of the environmental sector in the scheme with which he presented us. This helped us look at such things as the development in underdeveloped areas of common attitudes towards certain international problems; and helped us to understand some of the processes by which friends and enemies in the international community are identified.

Professor Binder also pointed out that it helped with certain problems in relating bipolar and other kinds of international assistance to such problems as foreign aid and technical assistance, and changes in nuclear capabilities among various countries in the international system.

We talked, somewhat in this context, about various types of economic cooperation. I had the feeling that that did not lend itself as readily to fitting within this same systematic frame as some of the other problems, but that may also be because of the context in which we came to it.

Even rogues and rascals seemed to lend themselves to some kind of systematic analysis. The notion of the dispersion of privilege appeals to me in this direction.

Notes

1. United Nations, Statistical Office. Statistical Year Book, 1962 (New York, 1963), p. 58.
2. This scheme is discussed in detail in Robert T. Holt, and John E, Turner, *The Political Basis of Economic Development* (Princeton, N.J.: Van Nostrand, 1966).
3. Robert Alan Dahl, *Who Governs? Democracy_ and Power in an American City* (New Haven: Yale University Press. 1961).

Session IV

Economic Growth in Newly Settled Areas as Contrasted with Old Settled Areas

Chairman HENDRY: The discussion leader tonight is Professor Theodore Morgan of the Department of Economics of the University of Wisconsin. I suspect it is not necessary to go into the details of his wide experience in the problems of developing countries, but the range with respect to geographic area is Ceylon, Indonesia, and Kenya. Professor Morgan has referred to himself earlier as one of the refugees from Indonesia. He has also acted as consultant to the Ford Foundation and the World Bank.

The discussants include Professor Baranson of the University of Indiana, International Development Research Center, whose main research interests are in technological transference problems and primary regional interests in Latin America and Central America.

Our other discussant is Scott Johnston of Hamline University, the Political Science Department. His major area of interest is in the Middle East, and I believe his research has centered on the development of political parties in Israel.

Mr. MORGAN: I think the first thing I should do, and briefly, is to try to put sense into the title, "Newly Settled Areas as Contrasted with Old Settled Areas." The problem is that of the effect of European exodus during the last several centuries into other parts of South America. They also went to areas that were either initially or eventually, through disease or fighting, thinly settled: among these, Australia, New Zealand, North America, and perhaps a few other areas.

Obviously, there has been a tremendous difference in the experience of economic growth in these areas. I suppose the extreme contrast is India and the United States. At this point you may feel it is all too easy to explain the contrast.

I.

1. First of all, I should like to say a few words about the context into which explanations fall. One tries to explain economic growth; those of us from different disciplines have different kinds of emphasis. What sorts of causes do we talk of: human resources, natural resources, produced capital, technology, the value system, social organization, political factors,and no doubt still others. I think we would agree that, broadly considered, all of these, have relevance; they are all influential. The question is not, therefore, a matter of "either-or." It is more subtle, it is a matter of the relative importance of each of these and perhaps of their interrelationships, both in timing and in causation.

There is involved also the extent to which these are necessary or only conditioning—only supplementary—causes of growth. There is the extent, Gerschenkron will emphasize, to which you can get around blocks to growth. You may have a society growing despite what, a priori, you might have argued to be effective blocks to development. This is the pattern. What I say is not to throw out X or Y cause, It is simply to argue for a particular supplementary cause as being—on prima facie evidence and not final evidence—an important cause.

II.

I do not want to spend very much time on the two main usual explanations of diverse standards of living in, let us say, Australia, New Zealand, Canada, and the United States, and perhaps Hawaii, South Africa, Uruguay, and Argentina; as compared to India, Pakistan, Ceylon, Indonesia, Burma, Malaya, the Andean countries, the Near East, and most of Africa. A Ricardian economist would think of the ratio of labor and, in the longer run, also of capital to natural resources. And so Marshall[1] suggests in his chapter on "Economic Progress" that the "field of employment" any place offers to capital and labor depends first of ail on its natural resources. But he does not consider the resources-proportion explanation as the central one. Instead, he picks out trade as the chief cause of the modern prosperity of new countries. "The causes that determine the economic progress of nations belong to the study of international trade...." (I suspect that to all of us who are not economists, that sounds very limited indeed, and probably that reaction is right.) Within the heading of trade Marshall emphasizes the flow of capital which exchanges goods and services moving into an area against the promise of an outflow later of local products.

Nurkse talks of the nineteenth century as a period in which international investment scored its greatest triumphs with strong emphasis on the great importance of international investment for the growth of what I call here the newly settled areas, Millikan, Rostow. Rosenstein-Rodan, Leibenstein, Nelson, and the studies that Chenery—well, Chenery's office, really—the laborious and impressive studies that his office is making for AID—place emphasis upon import coefficients and export projections for predicting foreign aid needs, and their possible and hoped-for tapering off as time goes on.

The savings-investment emphasis is presented in Nurkse's Wicksell lectures,[2] and in an excellent study by Douglass North, *Economic Growth of the United States.*[3] It is developed in Haberler's Cairo lectures[4] as a cause for growth in a dynamic context. Contrary to Myrdal and Prebisch, Haberler finds a number of ways in which trade, over time, stimulates the growth of nations, Perhaps I should list them; it provides them with capital goods, machinery and materials; it facilitates the flow to them of financial capital, disseminates knowledge, serves as the means for importing skills and talents and. checks monopoly. This is an impressive list. Meier follows much the same position in his attractive book, *International Trade and Development.*[5]

III.

The theory of investment in physical capital as the central cause of growth has been subject to criticism by Schultz and his fellow investigators, also by Abramovitz and others at the National Bureau of Economic Research, and by Solow and Denison in econometric and statistical studies which suggest that physical capital explains from one-eighth to one-quarter of growth, and that the "residual" or non -measurable inputs account for from one-half to seven-eights.

Tables 1 and 2 compare, for the half-century before World War I, the value of investment capital and of human capital outflows from Europe to overseas. I have spent so much time on them that I have, perhaps, amyopic view, I think they are worth considering seriously.

You can get—this is a judgment—data good enough to give you orders of magnitude on the value of the flow of immigrants as compared to the value of investment flows. To illustrate: what is the economic value of an immigrant? First, estimate the working life span of individuals once they arrive in this country. This is taken from life-expectancy tables for the period in conjunction with data on the age at which people came to this country. Find average earnings in this country and discount them back to the time when they got off the ship at Ellis Island, The data we have from both British and American sources is that, on the average, some 102,000 people per year were coming over from the U.K. They are valued, in addition to their discounted product here, at the cost of bringing them up in England,

Then you can do the same thing for the value of investment flows. Their current amount comes from Imlah data.[6] Their contribution to product relies on marginal-capital-output-ratio estimates taken mainly from Kuznets' studies. The range is wide; undoubtedly the actual range might well be wider than that.

Mr. HOLT: Are those annual figures?

Mr. MORGAN: That's right; averages per year for the period,

Mr. HOLT: In what, 1964 dollars or in 1800 dollars?

Mr. MORGAN: Valuation is taker, as of the time of the inflow of capital and migrants. The median point is around 1890, approximately, in both cases; not quite that, but almost.

Consider the viewpoint of people who emphasize the importance of investment inflow into the New World, or into overseas generally, as explaining economic growth. Here is *an* attempt, if you like, on the side of heresy to ask, "Is that really true? Can we get some figures that will measure the value of immigrants side by side with the value of capital inflow?" What is the outcome of the comparison? I think one should conclude that the orders of magnitude are in general roughly the same in Table 2.

But for the U.K.-U.S. the orders of magnitude favor the immigrants— they were economically more important. You might well say that if the figures are worth taking seriously at all, the greater importance of immigrants to the United States was probably not a matter of chance. The relative importance of immigrants probably is genuinely a part of the reason for the unique economic growth of this country.

These figures, by the way, do not give a complete comparison. They take no account at all of backflows to Europe and the U.K. from immigrant remittances on the one hand and amortization and interest on the other. These are not included because I could not find data for them. To that extent these figures are imperfect.

If it is true that the immigrant flows have a value equal to or greater than that of investment flows in the half-century before World War I, then I submit that there is no doubt at all about the relative economic magnitudes of these two flows a half-century further back, or a century further back. Investment, outflows from England and from Europe were hardly beginning before the early part of the nineteenth century, but people were coming to this country and elsewhere voluntarily or involuntarily, a long time before.

Table 1
Average Annual Value of Immigrants and Value of Investment Flow, into the United States from the United Kingdom, 1870-1914
(Rounded to nearest $10 million)

A.   Value of immigrants
    1.   101,800 immigrants, valued at their 25 years' product, discounted, of $8,702—$890 million
    2.   101,800 immigrants, valued at the cost of their rearing in the United Kingdom, $1,306—133 million
B.   Value of investment inflow
    3.   Investment inflow, valued at its discounted net product—150-500 million
    4.   Investment inflow, valued at time of flow—70 million

Table 2
Average Annual Value of Immigrants and Value of Investment Flow into All Overseas Areas, from Europe, 1866-1915
(Rounded to nearest $10 million)

A.   Value of immigrants
    1.   456,000 net immigrants, valued at their 25 years' product, discounted, of $5,801—$2,650 million
    2.   456,000 net immigrants, valued at the cost of their rearing in Europe, $1,088—496 million
B.   Value of investment inflow
    3.   Investment inflow, valued at its discounted net product—1,030-3,530 million
    4.   Investment inflow, valued at time of flow—500 million

IV.

The next point to mention is that sizable foreign investment seems historically to have come relatively late in the development process. The logical argument is that it is justified only when you have a foundation already built, when you have an economic and social structure that makes the bet a good one.

Mr. FATOUROS: In "foreign investment," do you include direct arid indirect?

Mr. MORGAN: Yes. The data here comes in large part from Berrill's paper given at what we think of as the Rostow meeting of the International Economic Association.[7]

Mr. NASH: Was there any U.S. investment going out of the country at this time, too, do you know?

Mr. MORGAN: There undoubtedly was some. I don't have any data on it, I assume it was very small.

Mr. FATOUROS: There was some in the late nineteenth century. According to the U.S. figures there was some in Latin America—direct, rather than indirect.

Mr. ANDERSON: What is indirect investment?

Mr. FATOUROS: Portfolio investment, securities.

Mr. MORGAN: Floating bonds, for example.

V.

Now, a word or two on trade as an engine of growth. This explanation has had various emphases: Nurkse thought that the engine, was running down; Prebisch thinks that the engine always has worked bsd~ ly, because it has always been transferring part of the gains from technical progress from the low-income to the high-income countries; Haberler feels that it has worked effectively and is working effectively now to the extent that it is allowed to work.

Evidently the expansion-of-trade mechanism as an important cause of growth must have worked imperfectly. There has been many an export boom, but among the countries of the world only a few, outside of Europe, have become developed. Economies have gone on developing—the large continental areas of the United States and Russia being the chief examples—without necessarily having external trade booms.

It is interesting to note, side by side with the trade or export boom theory, the Chenery cross-section study of 51 countries in the eariv 1950s. The results of this study turn the expansion-of-trade hypothesis upside down. The main single cause of industrial growth, amounting to about one-half the total causation, is, according to Chenery's findings, input substitution. It is replacing goods that used to come in, the squeezing out of trade as the growth of local production outruns the growth of local demand. At a certain stage in their growth countries become less specialized, according to this study. Of course, the 1950s experience need not necessarily be valid for earlier years, yet it, is suggestive.

Where trade expansion does not lead to growth, you can set up your special explanations. Robert Baldwin has an interesting analysis in *Economic Journal*.[9] You can think also of Rosenberg, or Hagen, or of Meier or Sinai's hypotheses to explain wiry external stimulus does not take hold within an economy.

VI.

What I would like to do now is to present a supplementary hypothesis for the differential growth of the two kinds of areas to which Europeans have gone. I start out with the generalization that people who go from the West to low-income countries usually come back vividly impressed by social obstacles to growth. Their judgments are not subject to quantitative test, but the concert of these judgments obviously should be taken seriously. The usual non-economic emphasis holds that European culture, in certain defined ways, encourages economic progress; and that indigenous cultures outside of Europe in general do not. You can talk of the Hebrew-Greek-Roman civilization, the Renaissance and Reformation, democracy, social discipline, a propensity to save and invest, better technology, better health and energy from superior knowledge, sanitation, medical care, and so on; and you can variously combine these explanations of why Europeans were effective in economic activity.

There is some weakening of this hypothesis from the fact that people, have moved out of their home areas from other places than. Europe and distinguished themselves abroad. Jewish people have gone to many areas in the world; Arabs to the East Coast of Africa; Tamils to many parts of South Asia, East Asia, and the Pacific; Chinese similarly to the Philippines, Indonesia, and other parts of the world, and so on.

Now it is obviously true that the Europeans did carry with them superior techniques and very likely possessed superior ability to organize in economic ways. These advantages served them well. Many of the people who moved were also self-selected for their energy, hopefulness, and ambition, which clearly are highly important kinds of assets for migrants between areas, between, different countries, and between sections of countries. Such qualities of migrants tend to disperse regional rates of economic growth, because people move from less attractive to more attractive areas.

Many people, however, moved out of Europe by compulsion, as slaves or convicts; or they were forced out of their homelands by personal ill-success or general disaster. Carter Goodrich has made some special study of this and has estimated that well over half the people in the Colonies at the time of the Revolution had come to the New World as slaves, convicts, or indentured servants. This weakens the personal qualities argument for the effectiveness of immigrants in the U.S., although I should guess that the balance is still probably favorable. There is a further argument. I suggest, for the brilliant economic success of the newly settled as compared with the old settled areas. It is a variant of the pioneer society hypothesis, and is the supplement I am proposing to add to the other causes of growth.

Consider the values and objectives of people who live in old settled parts of the world in comparison with those who have grown up in new settled areas. In other words, what are the sources of status and prestige in one area as compared with the other? In every society, the people at the top of the social structure influence value, systems, so far as they can, to sustain most effectively of all the social groups—have an interest in evolving and maintaining a value system that gives them maximum status.

This interest implies that, they will not set up "accomplishment," by any definition, as the criterion of social merit—physical or mental energy, ability in production or trade, or courage or skill in battle. Only in the remote, more primitive days, when violence was a way of life and more stable societies were only gradually being evolved, did the criterion of "accomplishment" hold uniquely. There are the father images of Romulus and Remus, King Arthur, and Charlemagne as examples.

For the top social group, one shaking up of the social heap in a millennium is quite enough. They cannot accept accomplishment and ability in general as the criteria of social merit; neither can they point to exceptional personal merit within their own group as justification for their status, for in every social group and generation high ability of any sort is rare.

Income, of course, can be a support for status. Everybody wants it. The high-status people have historically obtained it through land rents, taxes, ransoms, robbery, regular charges to merchants passing through, or through ceremonial or customary gifts; and these have sustained their position. The search for a justification for status leads to a last-ditch and, in a sense, conclusive argument, that one deserves eminence because of who he is. He doesn't have to earn it; he has it. He has his personal right, or he is a member of a family, all of whom have status.

Given the tight hold of such a status structure, an able and ambitious individual without initial status can hope to achieve it—how? If the structure is holding well, only by fitting in. For example, you can produce goods for the king or otherwise serve him, and so share in his status. But when this kind of society is losing its grip, then there are chinks in the status-armor, and prestige can be obtained in some measure outside the pattern; perhaps by becoming eminent in law or medicine but especially by achieving success in politics.

A traditional agrarian society with a folk memory of conquest and predation as the normal route to acquiring status, power and wealth encourages energetic young people to seek political success as their way up.

The route of politics is a flexible one, with great advantages. In a fairly stable status structure the successful politician assimilates himself into the existing hierarchy, supplementing and supporting it. Where there is more instability, the most promising task for the ambitious politician is to pledge reform or urge revolution. His aims may turn out, in fact, once he gets into office, to involve making the best of both worlds: an optimum compromise—to assimilate with the old hierarchy to some extent while reforming or supplanting it.

In the traditional low-income areas of the world, the demonstration effect in its widest sense will continue to foment political instability. As communications continue to improve—as they have improved fantastically by historical comparison, in the last 20-odd years—there will be increasing awareness of the wide gap in standard of living between the low- and high-income countries. Absolutely, and probably relatively, this gap continues to widen. In such societies, if the inevitable tensions lead to increased political turbulence rather than to increased economic effort and accomplishment, then economic advance will be slowed down,

You have, of course, a potential vicious circle. The rate of economic progress may be shifted still further toward low or negative levels, if the canons of status in these societies discourage energetic and creative activities, the sort we have spoken of earlier today: if it is no credit to you to do physical work, or to be able to solve mechanical, chemical, practical problems.

If innovatory production and trade activities, the close calculation of money gain and loss, and business preoccupations and huckstering merit contempt in society, then what will the ambitious youngster do? With complete rationality he will look for a better field of activity. He will not go into private business life, nor will he want to work for commercial or industrial organizations of the government. He will direct his energies to where they will do him the most good; this may very likely be in the political area. The maximizing calculus leads away from economic effort: the divergence between private and social marginal product is wide.

In its pure form this logic of ambition in low-income societies is illustrated in the student centers of political dissidence and intrigue in Latin American universities and, to some extent, in the student strikes and revolts in Near East and South Asian universities and schools.

With the disadvantages for growth in this kind of society. I should like to contrast the overwhelming economic advantages found in the newly settled parts of the world: North America, Australia, New Zealand and parts of South America, where the native populations were too small to submerge the newcomers in the old system, or to enable the newcomers to set up a new superior-inferior status sytems which would discourage effort.

In a pioneer environment, survival and real income depend on personal qualities of strength, wits, and courage. Since these qualities are valuable, they are the self-evident basis of status, "Who you are equals who your family is" is no longer relevant. The younger son of a distinguished European family, out in the prairies or in the Rockies, had to pull his own weight if he was to win the local respect that counted. The acceptance of personal accomplishment as the source of status was invaluable for favoring economic and other progress, lasting for some generations beyond the pioneer environment that gives rise to it.

What about post-pioneer influences on such a value system? A commercial and industrial environment tends to sustain it, since energy and (business) ingenuity have their rewards and indolence and business folly have their punishments. So there is constant shifting over the years, or a few generations, in the persons and families of the elite.

Progressive taxation and effective practical education tend to sustain such a status system. War also offers, in its way, a stimulus to growth, offsetting a considerable amount of physical destruction through the prestige given in conflict to strength, wits, arid ability in the achievement of concrete results. The survival value of these qualities tends to raise their prestige in all pursuits.

In contrast, an agricultural environment tends to destroy the status-through-accomplishment system, in that ownership rights, clung to zealously, have sufficed in many places and times to support a fixed elite group, generation after generation. The modern practice of professional property management also tends to destroy it by facilitating the continued high incomes and status of people who have no need to be other than unenterprising and unimaginative. There is a modest offset in that professional managers are chosen, presumably, for ability. This offers a small leaven of social mobility to the class structure.

This, then, is the argument. It does suggest that policymakers should have conspicuously in view the non-trade and non-investment conditions of growth, and they should look to the feedback effect, of specific economic and other measures into the status structure. The question left with us is how to give prestige to the qualities and habits that are useful to economic production, and to channel the efforts of the ambitious and able in an economic direction.

In the unitary kind of society that is normal in the low-income areas, class divisions are deep. They are conspicuous; they cut through all aspects of life. In such a unilinear society you must diminish prestige for the upper groups if you increase it for the others. But existing prestige holders do not willingly abdicate their prestige. You have the problem of developing the delicate arts of political compromise and reform, perhaps along the uncertain road suggested by Hirschman. He says you cannot bet on successful reform, but it is possible. Change can occur by slow degrees in the existing status and power structure; or else, in a harsher gamble, there can be a drastic overthrow of the structure in whose debris, under favorable circumstances, the ambitious and able may seek status through economic activities. But the debris following violent change is all too likely to advertise to the ambitious that their best chance lies in repeating the example previously given: of seeking success through a new political overthrow.

An alternative, for a policymaker or for anyone else who can influence the situation, is to attempt to move toward a plural kind of society in which there are many channels of activities and competition, so that an individual can get a sense of worthwhileness, of significance, of success, in many different lines. The ordinary and correct argument against, deep class divisions is the static economic argument, the bad fit between abilities and existing opportunities. We have added to this static argument a dynamic one: that the plural society blurs the class interest of individuals, and so weakens the conservative impulse to hold on to the present status pattern, and makes possible more reforms that are requisite for economic growth.

In fact, the traditional status holders may even not be sure, as more and more channels of competition are developed, that they are really injured by a given change. Their interests are complex and mixed. This reasoning holds also for other people below the top level in the society. They may tolerate reforms or even welcome them on the grounds of a more stable social structure developing, or perhaps because of the social approbation to be gained through favoring reform.

Mr. BARANSON: I feel that in one way this is a very challenging paper. It covers the gamut of the kind of things that concern us in development. If I may briefly summarize the paper, as I understand it, you are looking at the engines of growth during the nineteenth century. You alluded to the heavy reliance upon investment and trade during the nineteenth century as engines of growth. Development policy people today-place a large emphasis on capital resource mobilization.

You then offered as an alternative hypothesis that there is also an essential human ingredient built into immigrants who brought, skills and know-how with them that is just as important, as the material capital. The hypothesis here is one of human resources development and the particular protestant ethic or pioneer spirit that people brought with them.

I would personally be inclined, to redress the balance of importance between human and physical capital. I would weigh somewhat differently investment and trade in terms of their relative importance. I would place more emphasis on the importance of trade. With respect to investment, I think this is an interesting difference between underdeveloped areas today and underdeveloped areas in the nineteenth century. In the nineteenth century the real dearth was savings. There were markets in the developed world and investments went out to finance undertakings that could supply those markets. Foreign capital provided an essential growth ingredient in those days.

Among underdeveloped areas today, it is becoming increasingly clear that the deficiency is not savings but lack of viable investment opportunity. If domestic savings are deficient, there is a good deal of international finance capital from private and intergovernmental sources. But the banks *today* have a real problem in finding suitable investment projects. So the real dearth is in investment opportunity rather than in savings.

With respect to the importance of trade to development, I would offer certain qualifications. I feel that part of the business of providing viable investment opportunities is exploring more intensively and imaginatively the trading opportunities of underdeveloped areas. Much of the recent emphasis has been upon developing regional markets. To the degree that these regional arrangements do not end. up in high-cost industries and monopoly situations, expanded markets are unquestionably an essential ingredient of industrialization and growth.

Ted Schultz has argued for developing market opportunities in the mass markets of industrially advanced countries. For example, Mexico now furnishes part of the vegetable and fruit market in the United States—an excellent opportunity to earn income abroad. In a sense this is going back to the classical economists' thoughts on the international division of labor; this is one kind of trade that can aid development considerably.

I myself have worked on international manufacturing and. interchange systems. Any industrial complex, you will find, when it is broken down, depends upon a wide range of components and parts. Within this range there are alt-jays some elements that an economy is more ready to produce than others. For example, in Diesel engine manufacture: given the labor and managerial skills, a country like Mexico or like India is more capable of doing certain kinds of milling and lathe work than turning out the more sophisticated parts in fuel injection systems. Here again, is a trade opportunity, and I think there are. many others that underdeveloped areas can fruitfully pursue.

The pioneer spirit hypothesis, I think, like the Weber and Tawney thesis on the Protestant ethic, has its limitations as a growth theory, I think both trade arid investment patterns today have to be re-thought and reworked. I think the emphasis should be on markets and upon finding viable ways to engage in industrialization and trade. The concomitants of social conditions and human resources that you refer to are also essential ingredients. I have recently been concerned with the problem of technological transmittal and adaptation. Technology has been regarded largely as a passive growth factor, adjusting to local factor prices and resource availabilities, I have looked upon technology as a creative element, whereby you can adjust factor proportions and use levels of skills and resources as you find them. Technology becomes a creative element in the process of adjusting.

I think more than anything else that this is what an approach to development needs: a sizing up of the situation at hand. How do you develop in an underdeveloped environment, given resources as they are, and given the stage of development? The approach that social development or a social ethic is the prerequisite to growth may be a false start. Innovation in trade and in industrialization patterns to adapt to emerging conditions is what is needed. I think that is the kind of innovation that the already industrially advanced countries can bring in terms of know-how and insight.

Chairman HENDRY: The issue has been partially joined, not with rejection, but at least with modification, of the skepticism concerning the old pioneer spirit.

Mr. JOHNSTON: I should like to suggest a few items concerning economic growth in newly settled areas as contrasted with the older settled areas in the one country I feel I am familiar with, namely Israel, where I have been interested in a study of the political party system.

At the very beginning of the session tonight Professor Lewis's observation as to economics being a trivial explanation of economic growth was recalled. I have thought over the application of this observation concerning Israel as to the matter of economic development and even what kind of society it has been, in terms of the problem of typology. Israel is a society indeed where a very large number of non-economic factors have been involved as to programs of economic development. It seems to me that there is some value. In examining some of the different types of situations that have developed in Israel, and comparisons that might be made.

Let me just suggest some of these problems in terms of this particular society, a society which indeed does fall into an interesting pattern of being both a newly settled area, such as the Negev desert region, with projections for further development there, and the older areas related to the coming of the Zionist, immigrants in the late part of the nineteenth century. These include the coastal plain area and Galilee. Even concerning the coastal, plain there were indeed areas which had not been used significantly economically for several centuries since the coming of the Turkish occupation.

Now, non-economic factors which are associated with development plans involve a point which was brought out earlier today within another context, the point of defense. Concerning the location of the very small number of Kibbutzim that you have in the central and southern Negev area, these collective settlements constitute among other things, militia centers, a factor related to the surrounding Arab areas. This is obviously a matter of major importance from the Israeli point of view with economic consideration being clearly of a very secondary nature.

The paper just delivered includes the observation that the founders of new societies are certainly most concerned with the maintenance of the original values. This to me is one of the most Interesting things that has taken place within a discussion of Israeli politics and economic development between the older generation, who had a pioneering socialist

Zionism which involved settlement work and who find themselves being increasingly challenged by modern administrators like Moshe Dayan and others who *say:* now, the original plans and original concepts as to such things as the development of the Kibbutzim, reforestation, location of these new Industries and various types of economic enterprises no longer make sense. This instead is the kind of society and the kind of economy we have. It would be better to have the dairying industry closer to the Tel Aviv metropolitan complex rather than in the far reaches of the Negev. A whole series of observations of this nature are made by the newer generation of practical administrators and technicians.

These technicians and this newer generation of administrators are increasingly rejecting aspects of the traditional Zionist ideology, including the older fundamentalist socialist pioneering and are moving on to something else for which they are very much resented by many in the older generation.

Ben-Gurion is in some respects an example of this type of thing. He has had some very grandiose plans as to a population of several million in the Negev, and his own personal example has included living part of the time in a small and not economically prosperous Negev Kibbutz. It should be added, however, that Ben-Gurion also associated himself on some issues with the newer generation of modernizers and administrators.

Let me move on to other non-economic factors. There are religious factors. For example, there has been a controversy between the orthodox political parties and other groups in the community within the last series of months as to the location of licensed animal slaughtering. For example; there is the matter of where you may have pig raising in the country, and a law has been, passed in the last, year and a half on that, which has nothing to do with economic factors but has to do instead with a type of arrangement made within the cabinet coalition between one of the major religious parties and Mapai, the party of Eshkol and Ben-Gurion.

There are other non-economic factors dealing with the question of where you place the new immigrants, The new Oriental Jewish immigrants, to a rather considerable extent, are sent to the least desirable areas because there, is less available for them elsewhere. There are also, I believe, factors here as to the people who are already present and their strength within the society and their being able to influence to a considerable extent this pattern of the location of people.

There is the role of political parties, as to their stake in development programs. I see problems that are present here within the political system concerning the newer development areas now and certain elements of change and even of instability within the party system that are beginning to turn up and which deserve greater study. There is the weakening of party discipline in newer development communities and municipal difficulties have turned up which have called for special elections in a number of these communities, There are other problems which I think represent issues that are present in the party system which are going to appear increasingly in the decades ahead. These are in important respects even more to be seen in newer areas where older patterns of life, older patterns of the society, and the older traditions are present or lacking in varying combinations.

These are just some thoughts I have had and some things I have perceived, which occurred to me in terms of this one country.

GENERAL DISCUSSION
Savings vs. Investments

Mr. MORGAN: We are dealing, I suppose, with matters of emphasis. The concept presented by Mr. Baranson, that investment opportunities were abundant in the nineteenth century and are relatively scarce now in growing areas, is an interesting idea, I think it rides on the back, of the notion that, investment opportunities are opened up by complex social and economic development. You have to have these developments initially—which seems reasonable.

Of course, I am sure that trade is often a thoroughly useful stimulus to an area, as it may well be in Mexico. I just do not know how to comment on the Argentina-Brazil case. It seems to me that it is a mixed case, and probably one ought to look awfully hard at the specific facts if he is going to interpret the mixed experience of European—

Mr. KREININ: Mixed in what sense?

Mr. MORGAN: Mixed in the sense that, sometimes native populations lived in the new areas in large numbers, and sometimes not—mixed also in Sanford Mosk's sense: in a brilliant AER article[10] he compared Latin America with the United States and found differences in their growth experience which reflected differences in people, their values and organization. In Argentina, the large estates and haciendas are at the center of the aristocratic tradition that Mosk emphasizes. Elsewhere in the Americas, there have been the foundations of a different kind of economy and society, with more potential for economic advance: small men pioneering.

It seems to me that we probably ought not to talk—perhaps we do not any more—of a theory of growth. We ought to talk of theories of growth; and then we ought to ask ourselves which theory best fits a given problem, at a given time, in a given country. We should have at hand, as Joan Robinson has suggested, a kit of variously shaped tools when we are trying to say something useful about growth possibilities.

I might mention in connection with Mr. Johnston's comments on Israel that I had an opportunity of looking at the views of Governor Horowitz of the Bank of Israel on the problems of underdeveloped countries. I think Florowitz is, with the best intentions, considerably astray in his interpretation. He is immersed in banking concepts, and sees growth problems as turning centrally on the amounts of money flows, Prebisch's theory of the terms of trade is very prominent in his mind, He sees Israel's remarkable recent success—it has-been, the outstanding country in the world for rapid growth in recent years—as turning on the volume of capital investment matters. In addition, I suggest one might analyze the morale factors and skills of immigrants to Israel, and perhaps the shaking up of old status patterns that occurred as they were resettled.

Mr. SCHWARTZ: Mr. Baranson has made the point that in the nine-teenth century the deficiency was savings. He maintained that there was a sufficient number of opportunities for investment, whereas, in this century, the problem is not so much savings as, a deficiency in "viable investments" or "bankable investments."

I think this has to be at least very strongly qualified by the following: very much of the investment in the nineteenth century was in the area of transportation and public utilities. There is still tremendous opportunity for investment in transportation, and even more in some of the public utilities such as electricity. The problem is that this area, which was so attractive to private sources, either for direct or portfolio investment, has been regulated to death or simply taken over by governments. And the governments have not invested here for one reason or another. Either they hoped that they might be able to obtain the necessary investment goods with an International Bank loan or they decided upon some show—and I will not say marginal cost—price solution: some kind of a show low-price formula which did not leave them with the funds—or they decided they did not have the funds—from alternative sources to make additional investments. I just wonder, if you were to consider transportation and public utility investments in this light, whether you would come to the same strong conclusion about the relative lack of investment opportunities in this century compared to the last. I very seriously doubt it.

Mr. FATOUROS: Is it really true that today what is lacking is investment opportunities and not savings?

Mr. BARANSON: Yes.

Mr. FATOUROS: I think one argument was already raised, the fact that the kind of investment opportunities that existed in the nineteenth century also exist today in pure economic terms, although they do not exist in political terms. Public utilities, for instance, are either regulated extensively or taken over completely by the state in many less developed countries.

In addition to that, is it true—and this is really a question—is it true that the possibilities for profitable investment today in the developed countries, are much higher than they were, for instance, in. the nineteenth century, as compared to the profit possibilities In the less developed countries?

There is, I understand, high profitability of investment in direct investments in developing countries today, but the difference is relatively small, while back in the nineteenth century the difference was greater.

Mr. BARANSON: There is a very recent article on this which I just read a couple of weeks ago. I cannot remember whether It is in the AER [*American Economic Review*] or whether it was in the SID [Society for International Development: *International Development Review*], but it is on this question, and it was very well documented, I thought.

I go by the experience of the banking community today, the World Bank and the Inter-American Development Bank, and these international banking institutions. They all say they have more money than they know what to do with.

Mr. MORGAN: But they are fussy,

Mr. BARANSON: Sure, they are fussy. They have to know what they are doing.

Mr. HOLT: Well, if you are going to be too careful about the way you spend your money, you are going to find yourself with lots of money on your hands,

Mr. KREININ: I think there is evidence that profitable opportunities for investments in underdeveloped countries are pretty good, but there is also a fairly high level of risk, coupled with, the balance-of-payments constraint which makes it difficult to take earnings out of the country. When you speak of profitable opportunities in percentage terms, in terms of local currency, that is one thing, But to transfer earnings to American dollars and get the money out of the country is quite another. Coupled with this factor is the risk, either real or imagined, of expropriation and all that, that reduces the profitability of the investment.

The Frontier and Development

Mr. ANDERSON: There is a certain appropriateness in a Wisconsin professor picking up Turner's frontier theory and extending it. As nearly as my memory brings back to me the comments and criticisms of Turner, I think I would find the new version also shaky. For instance, if one were to compare, say sixteenth-century Europe and nineteenth-century Europe, or Europe and the overseas countries, I think you could ask: is there in modern Europe or in overseas areas actually more mobility between social classes? Is there more instability of fortunes? I am doubtful.

I am inclined to think that the absence of development is not due to the presence or absence of general characteristics of the society, and particularly for the countries copying Europe, but to the presence of specific cultural traits with certain clusters. I take a dim view of the whole line of reasoning of the frontier theory and related broad, sweeping conceptions of social structure—even as a sociologist. I think you had better stick to your international trade theory.

Mr. NASH: For what Mr. Holt calls settled societies, those with dense land-man ratios and complicated social structure into which foreigners come: for societies such as these the lack, of development has been pretty well explained, Jonathan Levin's book, *The Export Economies*,[11] treats Burma and Peru and the development of a foreign factor economy which leads to about 30 years of expansion, but such a distorting of the factor proportions in the economy that, when the guano runs out, or when other countries get into the rice business, you are dead; you have no flexibility to shift over and no skills to do anything else.

That is a case of the settled societies, where the foreign influence led to about 30 years of development and then stagnation; I think we have a pretty clear picture of how a foreign factor economy works to eventually lead to a blockage of development.

What bothers me is that, pioneers do not necessarily build social structures which are useful. I think I remember a little more about the Turner hypothesis, maybe because I went to school later; it was not the pioneers, the people out west, who made America great, it was the people staying back home in the dirty old slums, with the old customs, with the European ethnic groups. It was the offshoots, the nogoodnicks, that were going out there and boozing it up out west. The land-man-space, the pioneer ethic were not conducive to economic growth in America. What really made it grow were the settled traditional glass blowers from Antwerp and all these kinds of people who had all of the rigidities and turned out to be the people who gave America most of its development, I think Oscar Handlin documents it very well.

Mr. GINSBURG: I want to raise a point of caution by looking at the colonization period in North America and southern. South America and comparing the situations we observed there with the situations we observe today. Let me explain.

In the first place, when the Americas were settled, and I am thinking particularly now of North America and southern South America, there was a kind of "open world" system. In other words, there were possibilities in many places for frontier settlement, but in fact it did not appear everywhere. Now, of course, there is a relatively closed world insofar as colonization opportunities are concerned.

But at that time could, conceivably, settlers have gone into the Amazon? It was unsettled, heaven knows, and still is, but they did not do it. Where did they go? Where were the frontiers of settlement established in the seventeenth and eighteenth centuries? For the most part they were established only in certain types of world regions.

These regions offered sets of conditions which were amenable to treatment or modification, or which one could adjust to by means of the cultural apparatus that people brought with them. In other words, the settlers that went from Western Europe, and particularly Britain, to the east coast of North America were not moving to environments which were substantially different, from those to which they were accustomed. The same kinds of technology that they employed in their native environmental settings were, for the most part, applicable to the new environment.

Later on—much later—as the frontier moved westward, these conditions did change, but initially they held true.

Also, at those particular times, certain kinds of resources could be exploited in these new environments for which markets already were in existence. For example, Britain was pretty well running out of timber for ship building. The east coast of North America was a God-given area for the British ship-building industry, and this was an important factor in the settlement of that great region.

My point is that for the most part the lands that were settled by Europeans were empty lands which were amenable to development by means of the technology available to Europeans at that time. They did not go into the tropics where there were vacant areas. They went to areas which were familiar to them and with which they were able to cope.

Now, one can ask, "Well, what about developed areas?" The fact is that there really were no already developed densely settled areas in the world that were accessible to Europeans and which presented environmental conditions to which the European technology of the time was adaptable, or which presented possibilities for exploitation in terms of markets already existing in Europe. China might have been such a case but it was closed to Europeans.

If one looks at India, for example, even apart from all the people, it was exceedingly unlikely that European settlers would have gone there. They also could have gone to Java but they did not; and they could have gone to sparsely settled Borneo, but they did not—although these were a long way, I grant you. There were, in short, good reasons why they chose to go where they did.

I am not sure what my conclusion is, but although I do not object to the frontier hypothesis as you stated it, I would argue that it may hold better under some circumstances than in others.

Social Structure and Economic Growth

Mr. HOLT: I was very much taken by Professor Morgan's treatment here of social mobility and social status as elements that might be involved. I have done some research on pre-modern Britain, France, China, and Japan, which I think is probably very relevant to the comments he was making.

One of the interesting factors that links England and Japan as similar cases and contrasts them with France and China deals with this factor of social mobility, but it is a little bit different than the one you are suggesting. You find that in England and Japan there were very rigid legal restraints on mobility from the middle classes into the titled aristocracy. Where mobility was essentially blocked in England and Japan, it was actively encouraged by the government of *ancien* France and Manchu China, so that you will find, if you look at the figures, that the sale of titles ran rampant in France throughout this entire period. From 1600 to 1642, for example, about 28 per cent of the total French government revenues came from the sale of titles, and this was during the period in which the French kings were collecting about five times *as* much tax per capita as their English counterpart. You will find, if you examine the scholar-gentry class in China in the late eighteenth and the beginning of the nineteenth century, that it reached a point where almost 30 per cent had purchased their academic degrees rather than working up through the regular examination system.

You get a view here, that where you have societies in which the middle class, the merchant and entrepreneurial groups, are blocked by law from achieving these upper-status positions, they tend to stay on in the entrepreneurial or merchant kinds of role, whereas in France and China they purchase a title and then use what capital they have, after the purchase of a title, for the purchase of land.

Mr. GINSBURG: If I may just comment on the last remark, I do not know what the situation was in France, but I do not think your reference to China holds in the same way, because, although there was corruption as measured by the purchase of posts in the civil service of China, these posts were not inherited; in other words, no title went with them that could be passed from father to son. Only one generation was involved and this is an important, difference.

Mr. HOLT: This is one differentiation, yes. But if you look at the gross numbers, it is an exceedingly impressive number.

Mr. KING: Mr. Holt made the point, as I understood it, that there was considerable social mobility in China, that in Manchu or nineteenth-century China there was insignificant economic growth, and he tried to connect these factors. Yet it was a particular kind of social mobility that existed in China. It was a kind in which a peasant, through education, through hard study, might very well, become a leading official, His power remained, however, completely subject to the whim of an authoritarian state. The social mobility that occurred in England occurred in a free society and is hardly comparable. Historians have concluded that there was little social mobility in England (based on Cambridge University graduates, for example), yet, when the few lower-class university graduates entered society, they moved into a position of independent authority and independent action,

To turn to China again, those who bought degrees, who changed to the gentry status, did not necessarily take, official positions and many of them were numbered among the few entrepreneurs that China had.

Mr. HOLT: I was talking very specifically about mobility into the aristocracy. I was not talking about mobility in any other place in society.

Secondly, I did not address myself to the phenomenon of downward mobility out of the aristocracy, which I think is an additional part of the argument here. One further comment. When I am talking about social mobility here, I am talking about it solely in terms of prestige and not in terms of power. What was purchased in France and China was prestige. The intendances and the authoritative counselors to the King of France were not for sale and the crucial position of the District Magistrate in China was not for sale.

Theory Formation

Mr. BARANSON: I hear so much of this business of the Meiji Restoration and the Chinese societies and all these other things, and I am delighted; I think it; is good intellectual exercise, but what in the world does this have to do with development? Do you mean to tell me that you are actually going to take some of these analogies and you are going to be sort of a Toynbee? Are you going to reverse historial challenge and response and project it into the future to induce social mobility? What is this all about?

Mr. HOLT: If you are talking here about what kind of a social or political engineer I am going to be, I am not going to be one at all. All I am concerned with here is the analysis of a particular phenomenon of political arid social development.

I find a rather interesting pattern in the contrast between the development of England and Japan on the one hand and France and China on the other hand, and I think it is worth looking at these particular cases because it is very difficult to believe that the similarities between France and China come from a prolonged period *of* culture contact. If, indeed, you do find 12 or 14 different dimensions on which China and France resemble one another and on which England and France are different, it seems to me that you may have your hand on data that aid in the development of a set of hypothesis that are worth looking at in developing areas today. That is what I am concerned with. This information may aid in the development of a scientific theory of development. The careful formulation of good hypotheses is an essential part of the process of theory creation. If I find a number of patterns that prevail in societies that developed successfully, which are in contrast to those that prevail in countries that had great difficulty developing, I have the empirical basis for some hypotheses. If, further, I find that similar hypotheses could be deduced from existing theories in the social sciences, I have a good justification for spending money to test the hypotheses by examining contemporary developing countries.

Mr. BARANSON: What do you do, for example, in the case of China, where this was, say, an 83 per cent weighted, factor that you explained as a necessary and sufficient cause, but in the other society you do not know if it is one, two, or eighty-five?

Mr. HOLT: I think this is the kind of a thing you have to begin investigating. This is what is worth finding out.

Mr. BARANSON: Well, as a tool it is useless, then, and this is what I am concerned about. There has been a lot of these kinds of analogies and the further we go along the more there are of people who are attracted to this kind of thing.

I am talking about comparisons of the Jews in Romania to the Chinese in Manila, and things of this sort. (Laughter.) It is interesting, it is delightful, but considering the objectives to which we should be devoting ourselves, it is rather incredible.

Mr. HOLT: But the relevant question here is: from whence cometh your hypotheses? Are they hunches that come rolling out of the back of your head?

The argument is essentially as follows: One, I find the empirical patterns and I can, from these patterns, generate a hypothesis. Two, I find a body of theory in the social sciences from which I can also deduce the same hypothesis. This makes it worth testing in my mind, and you find in the developing countries to today the laboratory in which they can be tested. This is no argument from analogy.

Mr. FATOUROS: A footnote to your argument is that, of course, there are all kinds of problems that are created out of such a study. For instance, in France, and I suppose—I do not know—in China, this method of selling prestige and keeping power was certainly used by the governing class in order to stabilize the government. The same method was used to some extent in England by the sale of commissions in the army. This last was, to a great extent, a very conscious effort, not to have the kind of army that led to the creation of a Napoleon, and this was the reason it was retained for so long, up to the middle of the nineteenth century. How do you account, though, for the fact that the relative rigidity of entry from the non-nobility to the nobility in England did not lead to a lack of stability for the government?

I think the problem with such analogies is that you have to bring in more and more factors to explain why the analogy does not work in another case. There is an analogy between A and B, but when you consider another aspect of A, say C, it does not gibe with B.

Mr. MIRACLE: I want to refer to the general priority that should be attached to a hypothesis like the one Professor Morgan has given us. It seems to me that as a hypothesis it has a lot of plausibility. That is, when you talk about, ability and achievement spurring people on, driving the developing mechanism, and when one thinks about looking at historical cases and trying to work out the path or see if this happened. There has been doubt expressed about whether this is the single explanation of the particular case, but I wonder if we have a better hypothesis to explain the particular division that he has pointed out?

It seems to me that it fits pretty well in the countries he mentioned, and you can add one or two more. Most of the African cases fit this business of either having a large native population—as they do not like to be called any more, but indigenous population—or an imported social system in which one does not really have to achieve very much.

This was just a plea, perhaps, for some interdisciplinary attack on how in fact achievement and a variant of this within existing underdeveloped countries can be successfully carried out. I am thinking, for example, that in some places there are 50 to 100 ethnic groups within a national boundary and there are very-great variations in the amount that individuals are allowed to achieve. There are people who think they see, in many cases, considerable differences.

When you hear that this tribe or this group are more aggressive, that they are the economic men more than certain others, that they are the ones who are getting ahead, is there not some way that we could, get another check on this hypothesis, either with data that are already in but in the hands of anthropologists or sociologists and not available to economists—or by work of historians?

It is really a question of whether we could not make a fairly quick check on this from some other sources; at least it would be rather interesting to try.

Mr. NASH: Every once in a while we oversell anthropology; we teach everybody about culture and its constraints and its values and we leave out the situational role performance criteria. Lebanon is a pretty poor country and overpopulated. The West Indies, for example, is not overpopulated for Lebanese with the same culture. Whenever they go there they get prosperous.

We see this phenomena in many places. India is pretty poor for Indians, but when they go to Africa they prosper. With the same culture, the caste system, and all the things that are supposed to be barriers back home, they do very well in their new environment. So I think culture and values are very important but, if you do not take any role performance or economic opportunities into consideration you have less than the shadow of the story.

Chairman HENDRY: In Vietnam the Chinese are considered to be the dynamic people and in Cambodia the Vietnamese have become the dynamic element in the society.

Transformation and Trade

Mr. KREININ: Whether or not trade can be a stimulant to development depends on what Kindleberger calls the ability of the economy to transform. Most underdeveloped countries have a very limited ability to transform. Therefore, while some trade might be a prerequisite, I do not know that trade can be the major factor in the developmental process.

It is more likely that countries will develop through import substitution than through export-led growth, The ability to transform is something which affects not only the underdeveloped economies; it also affects the developed economies, where, for one reason or another, institutional or otherwise, they either are unable to readjust themselves to changing export market conditions or their factor remunerations have come to be out of line with factor endowments.

We see that in England today, where part of the external imbalance can be traced to the inability to transform. I suppose it might be argued that, the pound is overvalued, and there are a variety of other reasons, but inability to transform is one reason.

The balance of payments constraint on the development of underdeveloped countries and on the growth of developed countries—I suppose this is a difference in terminology—exists wherever you are.

It is true that there are other non-economic factors in the Israeli situation and therefore it is really not a good example for any development case. But economic constraints exist in Israel much the same as they exist elsewhere, and Israel is facing a severe balance-of-payments problem despite the huge inflow of capital.

I do not know that countries can really count on trade as the major stimulant for growth. It might be a subsidiary prerequisite, but let's take a look at the very few cases where countries have shifted, in the postwar period, from underdeveloped to developed status. We talk an awful lot about development but, let's face it, we have had 20 years of talk, and the number of countries which have actually developed can be counted on one hand.

Israel is one country that was so transformed but it is a poor example. It is an unusual case from which few general conclusions can be drawn. Japan, I suppose, is another case, and so perhaps is Mexico. When you start studying what the elements were in the engine of growth, you would like to determine why some countries developed and others did not, but it is very difficult to find examples. Take the Mexican case: would you say that Mexico experiences an export-led growth? I am. no expert, on Mexico, but I have a feeling that import, substitution played a more important role there.

I doubt, therefore, that the developing countries have the kind of ability to transform that would make possible export-led growth. Do not forget another thing: without rapid transformation, countries often get a huge deterioration in the commodity terms of trade, What I am trying to suggest is that they lose some of their gains from growth in technology, as a result of deterioration of their terms of trade,

I suppose with export-led growth more is lost than with import-substitution. Although Ted Morgan might dispute the idea that anything is lost that way, I think there is some loss involved, and it would be more with export-led growth.

Mr. NASH: In the case of Mexico, which I have followed with some interest, a tremendous amount of its economic development has come in agriculture with irrigation in the north Pacific states.

I think there is a moral to be learned from that and the moral I learn is, don't ever mess around with traditional agriculture. If the people are already settled peasants, let them starve and then start somewhere else; this way you will solve your food problem—otherwise, they are unsavable.

There are, however, great economic opportunities in modern agriculture and Mexico has done a lot in this area.

Sister THOMASINE: We are in a position, now, after 15 or 20 years, not only to reassess export-led growth for this period, as Mr. Kreinin says, but also to contrast it with the export-led growth of a century ago.

It is pretty hard to be a country now, in my opinion, and to be forced to depend upon exports. Despite what Mr. Lewis said, I take a dim view of the export position of many of these countries: what could they do even if they wanted to export? I really do not know where they would get rid of their exports, to be frank about it.

Mr. KING: Mr. Kreinin stated there was Imperfection in trade as a weapon in the development process. But in the nineteenth century the export economies were more passive. When there was a boom, it was regarded as a fortuitous circumstance. There was no reason why the rest of the economy, why the state of thinking in the economy, or why the level of education would be at a point where developmental advantage could be taken of the export boom. This presumably is where the modern study of economic development is effecting a change.

When we consider the 15-year period and say that we should have expected more development, I wonder if we shouldn't recognize that 15 years is really a very short time. When you think of the first conscious planning of the use of export earnings for investment and development purposes you can only go back about ten years in many of the former colonies—especially in Africa. Even in Malaya the first development plan began in 1955-56. Before that it was merely a continuation of a government capital-expenditure program. Perhaps we may be a little overly pessimistic in this condemnation of the failure to take advantage of the trade benefits.

Mr. SCHWARTZ: In any event, with respect to export-led growth and ability to transform, I do not know that you can deny how important export-led growth has been to so many economies and what a significant first step it certainly could continue to be.

Having said that, however, I would note, that, in most cases where there was some tremendous export opportunity which was not accompanied by a significant ability to transform, little more came of it. I guess the most famous case is that of Brazil, which had a sugar boom, a rubber boom, and a coffee boom: three export booms in a century without much in the way of continuing development.

In the postwar period Ecuador did not experience a very substantial change in its level of economic development—despite a very substantial export boom.

Mr. KREININ: In what product?

Mr. SCHWARTZ: In bananas. Not too much resulted from it, and I think this was in part due to this inability to transform that you are speaking of.

I do not think, therefore, that you can deny the stimulus and potential which export situations can lead to, but: I think the other is probably a necessary condition.

Mr. BARANSON: I would like to add a footnote to this business of transformation and trade. Kindleberger has some sophisticated thoughts on this subject of transformation and export and import-displacing industry.

I have done some work on industrialization in Central America. It is much, more difficult to set up a paint and copper wire factory in Honduras, which is an import-displacing industry, than to provide a range of copper wire products. You ought to see how many supporting industries you need in order to get a copper wire plant, started. It is much more of an undertaking than some people might imagine.

I gather from one or two remarks here that some people think that import-displacing is relatively simple and export industries are more difficult to develop, In most of the cases I have looked into, it is just the other way around. As a matter of fact, the worst choice you could make, in terms of what the economy can handle may be what they happen to import now, be it copper wire or paint. You may end up with the worst choices of industries operating at high production costs.

Mr. KREININ: Concerning the earlier point of ability to transform, we are again talking about the same thing we talked about yesterday: it depends on which industry. Certainly there are import-substitution industries which are more difficult to develop than some export industries.

This is not the kind of import-substitution under discussion, and the ability to develop industry—export industry per se—is not the sole problem of transformation. The problem of transformation involves also the diffusion of the benefits from that industry throughout the economy, and that is more difficult,

It depends, therefore, what industries you are talking about. If a Latin American country wants to develop production of electronic equipment, certainly it would be very difficult, whether for export or for local use.

I wonder whether, from your experience, you could tell us how you would characterize the Mexican growth. Would you characterize it as export-led or more import-substitution?

Mr. BARANSON: You would be hard pressed in most underdeveloped countries—even Brazil or Argentina—to find an industry that does not have to be hot-housed with a tariff. If you establish a high enough tariff level you can have any production cost base. The, real thing you are talking about in transformation is the ability to carry on an industrial activity at fairly efficient costs.

In the case of Mexico, and this is part of the Prebisch argument, he argues for instant industries and he argues that the only way to get started is to hothouse them; there is no question but what this is how Mexico got started.

Mexico and Brazil both are well on their way now. I am familiar with the Diesel engine industry. A Diesel engine has 750 parts. It takes about 200 plants in this country to build one engine, that is, 200 plants to provide the 750 parts. In that, range there are probably about ten parts Mexico can produce competitively because it is a particular part that uses a high amount of relatively unskilled labor. Thus they can use the kind of machines they can get without using up too much. foreign exchange.

I am suggesting here that there are many more low-cost activities that should be the leading areas of industrialization, that could be developed for trade and export. This other path, which is essentially a way of artificially creating markets through tariff barriers, either in the country or through regional arrangements, is one thing on which I really felt I should take exception to Professor Lewis. This business of talking about the kind of things that they can trade with one another is vitiated by the fact that they can set up direct trade barriers. I know that today one of the big problems is that Mexico does not want to be supplied with certain parts from Brazil; she wants to get them either from Denmark or from Belgium or from the United. States where she gets both the price and the quality she wants. It is only under artificially contrived conditions that you are going to get this kind of industrial trade.

Mr. MIRACLE: This very neatly touches a point that I was going to address myself to. It is really a footnote to what you called a footnote earlier, and that is, that a lot of the trade is agricultural, and in many of these countries it is very highly concentrated, In fact, this is one of the characteristics of the tropical, belt: its high concentration in one or two exports, and in many cases a single export crop. This then means that we do have *theories* rather than *a theory* trade, and *vie* have to look somewhat differently at transforming an export crop when there are few alternatives, particularly if it is an export crop that is produced by plantation methods, where it is very difficult to redistribute this capital to something else,

The Concept of Technological Breakthrough

Mr. NASH: Since we seem to be seeking sort of *a* magic key either in migrants or given capital, or trade, I will put up a candidate, I think economic, development takes place when there is some investment which is a technological breakthrough. Now, nobody knows what a technological breakthrough is until it occurs, but the search for it and the investment in it gets you over some critical hump which has a whole lot of—I wish I could use the language better—link effects, et cetera.

Mr. BARANSON: Multipliers.

Mr. NASH: —multipliers and linkages which change the character of the economy. Look at Mexico; they found two or three high payoff technological breakthroughs and invested in them and it has been going like crazy. The problem, or the dilemma, of Mexican economic development is that they always have to find the next one.

Economic development is having your society geared in such a manner that there are people always searching for and anticipating a technological breakthrough and having the investment to make it. In the twentieth century it is not hard to get the money. The problem is to find the technological breakthroughs. That is my candidate for the most influential factor in development.

Religion and Economic Development

Sister THOMASINE: As a person who has done some research on the place of religion in economic development, I would not discount it, I am thinking of Latin America. I know a little bit more, about that.

Taking my own Church: I think it has proved an obstacle to economic growth in Latin America. I think a change has come now, a change in the Catholic Church, which is very fruitful. In my opinion, however, the Church in Latin America held back development; it was not the missionary in a California spirit. In Latin America economic growth was held back by the colonial spirit of Spain and the Church. I do not think there is any question about that. It has changed now, however.

Mr. SCHWARTZ: I want to make three summary comments. One is in relation to the church item. In Argentina 3 the Chubut River Valley in Patagonia was set-led by Welshmen in the middle of the nineteenth century—at a time when even parts of the province of Buenos Aires were Indian territory and dangerous for newcomers. The settlement prospered at first, but for many years in the twentieth century the Valley has been experiencing a rather slow rate of economic growth. When asked about the reason for this, one Argentine church official replied, "Well, they're all Welsh." (Laughter.)

There are *many* people in Chubut who would object to this line of reasoning, but at any rate, it is interesting that this kind of provincialism exists everywhere. I think it is, to some extent, too strong to think that Catholicism has different consequences for economic growth, e.g., according to whether it comes from Northern or Southern Europe, or that Catholicism would necessarily lead to this kind of result. But; at any rate—

Sister THOMASINE: If you were on the inside, you would know the difference. (Laughter.)

Foreign Factor Economy

Mr. KING: Let me just comment on the foreign factor economy. It does not seem to me that it is today completely at variance with the idea of, or need for, technological change. The difference between the nineteenth century and today lies in the fact that the local population of a foreign factor economy was long unconscious of the potential for change. When it did become conscious, the foreign factor economy could be used to further development goals—this is the difference. People are now conscious of the potential for change and therefore they can use these export booms if they are wise; they can use the resources they gather during these brief periods in order to implement a beginning development plan and to achieve that first technological change.

Mr. MORGAN: The Chairman asked me whether I wanted to say anything in conclusion and I said I probably should, because otherwise I would be taken to feel, that the argument had failed.

It seems to me that In summing up all of these comments, what we have been doing is to give out of our own individual experiences the degree of emphasis we think ought to apply to this and that cause, and this and that block to causes; in that sense there is not so much conflict as supplementation in our discussion.

Notes

1. Alfred Marshall, *Principles of Economics: An Introductory Volume* (8th ed.; New York: Macmillan, 1949).
2. Ragnar Nurkse, *Patterns of Trade and Development* (Wicksell Lectures, 1959; Oxford: Basil Blackwell, 1962).
3. Douglass C, North, *The Economic Growth of the United States, 1790-1860* (Englewood Cliffs, N.J.: Prentice-Hall, 1961).
4. Gottfried Haberler, *International Trade and Economic Development*(National Bank, of Egypt, Fiftieth Anniversary Commemoration Lectures; Cairo: National Bank of Egypt, 1959).
5. Gerald M. Meier, *International Trade and Development* (New York: Harper and Row, 1963).
6. Albert Henry Imlah, *Economic Elements in the Pax Britannica: Studies in_British Foreign Trade in the 19th Century* (Cambridge, Mass.: Harvard University Press, 1958).
7. K. E. Berrill, "Foreign Capital and Take-Off," in W. W. Rostow, ed, *The Economics of Take-Off into Sustained Growth; Proceedings of a Conference Held by the International Economics Association* (New York: St. Martin's Press, 1963), pp. 285-300.

8. H. B. Chenery, "Patterns of Industrial Growth," *American Economic Review*, vol. 50, no. 4 (September 1960), pp. 624-54.
9. Robert E. Baldwin, "Export Technology and Development from a Subsistence Level," *The Economic Journal*, vol. 73, no. 289(March 1963), pp. 80-92.
10. Sanford A. Mosk, "Latin America versus the United States," *Papers and Proceedings of the 63rd Annual.Meeting of the American Economic Association*, Chicago, Illinois, December 27-30, 1950, *American Economic Review*, vol. 41, no. 2 (May 1951), pp. 367-83.
11. Jonathan V, Levin, *The Export Economies: Their Pattern of Development in Historical Perspective* (Harvard Law School, International Program in Taxation; Cambridge: Harvard University Press, 1960).

Session V

Cultural Change in Development

Chairman KING: In view of the fact that the economic solution to development is trivial or simple, we economists have solved our own problems and we can now turn to look into the problems of the anthropologists in this session.

The principal discussant this morning is Mr. Manning Nash, whom obviously you know very well, who has done a great deal of work in Guatemala and Burma, was recently editor of *Economic Development and Cultural Change*, and is author of works too numerous to mention.

I suggest that we move right into the discussion.

Mr. NASH: In thinking about "Cultural Change in Economic Development," anthropologists typically do it through two lenses. The first lens gives a very, very long view and the long view tells you just what sort of change—social and cultural change—the process of development in modernization is.

I will sketch about two minutes of the long view and give you some of the yield from that and then move on to the short view. If you look at humanity as a single human career, from way up with the bird's eye, there seem to have been three major transformations. We call them revolutions: the Neolithic Revolution, the Urban Revolution, and the Industrial Revolution. In the long view, the societies which, have undertaken self-sustained, economic growth are those societies which have invested or participated in the Industrial Revolution. Economic development then is the kind of transformation which allows you to do a very simple thing: to take tested, scientific knowledge and apply it to the daily life of a society in continuously new increments.

When a society is structured to apply tested knowledge normally to its productive process and to a lot of its daily life, it will get rich. What kinds of societies are able to do this? No society is fully adapted to do it. Look at our calendar and our measuring system; we know a lot better but we do not do it. There are cultural constraints even with respect to those things we do know, but we know a society has to have at least these general features: it has to have a high tolerance for ontological uncertainty. The world has to be pretty loose and a lot of people have to be able to have the personalities to live with a loose world.

It has to have a social structure in which economic performance is important in conferring real material rewards and status, It has to have a lot of mobility, both spatially and socially, and it has to have a political system which is not dedicated to order alone, but to some equalitarian or redistributive economic goals.

At least, that is the way I look at the larger parts of the social structure and value system which have been characteristic of those societies which are able, continuously, to put novel scientific stuff into their daily life.

This long view does not tell us anything about economic development at this particular moment. If we elaborate it and spell it out, it gives us historical perspective so that, when we look at societies now, we may be able to tell whether they are changing in the direction and toward the kinds of societies which have economic growth as part of their constitution.

Let me restate what the long view teaches you, or has taught me, in one sentence. It has taught that there is a sort of society which has two major characteristics: it grows economically in consequence of its daily operation, and it has a social structure which generates and absorbs change without disorganization.

Now, let me move to the short view. The short view is used to look at societies now undergoing, or attempting to undergo, the process of modernization or economic development. When you look at societies in the short view, you get more microscopic, and I think you ask three kinds of researchable questions.

The first thing you want to know about any society from the social and cultural point of view is: who is likely to undertake a course of modernization? By "who," I mean what social segment in the society? For which social group is economic development a viable, an actionable set of goals?

There are techniques for identifying these groups in a society with some good probability. Maybe you can point to a society and say, "Nobody. This society does not have a segment, that will undertake economic development." If so, the social and cultural anthropologist has nothing to study there unless he is interested in kinship, but from a social change point of view, there is nothing. The first thing, therefore, is to identify those people who will undertake change in the direction of modernization.

The second question is, whom do they face? What other segments do they face as they try to do it? This is one of the things I argue with Hagen. He has not *a* good, not a bad, but a moderate technique, for identifying the groups that are likely to undertake social and cultural change, but it never puts him in an honest-to-goodness social structure. He never tells you whom they face. Once you have the group, you are off and away, and I think that is naive because you have to deal, with a social system. Whether you diagram it in triangles as Mr. Holt did (Fig. 1), or any other way, there is a social structure and a culture pattern, and any group attempting change does face all sorts of other groups.

In the modern world, just as an aside, one of the interesting things is that economic development takes place against groups which have vested interests in a kind of economic, structure which never existed prior to the Industrial Revolution. In Latin America, when a group tries to industrialize it already faces an organized, entrenched working class. It does not create a working class. The working class is built, in and has some vested interests in a kind of technology, in a kind of arrangement with the government, and in a kind of rent capture on their wages. And we could, find other things, the other organized groups, that are in the social structure.

So you want to know: who are they and what will they face? You also want to have some sense of the possible outcomes of the courses they will take. This requires you to have at least a stage theory of economic growth.

The first two parts of the. short view, I think, are very well laid out between anthropologists and sociologists. The third part, the minimal temporal length sequence, which gets you from the state of transition to modernization is blank—at least in my reading. I know of no convincing set of stages—not taking seriously Rostow's Airplane Theory of Growth; there are too many airports and too many consequences. We have no minimal set of temporally defined sequences, and I think, if we need research priorities, this is one I would suggest.

Mr. ANDERSON: What is the significance of your inserting the word "temporally" in the term "temporally defined"?

Mr. NASH: Because it is a process over time, and a cross-sectional analysis may or may not get you to length stages. If you want to know where you are going. you have to have some idea of what the process looks like.

In the remaining couple of minutes, let me say what some of the yield has been—at least in anthropology—in the study of economic development as an indicator of a modern society. I now prefer to use the term, and I think the word is better, "modernization," because the economy is only one segment of the changing society.

We have empirical generalizations on several levels, some of which have a truth value number assigned which gives you confidence, and some of which is funded nonsense or wisdom of the business which circulates it. I will just give you a couple of them.

The first one I think of—which is pretty easy to get—is something like the less the more: the less polarized wealth is in a social stratification system, the more likely it is that a segment will appear to undertake economic development.

Mr. ANDERSON: Now, that is opposite Hagen.

Mr. NASH: Right, only this is true. (Laughter.)

Mr. ANDERSON: Since you are my colleague, of course.

Mr. NASH: There are other lower-level generalizations about the formation of dual societies.

Mr. KREININ: Why do you say this? What is your evidence?

Mr. NASH: I will document it later. I think now I would do an anecdotal defense, but I do have it documented somewhere. If I just run through in my mind the societies I know, and if you tell me the societies you know, the generalization may not fit all cases but it has a good probability number on it.

Mr. MORGAN: By "polarized," you mean concentrated?

Mr. NASH: Yes, and sort of held in, too, by social constraints.

Mr. KREININ: This is what we would say: the less equal the income distribution or the wealth distribution? Is that what you mean?

Mr. NASH: Well, polarization is only one component in the status hierarchy. There are mechanisms of status conferral, career, modes of recruitment, and so forth. I do not intend to teach my colleagues anthropology and sociology, but the word is used to refer to a whole kind of social arrangements of power, wealth, influence, and prestige, which are parts of the institutional structure of the society as against the performance level of individuals. That is one component—and only one component—as wealth, is only one component.

Mr. KREININ: So you use it as an indication of mobility, of class mobility?

Mr. NASH: Well, mobility is one of the aspects, I am using it as an indicator that under conditions I have given, it is more or less likely that a group will begin to undertake economic development. Let us take a polar example such as Laos. On this generalization there are zero people in Laos ready to undertake economic development. Somebody might start it in from the outside, but I doubt it.

There are lots of other empirical generalizations on the formations of kinds of societies. There is a typical pathology now, in the middle of the development process, which results in a form of technological and economic dualism and a multiplicity in social organization, which keeps lots of societies on dead center and not able to move off. I think Indonesia is probably the hearth on which this model has been built.

Finally, we get a low level yield, but probably the most useful one for practitioners. This is the diagnostic yield. If you ask anthropologists and sociologists what to look for in the social order, I think they can give you a reasonable budget, of things, so that you do not have to do the mind-dizzying business of taking everything into account.

Some way or other I have seen sort of a checklist that conies out in books like *Cooperation in Change*,[1] Goodenough's latest book, and Lucy Mair's *New Nations*.[2] They are sort of checklists of what it is that anthropologists take to be the main factors to look for, and that might save the practitioner some time.

The last word is that, the minimal time span—and this is sheer opinion—of economic development is minimally a generation and probably two, because it is a process of cultural learning and resocialization and reformulation of a whole generation of people; the minimal temporal scope of the modernization process, I would guess, is about 40 years.

What good does this advice do? It saves planners, visitors and governments a lot of unnecessary anguish when they do not achieve modernization in five years.

Mr. KING: Thank you very much, Mr. Nash. We will next hear from our discussant, Mr. Daniel Wit, who has done field work in Thailand, and is the author of *Labor Law and Practice in Thailand*[3] and other works. He is now with Northern Illinois University, Mr. Wit.

Mr. WIT: I tend to approach this as *a* political scientist and so I approach it in two ways. First, I approach it intellectually: in terms of basic interest in trying to understand the interrelationship between the cultural and the political, along with the economic.

I also approach it operationally: in the sense that I am interested in problems of technical assistance and in what government can do.

Basically, I guess I have been indoctrinated to some extent by Mr. Nash's type of analysis because this makes sense to me. The question it leaves open, however, is the type of professional question with which I arc most concerned, really, which is: what can government do? This gets back to our big debate of yesterday, or rather, our rather lengthy discussion on the role of the political scientist. Is there some development strategy that can be employed, which recognises the necessity for taking into consideration the cultural factors and the need for cultural change?

I personally think that cultural change is a critical factor. I would include in cultural change not only attitudes concerning work, for example, where we have something very tangible in terms of ethnic differences, but I would also include motivation. I have been impressed by McClelland's efforts and other clinical psychological efforts to apply the whole concept, of achievement and motivation to the field. But what, then, can government do in this regard?

Well, I think first it has to realize the importance of culture. I have been very much impressed, operationally, by the extent to which both indigenous governments and sometimes American government agencies have not been really very concerned about this point. There is a certain pattern of assistance that we engage in, but just what does it really mean? In part, cultural differences are ignored because they appear to be nebulous to the operationally oriented practitioners, They do not know how to deal with them.

As I say, I am impressed by the need for government, to take cultural factors into consideration. I am impressed also by the many occasions in which economically sound recommendations or administratively sound ones—and I have been involved in public administration technical assistance—are completely worthless, either because they are ignored or because they are "handled," for reasons of political expediency, by the host government; the government wants the assistance or the money, but then intentionally circumvents the recommendations because, culturally, they do not make any sense.

If we have a government which is committed to development—which we often do not have—but if we have one, then it seems to me that what is required in this day and age is a strategy which attempts to blend a number of these factors.

I do not "buy" the notion, that one must transform the entire society before one can get on with the work of development, because this is a morass one sinks into, and also this becomes undirected effort to transform.

I also do not see a government as being capable, in itself, of conducting such a total revolution within any meaningful time-frame.

I do see, however, the possibility for government running a checklist of those cultural factors, including psychological factors, which can be counted as assets for the promotion of development, and running a research checklist of those factors which can be noted as obstacles and liabilities, and then building it into the strategy for the promotion of development.

In other words, I think that one stage in the formulation of strategy for development by a government must be the incorporation into the development plan of what can be learned from this type of sociological and anthropological research.

This has to be associated with the effort at scientific economic analysis which in turn, to be realistic, must also be adjusted to the political realities and the administrative realities of the society, apart from the cultural realities. Again, I am searching for what we were discussing yesterday when Mr. Blanksten put his finger on it for me in saying, "Can we mesh in any way?" Operationally, I think we have to mesh.

I see, therefore, government as being able to utilize this type of analysis of facilitators and obstacles within the cultural and the social sphere, just as it can utilize the political and administrative strengths and weaknesses of a society and associate them with the economics of development. I also think that it. becomes critical from the point of view of a government which is committed to development—I am only talking about that fairly rare bird, from my point of view—it becomes essential that it go through the effort of attempting to identify that group within a society which has either rebelled against or emerged from the traditional culture sufficiently to be potentially flexible and able to provide the necessary entrepreneurial spirit. Whether one talks just about managers, of which there are shortages, obviously, or whether one just talks about "attitude" without necessarily pinning it down to someone like a plant manager. I think these types of people have to be identified and have to be associated with the strategy of implementing a comprehensive plan.

I think, here, we can get help from the psychologists, combined with the anthropologists who are concerned with *a* given country, I recognize fully that *we* do not know much, for example, about mental health in many countries; it becomes very difficult, if you do not: know much about mental health in some countries, to know how one promotes development in them when development requires the tapping of psychological forces and eliminating psychological obstacles. But, I think this is the challenge. I also think that the very fact that these demands on government are so complex, is the reason for the *relative* lack of success of many governments in doing much about the generation of development, apart from the matter of time-span to date, which has been very brief. I see these several types of demand upon a government which is committed to the promotion of development.

There are other things, of course, that one could "toss in" as a political scientist, "Commitment" to development by the government is obviously not enough, either. It must also have certain types of capability. I regard administrative capability as a very critical factor.

I do not necessarily "buy" some of the public administration analysis of all world civilization as a product of successful administration, but, on the other hand, I do think that the administrative capacity of a government is critical. This, too, is a cultural problem, in the sense that much technical advice for reforming administration is totally meaningless, given the specific developmental stage of a society and its culture.

Parenthetically, may I just mention a very delightful talk which was given by a Filipino to a group of American foreign aid people gathered together in Manila. In that particular talk, the speaker took to task the whole American effort in the Philippines to introduce into government such things as performance budgeting, and also to get at nepotism and corruption, on the grounds that this is dysfunctional from the Western point of view. The whole "pitch" of this Filipino with a Michigan Ph.D. and all of the other Western trappings was that this is nonsense at this particular stage in the Philippines. At this particular stage in the Philippines, he claimed, if one attempted to achieve this American objective as part of the modernization process, all that would happen would be that, we would throw the Filipino administration into chaos. Why? Because we are dealing with a society in which people do not trust each other, or, if they trust each other, they trust their *compadre* only. Nepotism, he stated, is the only way in which you can get any decentralization at this time—which is also another administrative objective—and so on and so forth. So, scientific modernization in administration[5] like scientific modernization in economics, is meaningless without the attempt to develop a modernization strategy which blends cultural factors into it.

I am in complete sympathy with the types of insight provided by sociology and anthropology, but I also desperately search for operational means of getting that insight out of the conference room and into the field; this is the sort of thing I am personally wrestling with at the moment.

General Discussion

Chairman KING: I have "just one or two general comments. With respect to the estimate of the time-span as being 40 years or two generations, the questions that come up in my mind are connected with something that you brought up, Dr. Wit, namely: now that we are conscious of the problems of development, can this time-span be consciously shortened—perhaps by seeking to improve the political capabilities? Is it possible for a ruling class or a ruling group to willingly destroy itself or transform itself into another class that can be identified? Or can the ruling class give itself a new interest that can be better identified with the development process, and given this consciousness and this possibility of transference of interest, can the role of the civil service, which may belong to the ruling class by family ties and so forth, be given other horizons, perhaps other experiences, so that it can perform a role in the development process which will somehow shorten the time-span?

Professor Nash gave us two views, a long view and a short view. He stated general principles here which we can discuss as such, or we can bring specific examples to bear on their relevance or irrelevance to the development process.

Time and Signs of Change

Mr. SCHWARTZ: You were talking about economic development in a minimal period of time-span, in a generation or 40 years, and this seems to me a little bit in contrast with your stress on situational differences in other respects.

After a certain period of rapid development in some societies there is more concern, more consciousness of the need and desire for development, perhaps influenced by a relatively advanced degree of communication. In such a situation, a more curtailed time period might be all that would be necessary. But this could lead to an effort to do it in too short a period of time, which might cause a reaction against the development plans—particularly if the shortened timetable were not met. The result might be a consensus that the time necessary might be not shorter but, indeed, longer than originally estimated. In any event, I would think there would be differences from time to time, and from society to society, as to what the minimal development period would be, and that these might be as different as between ten and one hundred years. This would be the sort of thing which I would expect to hear, as a matter of fact, from the sociologists and anthropologists. Why do you seem to insist: on a generation?

Mr. NASH: I had in mind, when I said that, the new nations, the societies of Africa and Asia. I think Argentina could get off center in a lot under 40 years because Argentina is in many senses a pathological modern, if I can use that term. It has a lot of the institutions and markets, the people with firms, and the labor forces, which are absent from Thailand, Burma, Cambodia, and many of the African countries. That minimal time-span has to do with the transformation of the recently independent nations, which I think form a special category by themselves.

Remember, I said that as a matter of opinion. If you pin me to the wall with some fact in opposition to it I will give up that opinion.

Mr. SERRIE: Allan Homberg's project in Vicos, Peru, caused an incredibly basic transformation in an essentially peasant population characterized by fatalism and tremendous suspicion and fear of the outside; and everything in only ten years, not in your minimal span of 40 years.

This, of course, was only on a village level, but how would you deal with this kind of thing?

Mr. NASH: Well, I am not sure yet that if Cornell University pulled out of the Vicos project it would be a self-sustaining hacienda, and I would have to go look.

The literature of the Cornell School has not convinced me that the change is built into the social organization and the minds and hearts of the Vicosinos yet, and that doubt is widely shared in Peru; I do not think we have a clear instance there which would knock off my hypothesis. There is one other thing you must remember: with respect to communal development, when the time of the developers exceeds the time of the people living in the village, you have a bad investment, and I think that is what Vicos looks like. When the anthropological hours exceed the hours lived by the indigenes, it is not worth studying any more.

Mr. KREININ: It seems that you are in search of indicators—sociological indicators—so you can look at a country in much the same way the National Bureau thinks it can look at the economy; identify certain living indicators and say, "Now, the economy is going to develop," or, "Now the economy is not going to make it." I wonder whether this is essentially what you are doing, and, if you are, can you give us an example? Can you stick your neck out on this?

Mr. NASH: My crystal ball is about as cloudy as the National Bureau's, and I leave forecasting to the astrologers. (Laughter.) By the time I would make a prediction it would have so many OTE's [other things being equal] hanging around that it would not hit the case anyway. I do not think I should try to make a prediction now, but I think it is true that I am looking for a shorthand set, somewhere between the level of features that Talcott Parsons, Marion Levy, and other third-story theorists would lay out for a modern society and the bottom rung of the anthropologist who says that you have to take everything into account, culture trait by culture trait. What I am trying to do is become a second-story man, get off the ground a little, but not look up and let the skylight dazzle me—with apologies to Oliver Wendell Holmes.

Stage Theory

Mr. BLANKSTEN: I would like to comment on something Professor Nash said at the beginning of this session about the need for a viable stage theory of development.

I think it is clear that, if we do not have one, it is not because nobody has tried—as witness the airplane theory and some other attempts. Among the various things we have attempted, the stage theory has some special kinds of difficulty. There are problems in the definition of stage and how you use it in theory and so on, but the question I would like to put to you, Manning, is this: it seems to me that of all of the social science disciplines involved in this kind of effort, probably anthropology has had the most traumatic brush with problems of stage theory and evolutionism and so on. I wonder if there is anything that comes out of this experience, in terms of a kind of an intellectual history of anthropology or however else *you* want to frame it. What are the special things we have to be careful about as we try to develop the stage theory that you say we need? I am not asking you here to spin out a stage theory for us, or anything like this; but what do we need to do?

Mr. NASH: One of the things that topples the magnificent edifice of evolutionary theory that anthropology has is, of course, the facts. They made mistakes, I think, in laying out a kind of stage theory which could not be faulted. You could select things from it. They made the mistake of getting formal succession from stage to stage without ever any mechanisms of transformation. They went from savagery to barbarism to civilization, and they had formal definitions, but nobody was interested in how you went, or how you got there. Stage theory without mechanisms is a spectral mass of bloodless categories,

Take Rostow: he adds to our vocabulary, but not to our knowledge. He adds propensities. I think these are the special pitfalls in trying to construct a stage theory.

Ontological Uncertainty

Mr. FATOUROS: I would like to ask a question about another of the indicator requisites, and it is simply this: what is "ontological uncertainty"? I like the term, and I like its existentialist overtones. You mentioned that the military does not like it and that makes me like it all the more. So will you explain: what is it? (Laughter.)

Mr. NASH: Well, "ontological uncertainty" means that there is not a creed, or a dogma, or a set of cultural values held in an overcommitted way throughout the entire population. There is a lot of variety in the commitment to the values; lots of people in the society are loosely committed, and there are competing value systems.

Now, when I give a proposition and I give it in my own scientist guise, I am ontologically uncertain as to how it fits the world; if you give me reason to reject the hypothesis, that psychological stance and that value system, allow me to take on your new hypothesis easily.

Mr. FATOUROS: Would that have any relationship to the relations between cultural values, religious values, and political structure?

Mr. NASH: Surely.

Mr. FATOUROS: That is, if there is no direct relationship between the three, then you would have a higher degree of ontological uncertainty?

Mr. NASH: Possibly. The conditions for the creation of ontological uncertainty, I do not know. That is a researchable problem. How it is infused in a society—partly in the education system, partly in the family socialization, and partly in the kinds of groups competing with each other—makes for ontological uncertainty. It takes a special kind of person to live in that, sort of environment.

The Guatemalan Indians, by and large, are not ontologically uncertain about the most important things in the world. If you ask in Cantel, "Where is the center of the world?" they will answer, "Here." "Why is it here?" A saint was born here and lived in a certain cave. They have a structure which is hard to get through.

Mr. FATOUROS: Are the Antioqueños ontologically uncertain?

Mr. NASH: I haven't a clue. What I know about the Antioqueños is the hearsay I read in Hagen's book. (Laughter.)

The Case of Modernizing Oligarchies

Mr. NASH: I want to say something about the question that was asked about transforming groups. There is a kind of group called the modernizing oligarchy, which has empirically existed in starting modernization. These are the people who led the Japanese transformation, and the remnants of the princely class in contemporary Java, who are attempting to run business as modernizing oligarchies. The precise identification of the group which will take on modernization is a very, very difficult process, and it does not have any particular set of generalizable features, I think it is situationally specific, so that we are always slipping between—I am always slipping between—my levels of generalization and the diagnostic kickback for any one given society.

The linkage between *my* medical-like case skills in looking at poverty and constructing a general theory of health—if I can use Jack's kind of analogy here—is about as good as such generalization and prediction are in medicine. I am a little over the break-even point, but not much,

Mr. WIT: One additional thought that comes to mind with regard to this possibility, or what happens with the modernizing oligarchy, is rooted in my concern about Thailand. In the case of Thailand, one finds a situation in which whatever significant change has occurred in society, including significant modernization, the government has had a hand in, although they also have been very relaxed about non-regulated and undirected economic change in the society. But they have been so very relaxed about it because there has not been any significant percolation; the society basically being complacent, basically being quite happy—at least as far as the masses are concerned—with something close to the "traditional." Nevertheless, the oligarchy, the civil service bureaucracy and political leadership, have played a primary role and the society, in 700 years of continuous existence in Southeast Asia, has undergone several major transformations.

Very interestingly, one faces then the question of what sort of definition *of* change and development a bureaucracy provides. In that sense,

Thailand is a good case study. The definition it provides, or has provided, is one in which economic growth, as such, has low priority. I think this is very significant, because development in different societies is defined, obviously, in different ways, and a non-economic definition is sometimes the dominant definition.

In the case of Thailand, I have the feeling the following has been true: the ruling oligarchy, which is a bureaucratized oligarchy, has seen the necessity for modernization, usually in response to external stimulus (which gets us back to the discussions of environment): the threat of invasion, the necessity at the end of the nineteenth century of playing off French and British imperialism in order to survive. At that time, the country needed to look modern enough to Westerners to be allowed to retain its independence, so the oligarchy defined their development needs. But they did not define them in terms of economic growth, and they did not define them in terms of drastic transformation, either of the economy or the society or the culture. They did, and still do define them conservatively in terms of the necessity to save as much of that society which they enjoy and in which they are well embedded, as they possibly can. They create the least number of political problems and tensions for themselves by a very controlled economic growth which is not primarily oriented toward industrialization—or has not been—but toward bolstering the peasantry, helping to keep them satisfied, providing administrative services plus some of the selected trappings of modernity which, for reasons of cultural flexibility, they have been pragmatically willing to incorporate. All of this suggests, then, that bureaucracies can preside over a conservative development in which, perhaps, their definition of development is not primarily economic growth, but has to do with stability, control, and perpetuation of the role of the elites.

Now, how can a government get away with this form of controlled development? Well, it can get away with it, it seems to me, only in a certain type of society. In another type of society we may end up with the bloody rebellion that was suggested yesterday, as the only means of achieving a real transformation. But in a peculiar situation like the Thai, they can get away with it—although the world is now increasingly closing in.

Mr. BARANSON: There is one aspect of this that has always interested me. I was with the CED Mission, the Committee for Economic Development Mission, that went down to Central America about two years ago, and I remember that we met with, some of the modernizing oligarchy that you mentioned, the Mendozas of Venezuela and the de

Solas of Salvador.

The thing that struck me was that we have a predisposition for certain kinds of social change because there are kinds of people we feel we can talk to, who are our breed of man and understand what we are trying to do.

I was wondering if a group like this would have met with Lenin in 1917. I have often felt that as soon as you got 15 miles out of the capital city and you began to talk to the people, you find you are in another world, that the real thrust and pulse of social change was not in the rooms in which we were meeting and the people we were talking to.

We tended to meet with the kind of people we could talk to, and not with the social elements that might really determine the future. This is always something that has disturbed me.

I wonder if in your own experience you feel that there are groups in the country that think in some of these patterns?

Mr. NASH: Well. I have a professional bias to say yes to that. Anthropologists gravitate to the lowly hut, as we like to say, and look at the society from the peasant's point of view. We have learned to identify with and talk to the peasants, and to defend their interests. When we come to look at their modernizing elites, we find them to be very ignorant of their own peasantry, as being harmful to their peasantry. And when you come out of the village and go to the capital, you find that you are unable to seriously engage people in conversation about their own country. I think if you come as an administrator, clean from the United States and fairly ignorant of the culture and the society, you and he (elite) could exchange language in MIT-type syllables. But that has nothing to do with the development process in the country, and I think you are now in the third culture.

You start talking like university people, ex-changing those symbols—and many of us here have had this experience on these kinds of missions or in planning boards—with people trained in our own universities, who have the ability to play with the same kind of modern symbols we do, but not really to design programs which will get traffic moving in Calcutta or bridges up across the River Kwai, or whatever you really want to do, because they do not have much insight about their peasants, either.

Guatemala is my favorite case. The Ladinos of Guatemala—anyone who is not an Indian is called a Ladino, and they are about half the population—the Ladinos have about the same depth of knowledge, misinformation, and mythology about their Indians as most of you have about ours—only there they are half the population. They know what is good for the Indians and what the Indians are like and how to run them; but of course, they do not.

Let me give you one anecdote, and I will terminate. The Burmese government looked around, at the advice of the KTA mission [Knappen, Tippetts, and Abbett], and told them that up in Maymyo it is cool, which is true, and that there were cows, which was also true, and that the Burmese consumed condensed milk, which was also true. The mission then said, "You can put all these together and get a milk factory up at Maymyo and it will be efficient."

They built the milk factory and it has not squirted one drop of milk. Now, that is a combination of bad advice from Americans and ignorance on the part of the planners. If they had looked carefully at upper Burma, which is pretty dry, they would have seen that you need transhumance; the size of herds is very, very small and they go from place to place, they are not fixed; they could not stay big enough and in one place long enough to supply a milk factory.

What the herds do supply are hundreds of Burmese villagers who have bathtubs and who get the milk and cook it into condensed milk. This is a local industry done with a nifty production function which meets the needs. You do not need a factory and never did, but these fellows had been away from the villages so long they had forgotten that.

Mr. BINDER: If they practiced transhumance, how did they get the milk back to the bathtub?

Mr. NASH: It is not the same people who take care of the cows who do the cooking. They come near a village and they sell their milk to people who have bathtubs. When they move to other pastures, they sell to other people and these people cook as very much a part-time job.

Mr. KREININ: How about a bathtub factory? Would that go well there? (Laughter.)

Mr. NASH: Why not just continue to import the bathtubs?

Mr. KREININ: That is capital-intensive: a bathtub factory. When were you last in Burma?

Mr. NASH: In 1960-61. No Burman, by the way, has ever taken a bath in a bathtub.

Chairman KING: I used to hear that the coal miners in Wales put coal in the bathtubs, but this is *a* new story to me,

Mr. HARING: I wanted to ask about the Burmese milk factory, I was thinking of English cloth manufacture 150 years ago.

There was a dandy system for making cloth in cottages. Then we set up the factory system. Now, what would have been the difference in the anthropologist's analysis of the putting out, or cottage system, and the erection of factories which destroyed that system? What would be the difference between looking at that and looking at your Burmese milk factory?

Mr. NASH: Well, the difference is obvious. Those factories were more efficient and had some supply factors on their side and they produced cotton. In the Burmese case, they explored the demand side, using somebody else's language, and failed to take into account the technological constraints on the supply side in the scale of production.

Of course, nobody knew about these things. These are simple facts and you could have ascertained them on the ground. There is not there the size of herd, or the transhumance pattern, or the permanence which would allow an efficient, steady supply of milk to keep the factory going.

Mr. BINDER: Did they take the bathtubs with them when they went to get their milk?

Mr. NASH: No. The bathtubs were fixed in the village.

Mr. GINSBURG: Mr. Nash, with respect to the milk factory, it seems to me that you might be deriving more mileage from it than it deserves. Robert Nathan and Associates gave bad advice, perhaps because they did not have any geographers on the staff.

Which leads me to say something else: it is so customary to point to the separation between administrative elites—I made this point myself yesterday, I think—and the mass of the population, that one ought to regard the proposition with considerable suspicion.

Mr. Wit's remarks concerning the Thai situation suggests that this is not always the case anyway, that there are instances where an elite apparently understands well enough what is going on in the country as a whole so as to be able to keep fairly firm control.

My own bias, just to match yours, is one of great suspicion as to the peasant's conception of what is good for his country. In the first place, in many cases he does not even know what his country is. There is a tendency, quite understandable, for anthropologists who live in a particular village and come to understand quite well what its people are thinking to overestimate the relevance of what is being thought about in that microcosm to the general polity or economy of which it is a part.

Of course, there are cases which illustrate the other side of the equation. Certainly in Cambodia, the elite, however you define it—as a group or an oligarchy or one man—apparently knows what the people want pretty much, or so it appears, and the people seem willing to be led. But if you were in a Cambodian village for a long period of time, I am not sure you would really understand the situation any better. The same probably is true in Thailand and in Malaya. I do not know the situation in Burma. In parts of India it is the same, however, though in other parts of India it might be quite different. I hate to see you mouse-trapped into assuming something to be a general truth when it might at best be only a partial truth.

Mr. NASH: I think that is a very good sobering caveat, and perhaps the way to rephrase it is to unpack the societies. I have been talking about nation states as if they were unitary; when we get to a specific case we really have to explore the way it is hinged together in the different segments, what they know about each other and how they do in fact communicate with each other. The fact that, empirically, on the ground of my generalization, elites, by and large, do not know where the technological and economic breakthroughs are for their peasantry, is not to say they do not know enough to rule their country very well or cannot enlist and mobilize the peasantry.

Let me give you another example, from which I will not get so much mileage. They have an ARDC, an Agricultural Redevelopment Commission, in Burma and it goes around to villages. They give advice—the Burmese themselves—and they show movies of McCormick reapers, tractors, chemical manures, and so forth. I asked some of them, "Why don't you get small things like the Japanese plows for rice fields? They have a whole lot of technology that you can use," and they said, "Well, I don't know about it. I know these big things and that is what we have pictures of and that is what we are instructed in."

Mr. GINSBURG: Yes, but I would like to respond with another kind of story. The Rural Industrial Development Authority in Malaya is said to be making a hash of everything it attempts to do, which may be true, but there is a farm training center up near Ipoh, full of machinery lying on the ground rusting. What sort of machinery is it? It is great big Harvester combines, which are suitable for Kansas, not for Malaya.

Mr. NASH: That was my point.

Mr. GINSBURG: But it was not the Malaysians, or RIDA for that matter, who asked for this stuff. It was given to them by the United States; and they either had to turn it, down, saying, "Don't *be* stupid," or they had to take it, and that's what they got. They know very well what there is in Japan—no question about it, However, I do not know what generalization you can make out of that case except that it illustrates only one example of the stupidity of some American officials. Back in 1950 one American aid technician came to Java all fresh from Utah State and told the Javanese, that they had to grow hybrid corn all over the place. The Indonesian officials were very polite about it. They knew they could get more calories per unit of area out of hybrid corn, but in the Javanese value system corn was pig, not human, food. The elite understood it, the peasantry understood it, everybody understood it—except our boy.

Mr. NASH: A *very* good point. I just want to say that I will accept your proposition that they do know.

This reminds me of an American experience in the Depression of an extension officer coming to a poor farmer; he was going to give him an education in extension services. The farmer looked at him and he said, "I already know better than I do." (Laughter.)

Mr. WHITEFORD: I want to comment on the matter of the modernizing oligarchy that Professor Nash brought out. This is really one of the crucial issues, not only in Latin America but also in many other parts of the world as well. Somebody said that what we are trying to do at this point in Latin America is to convince our own best friends that they should vote themselves out of existence. This is a very difficult kind of thing but we must recognize the matter of generational change which is taking place. This reflects the result of the filtering in of outside influences.

If you get back into a Burmese village or if you get back up into a village in the Andes, the filter factor has been very much reduced; but if you are working with metropolitan communities, even relatively small communities, you find an amazing number of the second-generation members of the oligarchy have been educated in Europe or in the United States. They come back to their communities with a very different point of view from their oligarchial predecessors—from the viewpoints of their fathers and grandfathers.

In Popayán, for example, the sons—or the grandsons actually—of the men who resisted the arrival of the railroad are bringing back all kinds of ideas from their education in the United States and other places, about new methods of raising cattle, about new means of developing land resources and so forth. These people are much more receptive now to the development of industries in their own community than their grandfathers were. Furthermore, they are also aware of the total world picture, and, increasingly, they realize that if they do not make changes, somebody else is going to make them and they are going to be left out. There is, from what I have seen in this very traditional community, a changing process in the oligarchy which, in a sense, is an attempt to save itself, although not conceived of in those terms.

A situation where this did not happen is in Uganda, Among the Bunyoro, the traditional, group of leaders, was one stratum, one clan, the Bito. The Bito group, which had been the traditional rulers of the country, maintained, its own traditional position, while other people were going to Europe and being educated, or going into the missionary schools and getting educated. When a bureaucracy began to develop, the educated people were not members of the Bito. The educated men were the only ones who could fill the offices, but this matter of going to missionary schools had been below the attention of the Bito, so eventually the ruling clan, just "uneducated" itself out of existence as a strong factor in the society.

I do not think this is going to happen in Latin America.

Mr. WIT: A final thought on traditional oligarchies, since we have been wrestling with the problem of whether a traditional oligarchy can preside over development. It seems to me that we mentioned a number of problems of the traditional oligarchy in attempting to do so. However, one thing can help it considerably in its success in presiding over controlled development—which, in many cases, is really what American policy is angling for, since we cannot afford to destroy our friends if the replacements are obviously our enemies. One of the important facilitators, then, is the "opening up" of the oligarchy. What, has struck me, going back to the Thai experience, is the fact that the motivated people—at least those that are achievement-oriented in the society—get absorbed into the oligarchy.

Thailand is a society in which there is a clear-cut elite, and it is a bureaucratized elite. The nature of the absorption of achievement-oriented people is not necessarily conducive to economic growth, because they are absorbed into the government rather than into the economy. Nonetheless, these persons do find career satisfaction and personal satisfaction. This is one of the reasons why in Thailand you do not develop leaders for peasant revolts even if the peasants are of a mind to try revolt.

Mr. KREININ: Are you talking about ruling classes that might lend themselves, or identify themselves, with development? Let's take three examples, Nkrumah, Nasser, and Ne Win. I have no use for Nasser, you know that, but leaving emotional feelings aside, what do you think of them as possible people to associate with development?

Mr. NASH: Well, the only one I have any sense about is Ne Win. I think this military group has about as much chance of modernizing Burma as a snowball in Hades, for three clear reasons. The army colonels who run it have no accountability system and no feedback on their performance; when they ran the DSI, the defense service industries, they ran it the same way. They made, decisions, and, whether they were carried out or how they affected the agencies, they never got any feedback and there is nobody to dislodge them.

Secondly, I think the army is peculiarly unfitted for maintaining conditions of ontological uncertainty. The Burmese army, and maybe all armies, when they really get out on the street, want to get the betel nut sellers out, make you pull up your socks, brush the streets; all the useless junk that armies always get involved in. They have nothing to do with development.

Thirdly, they do not have the confidence of the peasantry. At night, I am sure, the country belongs to the peasants, and in the daytime it belongs to the army. They are in power because they leave the peasants alone. They bother the people in Rangoon, and they blow up Student Union buildings. If they start to bother the peasantry in any real sense, they will be out of power.

This [drawing snail-like diagram, Fig. 2, on blackboard is social structure and social space. This is my favorite shape. It is my ontological reality. Everything distributes that way.

In regard to cultural norms in a stable society, I think you always have something like this [indicating central, hump]: 80 per cent of the

Fig. 2. Social Structure and Social Space

members in any stable society are 'well built-in members; they take the culture, they live by the norms, they play their roles, and they have the normal troubles of living, dying, procreating and carrying it on. Ten per cent are over-committed. They provide the upholders of the norms, the readers of texts, the censors., everybody who believes that this stuff is graven in gold and stone.

Ten per cent are in the 3D category: the deviants, the defectives, and the delinquents. Part of the people who go in for social change are usually found in this category. Somebody out in this end of the distribution has to invent and discover something that will appeal to that large mass in the middle. As I envision cultural change, it is in part the creative solutions of some people in the 3D's, which then solves some of the problems of the well built-in members, The 3D's are deviant, defective and delinquent because they are having excessive troubles with the same problems which the well built-in members have as normal troubles. Then you get a redistribution and the curve itself moves over and you get another kind of society, and so forth.

Mr. KREININ: Isn't your representation on the board there in fact backward?

Mr. NASH: All right. We will put the head over here [indicating he would move 3D's to far right] and the tail this way [indicating he would put the overcommitted at far left].

Mr. BARANSON: I just wanted to comment on something you were saying about the oligarchy. In Honduras, I think it is well to keep in mind that the local culture will take from another world what suits it best and will utilize it in an entirely different way from what you had in mind.

I remember, down in Honduras, I ran into this one family. One son had come to the United States and brought back an MIT education, an American wife, a short-wave radio set to listen to the World Series, a Thompson submachine gun, and an idea of starting a General Motors distributorship, which he had tried to obtain for some time without success. So he and his brother finally got together and helped overthrow the government, and he got his distributorship.

We have one thing in mind and they take what fits their situation and rework it in their own way.

On the ontological viewpoint, a lot has to do, it seems to me, with who is involved in change. If they have at hand the means of using terror, if they have ways of shaking up ontological certainty, this is entirely different from gaining consensus through a democratic process. It also makes all the difference in the world whether there are social groups who are disposed to deal with ontological uncertainty and have the necessary means at hand. It makes a difference if it is a professor who is going down to teach the oncoming generation modernizing ideas, or the American government with only the CIA and economic aid to do the job.

Mr. NASH: I think that is a research problem which has not been touched, and Americans do not touch it, the substitutabillty between guns and ideology, or coercion and commitment.

Mr. BARANSON: Sort of a marginal rate of substitution occurs?

Mr. NASH: Yes, and we ought to figure out how much they are interchangeable, and I do not see any research on that. I think that, is an American middle-class bias of a clean-scrubbed democratic kid. They do not publish. (Laughter.)

Polarization and Change

Mr. HERLIHY: You said in the long view one of the factors that is necessary for modernization is equalitarianism, and then in the short view you were also talking about polarization; I think you were talking about the same thing. I would like you to explain to me just why this is necessary for modernization.

Mr. NASH: Well, one of the sustaining energies in modernization, for the people undergoing it, is actual distribution of real goods, and the actual distribution of real goods in a performance-oriented economy tends, over time, to lead to equalization. There has to be some commitment of redistribution of what comes out of the economic development.

Mr. HERLIHY: By "commitment," do you mean actual redistribution?

Mr. NASH: Yes; part of it government-sponsored and part of it not. I think all of these governments at least seem to be engaged in what has been called the politics of equality. They all have some sort of welfare notions, and they all have some notion of distributive justice apart from economic performance.

Part of it is that a modern economy tends, more than unmodern economies, to spread shares out more equally—and I think that can be statistically documented. Modern governments tend to play the game of the politics of equality,

It has taken us a long time; it has taken us a hundred years to get around to a War on Poverty—if we get around to it.

Mr. HERLIHY: But is this a necessary condition, then, of modernization?

Mr. NASH: No. This is one of the products of modernization,

Mr. HERLIHY: In other words, it is not a necessary condition.

Mr. NASH: It is what a modern society does, that is right.

Mr. HERLIHY: I thought you were saying something different, that this was a necessary condition.

Mr. KREININ: Yes. My understanding also was that your disagreement with Higgins was on the necessary-condition kind of thing.

Mr. NASH: Yes, but then I made a polarization kind of hypothesis. The other was a characteristic. Perhaps I spoke too rapidly.

The first was a characteristic of what a modern society looks like. The other proposition was that the less polarized the elements, and the status, and the stratification system are, the more likely it is, and so forth.

Mr. KREININ: That means a pre-condition, then.

Mr. NASH: Yes.

Mr. KREININ: In all likelihood it is a pre-condition,

Mr. NASH: Well, it. does not have to happen. It is a matter of probability.

Mr. HERLIHY: This was not true in Japan, was it?

Mr. KREININ: No. That is not what he is saying.

Mr. WHITEFORD: Could I introduce one or two instances which I think tend to support Mr. Nash's generalization. I would like to describe briefly two communities in Latin America in which I have worked and which are quite different from each other in many respects. One is a very traditional, highly stratified, aristocratic community, Popayán in Colombia; the other one is a more rapidly modernizing community, Queretaro in central Mexico, where the stratified system has broken down to a considerable extent.

In one situation, in Popayán, where the hierarchy, the oligarchy, has maintained its position almost completely unchallenged up until the present day, modernization is going on very slowly. Most Colombians and the Popayanejos themselves say that no change is occurring in the city. When I went back after ten years of absence, on my way down, in Bogota, Cali, and other places I asked about Popayan and they all said, "Nothing has happened in Popayan. Nothing has happened. It's always the same. It never changes." When I got there and spoke to the people themselves, they also told me that nothing had happened, that everything was exactly the same. But, after my ten years of absence, I was aware of a considerable number of changes that had taken place in the community; they were not major changes but they were there.

In spite of the changes, there had been no real dislodgement of the oligarchy. It was still there and still in. power. It seems to me that this suggests some validity in the generalization about the polarization of power and the polarization of wealth; as long as it continues to exist in Popayan, it will be one of the factors acting as a deterrent on modernization and change.

In the Querétaro situation, the first thing that happened, with the revolutions in Mexico and various other factors, was the breakdown of the old land-holding aristocracy. There are still remnants of it in the community which enjoy social prestige, but not very much power.

There has been emerging in the last ten or fifteen years a new segment in the society, partly by immigration, but also from middle-class individuals who have been getting education and who have also been alert to the developing possibilities brought in by the arrival, for example, of the Pan-American Highway and the necessity for garages. These people have started garages, they have procured the franchises for automobiles, and now they have taken over the franchises for pumps and various other things in which the remnants of the old aristocracy have not expressed much interest. As a result there has emerged in Queretaro a very potent upper middle class. Many of the individuals have moved into a position where, stratigraphically, they have to be recognized now as a lower upper class.

In the matter of social prestige we found that this group ranked in the community just below the remnants of the old aristocracy, but it has very much more power, very much more wealth, and even in the time since we were first there it was interesting to see the accumulation of political power that some of these people had attained.

For instance, one man who came from a middle-class family and who was a real entrepreneur managed to get: land and also franchises for Dodge and then later Chevrolet automobiles. During a period of two or three years he managed to pick up a number of other smaller franchises and, at the end of our period there, was in the process of being elected, as a senator for the state. He is very definitely on the way up so far as political power and financial power are concerned.

Mr. HERLIHY: It seems to me that there is a fundamental difference here between Arthur Lewis's position on the trade-union devil and equalization. We are now saying that equalization or redistribution of income is a necessary characteristic of a modernizing society or economy, We have also said that trade unions are a factor in this process of redistribution. And yet, if I understood him correctly. Dr. Lewis says that labor unions tend to hold back modernization.

Mr. HOLT: I would like to talk a little bit about this. It seems to me that this is precisely the area in which. Professor Nash's stage theory comes in.

In the studies I have done there is some indication that at a pre-industrial stage it is nice to have polarization, perhaps to a considerable degree, in the distribution of 'wealth, some polarization in the distribution of prestige, and relatively little in the distribution of power. Then as you move into the beginnings of a modernizing stage, the modernizing class should take over power (preferably by peaceful means) and the distribution of power should become more polarized.

You may have at the beginning, therefore a relative equality of power, as illustrated by the existence of various veto groups which cannot initiate policies, but which can prevent the adoption of an anti-modern-izing policy from an old aristocratic class and then move in at a later stage to positions of power, and here you have a disequalization of power; you have it concentrated in the hands of those people who are the modernizing force.

This is the point at which you might prevent labor unions from exercising power, whereas, at a previous stage, you might want to have them as veto groups. There are, therefore, definite stages and shifting in this respect, as I look at it.

Mr. WHITEFORD: Your point about the peaceful transition is important because in Querétaro there was a violent overthrow at one point, of course, but since the Diaz regime there has been a period of relatively peaceful transition which has been brought in by-changing transportation and industrialization. People have taken advantage of it.

In Popayán I have been very much concerned with the difficulties involved in this peaceful transition. In talking with young men of the middle class or lower middle class, I find that they are very much upset about it. They cannot see that the situation is developing in such a way that they can eventually attain anything for themselves, so they continually talk about the necessity of "breaking the ring." This is the communist appeal to them. They feel extremely frustrated.

In the past, people who became frustrated were simply drained off because they went down into the Cauca Valley and worked in Call, but today people want to stay in their own community. Apparently, they have a broader view and they would like to see changes brought about in their own native city but they feel frustrated because they do not see how they can break into the structure as it is now established.

Mr. KREININ: *I* think the point before us is of fundamental importance. There is, you see, an actual conflict here between the view of the psychologist-anthropologist and the view of the economist. I think that the conflict Professor Nash had with Ben Higgins can be traced hack to the same thing, if I interpret Nash correctly: talking about the requisites rather than results. The economist would say that non-equal distribution of income is necessary to produce savings, whereas Professor Nash says that income has to be equally distributed in order to produce—

Mr. SCHWARTZ: No, He did not say any such thing.

Chairman KING: Excuse me. Are you being correctly interpreted here?

Mr. NASH: No, I am not.

Mr. KREININ: No, no, no. This is what Higgins would say.

Chairman KING: Oh.

Mr. KREININ: He would say the opposite, you see.

Chairman KING: I see.

Mr. KREININ: I am saying that what Nash says is the opposite.

Mr. SCHWARTZ: Why says which?

Mr. KREININ: Nash says that he would like to see income, as equally distributed as possible.

Mr. NASH: No. I have fought with Higgins about other things, but not: about that.

Mr. KREININ: Well, this polarization: isn't that how it is reflected in the income distribution?

Mr. NASH: Part of it. I just said that, there is a point of polarization in the stratification system where there is little possibility that anybody will undertake economic development, there will not be a group available, and it is as simple as Mr. Whiteford said: the group that controls the resources, recruitment, and means of mobility has a good thing going and there is nobody else with enough power to change that good thing, so they keep that kind of society going.

If there were less polarization in that status structure, then they could not keep the society running in the same way. They would have to take account of other changes, other stimuli, so it is just that simple a statement. I am sorry that I picked that particular empirical generalization because I do not love it that much. I have others.

Mr. ANDERSON: That is a bad word, "equalization."

Mr. NASH: Yes.

Mr. ANDERSON: You had better choose another one. It throws people.

Mr. NASH: Yes.

Mr. SCHWARTZ: There is not necessarily a conflict between this—whatever you want to call it: drive toward equalization, or necessity for equalization, or correlation of equalization—and the Lewis kind of presentation of trying to hold back labor unions, among other groups, and hold down wage levels. There need not be any conflict between these two approaches because, as Lewis pointed out, there have been increasingly smaller additions to employment resulting from a given amount of investment. One of the examples he gave showed that, with a particular wage level, you could expect only a rather reduced number of laborers, whereas, at a different wage level, you might expect a much larger number. So, you are really talking about high wages for what becomes an increasingly small proportion of the population and, insofar as this is true, unionization and higher wages are not necessarily going to improve the equalization. While I do not necessarily agree completely with this point, there is not necessarily a conflict between this and the Lewis presentation.

Mr. KREININ: Could it be a matter of degree, too? That is, how much will it disturb the equilibrium? Perhaps a little higher wages is all right but too much isn't; a little would produce incentives but too much will hold back the process?

Chairman KING: This was his point. He said there was a differential, if I recall it, if we are talking about Professor Lewis,

Mr. KREININ: Yes, but the amount of the differential: could that be an explanation?

Mr. FATOUROS: Oh, yes. He did mention the fact that it could be higher up to some degree but not too much.

Mr. HOLT: Yes, but the implication of what he was saying there, it seems to me, again is lack of correlation between the income distribution and the power distribution. In order to reduce the ratio of wages to something he would consider desirable, it would seem to me that it would be necessary to clamp controls on the labor unions, and In effect to deprive them of power and, in a sense, increase the polarization of power and decrease the polarization in income. Although in some general survey analysis you would get a high correlation between power and prestige and wealth, what is interesting is that you may maximize the opportunities for development when they are not highly correlated.

Chairman KING: Is it not a question of checking the power of the unions, or a question of whether the government which has the power merely abdicates it or not. to the unions at a particular time?

Mr. HOLT: *I* think it is going to be very difficult for a government to get voluntary cooperation from the unions over a long period of time to hold wages down. Lewis himself said that in case after case the unions put a government in power and then the government turned around and kicked it in the teeth.

Mr. BARANSON: I think on this matter of indicators, as soon as you begin to think in terms of policy terms, the indicators you select and how you read them take on an entirely different light. It is not only a matter of the disciplines. Religious church groups, who are missionaries, want to introduce a certain kind of change: they may go in and teach the language first because, if they are going to bring the word of God, this is the first thing to do.

I know when the CED went into Colombia there was a Father Salcedo [Monsignor José Salcedo] who was working on the communist influence in villages. Father Salcedo tried to negotiate with Sears Roebuck in Colombia to provide small radios and drop them into the villages so that Father Salcedo could broadcast to them, The CED decided it was not the CIA, so we went back to our modernizing oligarchies.

I also remember running into a young agronomist in Colombia at Tibaitatá. The Rockefeller Foundation had one of the finest agricultural experiment stations in the world that they build outside of Bogota. The young agronomist who was from Minnesota had been there four or five years.

I asked him what brought him down there and he said he could not get facilities for experimenting with hybrid corn anywhere in the United. States as fine as they were at Tibaitatá. He also told me that they had *a* backlog of something like 20 years in innovations on improved strains of corn, rice, and potatoes. What the people really needed was ways to store potatoes and other crops.

The price range in one year went from something like three to over a hundred pesos, and the real difficulty was to find ways to store potatoes so as to help stabilize prices—not to develop new strains.

What I am trying to say here is that general indicators are poor guides to policy. You must have particular reference to the kind of social instrument of change you are working with, and pick your spectrum of indicators accordingly.

Mr. NASH: That must be true. I have never affected policy anywhere in the world. Nobody has ever asked my advice in that regard.

Mr. BARANSON: You never know.

Mr. WHITEFORD: I like very much what Mr. Baranson was saying about moving into a society where you are trying to analyze the situation regarding possible change. One of the things you have to keep in mind is the kind of change you are going to try to institute. It seems to me that, in many of these areas, one of the things we should try to determine, although it might be difficult, is: what kind of changes do *they* want? Frequently we go in with our own pre-determined concepts of the kind of industrialization or the kind of economic reforms a country should have—from our own academic background or our own practical background—without taking the time to really investigate the situation to see how applicable our program might be or how much it might be desired by the people.

In talking with Mr. Hendry yesterday about field research, we agreed that one of the factors which is always present is the time factor. You cannot determine these, things simply by doing sort of a helicopter survey, or, as Mr. Baranson says, by talking to the people in the top echelons, who speak your language, because they may be just as foreign to their own culture as you are.

I would, therefore, like to enter a continuing plea for prior, thorough investigation—research—in the areas where we are going to work in order to identify the groups with which we will have to work, and which may be the factors to institute change, as well as the groups which may oppose them; to identify the resources which *may* contribute to change; and also to examine the whole pattern of what is regarded as desirable by the people who are going to be affected by it.

Mr. BINDER: I have a number of notes with respect tc points I want to make. Actually, these began to occur in chain reaction with the excitement over the problem of polarization and the trade unions, but I will tie then; up with some things that were said later on, too.

One thing that I certainly hope we have not accepted, the one proposal that was put forward: that trade unions should be clobbered in developing societies. I do not consider it prudent.

I would suggest to Professor Nash, however, that this polarization concept, it seems to me, is best tc apply to small societies, or to these having obviously a relatively simple structure. I do not know how many people there are in Laos or Cambodia or wherever it was, where you said that the number of people who were going to institute economic development or cultural change is probably zero.

Chairman KING: Two million.

Mr. BINDER: Thank you. This is about it. Of course, there are societies with two million people that are much more complicated in their structure. I think probably Lebanon is one such.

I would like to give a very brief example of a similar polarization, not of a traditional society, but what I presume would be a modern society. I will not. name the place, but it is in Israel and it is a Moshav (privately owned land) and whatever cooperation goes on is on the basis of ad hoc agreements or contracts between the people who are going to cooperate, In this particular place I have in mind it was decided that industry should not be brought in, and by golly, industry was not brought in. I. suppose the Mapai, the labor party, was not brought in at the same time.

These were people who certainly were not traditionals, but the great majority of the original settlers in this town were from Europe, and. they had. higher education, or at least the beginnings of a higher education.

This leads me to suggest what I always suggest whenever I hear Mr. Nash talking this way: that one of the areas of cultural change has to do with the high and written tradition. This has a great deal to do with the import and export, of ideology, I suppose, but it is not only the unwritten traditions of the villager one has to be concerned with; one has to be concerned also with the high tradition that one finds only in the capital cities and perhaps only fully controlled by the traditional intellectuals. In the case of the Moshav, of which I have given you an example, these are not traditional intellectuals, but they are intellectuals who were also involved in the mass movement.

This high tradition and rich tradition is often that which is not shown to the foreigner by the administrator or the person in the capital city in the country which you are going to advise. He talks to you in these MIT symbols, but he perhaps has latched on to the high tradition, and he may very well know that he is not going to show it to you. But he does not share this with the peasant, except in a very vague way, and somehow or other you have to penetrate that rather special tradition of the upper classes, which is indigenous and not shared with the third culture, if you are going to bring about a change. Now, perhaps this is what Manning means, or what Manning is getting at, when he insists upon the importance of ontological uncertainty, That is, you somehow have to blast apart the high tradition, and you have to get at that by means that are not used to disturb the peasantry. That is, you might disturb the peasantry by changing the shape of the bathtubs in which they boil the milk, but you are not going to get at the high tradition except through intellectual discussion, through experience which is tied, perhaps, to some kind of philosophical exchange.

The problem then, I think, is one going beyond ontological uncertainty, because all the uncertainty does not give the motivation to bring about change; one has to also think about the value change.

Somehow or other the things that are associated with development have to be valued, and I think we do have a problem of connecting value orientations with this situation of ontological uncertainty, I do not have the answer, but I think that here is a profound problem that must concern us and it is a question of cultural change. It is connected with development: what kinds of value orientation are compatible with a condition of ontological uncertainty, or what range of ontological possibility being admitted in the culture would be compatible with certain kinds of value orientation that are compatible with economic development?

Again, I do not have the answers but I think the questions are worth posing.

Sister THOMASINE: With reference to some of the remarks about trade unions, I would like to side with Mr. Kreinin. I still think that what Mr. Lewis had in mind, and I hope I did not misunderstand him, was not a darkling thought of just clobbering the labor unions, I think he was thinking—at least I gained that impression from conversations before and after that that I had with him—of the *pace* of *change* and of the *degree* and *differences* in *change. I* think that is what he has in mind, and has very seriously in mind. It is this reflection that has changed his own thoughts on the subject. Whereas he may have given the more radical impression, I do not think that is what he meant.

Identifying Societal Segments

Mr. MORGAN: I was hoping to ask Mr. Nash about the two central points I understood he was presenting in his long-run analysis. One was to identify the people who would undertake modernization. I should be glad to have a comment on that. And then, whom do these people face? I guess we have talked *a* little about that, but perhaps something might be added.

Mr. NASH: How do you do that in a society? If you go to a place, you have to get fairly saturated in the knowledge about the country and find, out what groups have what sorts of goals—what they are aiming at.

If I were to diagram a society—and this recalls Professor Holt's social spaces, his round minus square—it would be made up of all sorts of role sets, to use our terms, What you would explore is: what kind of resources do these people command, what span of control do they have over other sorts of persons, and. what is it that they do in the operation of their roles? What are their goals? Are they out to expand, to do X, Y, or Z?

Then, from describing the society, you would find, let us say—as in Guatemala where I once tried this—that there are segments of the upper classes who are modern, willing to modernize, and who have tried it and keep trying it successfully. So, you have to identify the groups, and determine what they face. They face other groups in the society: the cosmopolitans, who run the large landed estates; they face a rural gentry with an absentee technique; they face the United Fruit Company with a foreign factor economy; they face the Indian population which is alien to them and whose problems they cannot solve.

In this kind of competitive system, therefore, your prediction always comes up to this: the tension between this upper literate segment of performance-oriented economic Guatemalan actors and the landholders, the rural gentry and the Indian population is always resolved—not always, but most frequently—by the *cuartelazo* [army revolt.]

When these groups start moving and the equilibrium shifts enough, this group in the background, the army, allies itself with one or another sector and stabilizes the situation. Sometimes, as in the case of Arévalo, they held the arena open and, for a while, they allied themselves with segments of this middle-mass and with the Arbenzistas, to get it down to the lowest level. But then they started to eliminate a big section of this middle-mass because they went left, the army disaffiliated, and Arbenz went out.

If the army had hung on, you would have had in Guatemala what you have in Cuba; they would have transformed it and thrown out the unassimilable part of that modernizing group. I do not know what they would have taken these people and the urban working class into the political process. That is sort of the way you use these diagnostic tools.

Mr. FATOUROS: So Castro's technique of breaking the army up, on the first opportunity available, would be, from his point of view, very well take.

Mr. NASH: Yes. The thing that strikes me about armies in underdeveloped countries is that they are very strange animals. By and large they exist for the slaughter of their own people and not for national defense, or whatever armies are for. I guess the Guatemalan army has fired a shot or two in anger at Salvador and Mexico, but, but, by and large, their war trophies are against other Guatemalans.

Mr. WHITEFORD: In answer to Mr. Kreinin—this Is ex post facto, of course—I think it would be possible to look at Popayán and determine on the basis of a fairly simple analysis where the locus of power lay and where the locus of wealth lay; to see that, for the upper class in Popayan, there was no need for further expansion. They felt no necessity for greater wealth than they already had, they were as wealthy as they needed to be; and you would, also see, if you looked, closely, that there had been very definite indications of rejection of modernization. For instance, the old generation resisted the arrival of the railroad. They did not want the railroad to come into Popayán; they tried to get it to stop in Cali. They felt that it would bring in too much change and they liked it the way it was.

Nestlé's came in with the idea of—I hate to introduce milk plants again, but this is a stock-raising area and they wanted to establish a milk plant. But the people who owned the milk producers rejected the idea; they just made it: so difficult even to get the place started that the company eventually gave up in disgust and went back down into the Cauca Valley to Cali.

There have been several instances of this sort of situation where the old generation not only failed to take advantage of modernization but actually rejected it. On the other hand, I think you could look at the societal structure in Querétaro and identify the rising entrepreneurs, the changing middle class, and certainly the greater spread of power and of wealth as compared to Popayan and, following what Manning has said, identify one as a situation conducive to rapid modernization and. the other as *a* situation which would be resistant.

As far as identification is concerned, I would say, although this is not what I have been concerned with primarily, that there are certain clues, there are certain factors, which can be identified: we might eventually be able, to say that some are indicators of greater potential for rapid development and others are not.

Sister THOMASINE: The subject matter discussed today which may link with our talk this afternoon was the subject matter of—I do not know whether you want to call it oligarchy, the elite, the high-thinking or what—and the filtering process that you mentioned, Mr. Whiteford.

I think, because we are either a semi- or completely learned group, we tend sometimes to be unrealistic and a little bit without hope. It is because we know not quite enough—but a lot. There is a great deal of hope in this filtering process. Let me illustrate this point by referring once more to the record of my own Church.

Fifteen years ago, looking at the future of the Church in the continent in which I am particularly interested, that is Latin America, I would have been very dismal. But I have seen a tremendous filtering process there and. for those of you who want to know the inside view, I will cover it very quickly.

If I were to tell someone who is not acquainted with this about what happened to the Church, and had to do it in two minutes as I am doing it now, I would say something like this—and there are millions of other things to be said, things you know that I do not know—I think what went wrong in the Church in Latin America, and by "the Church" I mean the Catholic Church, were three things. I will list them here:

There was the paternalism with which the Catholic Church started out because it was with the Spanish Crown, which itself had a paternalism that militated against leadership. It came over with the Crown, and looked upon not only the Indian but also the Spaniard and Creole who were born over there as being children. We should understand this in the United States. For we have done that. We looked upon certain people as children, as did the Church in Latin America and as did the Spanish government also.

Second, a sort of medieval concept came with the Church, an idea which is not wrong and which is shared by Protestantism in its right form; namely, that every state of life is good and therefore it is sort of fixed. Carried to its extreme, this idea ruined, you might say, the social outlook of the Church. Carried to its rightful place it has meaning, certainly, for people everywhere.

The landholding of the Church was very often acquired justly and often used well in the beginning—not always, certainly, but often used well in a charitable form. Yet these lands were looked upon as an elite would look upon them, as something that was due to the holders, something that went from Church generation to Church generation.

Then came the situation that Mr. Nash mentioned. Churchmen were put against the wall. After the nineteenth-century independence movement, the Catholic Church was put against the wall and deprived of its landholdings. When the Church came back to Latin America after this movement, it had no means of subsistence except what it could get occasionally from the wealthy groups. So it took, I really think, the infiltration of the changing Church, which you people recognize in the Council going on today, and it took communism—"for whom the bell tolls." It took that.

Now, in Latin America, remember that this is an established group. It is true that the vocations of the Church have come from the middle classes, from the educated classes and from some of the peasant people; but in Chile, as many as you know, in parts of Colombia and the Brazilian northeast, the Church is doing remarkable things. It is divesting itself deliberately. Perhaps you can say that this is because it is the only way it can last, true; but it is a good thing, and it is doing it wisely in many countries—wisely and well.

The Chilean example, I think, is the best. Before the lands were divided, Chilean experts were brought in to tell the people how to use their lands. What I am saying is that it did not come from any university directly, but it was an infiltration of immense importance.

This movement is not to perpetuate the Catholic Church in Latin America. It is to perpetuate, I hope, the good life. That, I think, is linked to education and I hope it is, in some way, what we will talk about this afternoon.

I did not mean to make a speech, but this is something you do not have an opportunity to know. This is the inside story as well as I know it.

Chairman KING: I think this is a most interesting summary and very useful.

Cross-Disciplinary Influence

Mr. MIRACLE: It seems to me that Manning Nash made a pretty convincing case that societies we call underdeveloped, and that are changing, have a number of dimensions to that change which are usually have been talking about them in this conference.

Some others, the economist Ted Schultz, for example, have recently lauded the contribution made by anthropologists and our understanding of how to transform peasant economies. I have also heard an argument recently by Aidan Southall, who is a British anthropologist, that economists working on underdeveloped countries should at some point sit in a village a while—if only a week or two—with the anthropologists, and maybe the anthropologists should sit with the economists somewhere—or something like this.

Chairman KING: This is what we are doing here, sir.

Mr. MIRACLE: My question goes to methodology. Should all of us be sitting in a village, or can we divide up the specializations and let the anthropologists alone go out to the villages? That is one question, and purely a question. What do I tell my graduate students? If they want to be the rising stars ten years hence in economic development, in transforming peasant economies, can they go along the way we have been going in economics or had they better get into Manning's courses at some point?

Mr. NASH: Since I do not get paid on a per capita basis, keep them home. (Laughter.)

Sister THOMASINE: I would like to make a roundup of comments and then perhaps one that will lead to the afternoon's discussion. At least, I hope it will. I have been in several meetings with Mr. Nash, and I never can resist making a few remarks about anthropologists. One is an old joke that I recall from my undergraduate days; but before I tell it I want to say that I think that anthropologists are changing—and for the better. (Laughter.)

Incidentally, I should add that I feel they are terribly necessary. The joke I recall was about the woman who was glad she married an anthropologist because the older she got the more he loved her. (Laughter.) Perhaps this is why I seem to like anthropologists more and more as time goes on.

Mr. KREININ: One point about anthropology and economics. You know, it is making progress. Economics—

Mr. NASH: Which?

Mr. KREININ: Anthropology. (Laughter.) Economics can be defined as the science in which everything is tangent to everything else. Once you introduce marginal factors of substitution in anthropology, you have it half-way. Now you have to find something for it to be tangent to, and you've got it made (Laughter.)

Mr. HENDRY: I am very much interested in this viewpoint of Mr. Nash's with respect to the idea of identifying groups responsible for change and the forces opposing them, trying to get indicators, and so on.

I would like to ask about something that has been touched on to have it made a little more explicit, and that is that many of the things which are introduced, particularly in peasant societies, just do not make much economic sense. I have in mind the kind of example where, in East

Pakistan, recommendations for fertilizer application, based on some rather questionable results at fertilizer trial-and-experiment stations, called for something like 40 pounds of nitrogen per acre, while farmers were using on the average, where they used it at all, something around ten pounds.

Well, some further experimentation, which has just recently been done, indicates that probably anything above eight pounds of nitrogen per acre is beginning to generate a negative response. The farmers had in part begun to appreciate this by their use of it and the recommendation at this stage is something which is contrary to an essentially sound economic judgment on the part of the farmers.

In addition to looking for these kinds of things, perhaps the sort of work Mr. Miracle was talking about where the anthropologists and economists sit down together would result in recommendations within an anthropological framework and an economic framework which would make a lot more sense than what we have had up to this point.

Mr. GINSBURG: May I interject and say that the last people I would like to see make decisions about fertilizer would be anthropologists or econmists, either singly or in combination. (Laughter.)

Mr. WIT: I had a couple of fragmented thoughts earlier, one with regard to Mr. Whiteford's proper call that we find out what "they" want to do. It struck me as also fairly obvious that we have to keep in mind some of the research which demonstrates that all segments of peasant societies do not necessarily want development. I think, for example, of Mrs. Nair's study, *Blossoms in the Dust*,[4] which is very enlightening in terms of the trials and tribulations of at least Indian planners from one perspective, the peasant perspective.

The other related thought that comes to mind from that same volume is the diversity among the masses. Apart from worrying about what the elites want, the fact remains that some of the masses may want development and some may not want development.

This, then, ties in with the comment that development defined economically is not necessarily the primary objective in many of these societies; or at least the disagreement about definitions of development and "need" is so great that any economically rational analysis is not realistic.

Then in terms of the comment made about the conflict between the groups who are motivated for change and those who are not: this to me, obviously again suggests something concerning the potential strategy of the "committed" government. The potential strategy is clearly to throw the weight of political and administrative power behind groups which it has identified as being committed to development.

The problems we all see immediately, too: many of the groups resisting change, even if they are not closely associated with and propping up the government, are nonetheless powerful enough so that, politically, they must be accommodated. This has a lot to do with why even well-motivated governments do not necessarily play out the strategy successfully.

Conclusion

Mr. NASH: If I can ask your indulgence for two or three minutes, I would like to place in some sort of historical perspective the evolution of economic theory and the evolution of culture change theory to show you why I think they have come together, and why the conversation will be a continuing one and a fruitful one.

Economists started thinking about economic development in its modern sense around the time of the Marshall Plan, and they saw the miracle achieved by pouring in capital to war-devastated Europe and putting it back on its feet. Economists are quick to learn, and they learned from that that the engine of economic development was capital and capital accumulation. It, took about 15 years, and a lot of money down a lot of rat holes, before somebody decided that it is not just capital but the form and the quality of capital. They went on then to develop education theories, technological theories, and so forth.

It took about another five, years before that wore out, and economists finally decided that they must confront the social and cultural systems head-on. The do-it-yourself efforts of Rostow, Hagen, and others are responses to the situation—and Professor Lewis's remarks, too, that the economic problems are trivial, that the confrontation is between decisions in a social and cultural structure. So the economists are now at the point where they have a lot of interesting problems in dealing with social systems and have begun to think about them.

Anthropologists and sociologists, the other part of the team—when it is a team—started out at a high level of index theory. There are 15 or 16 features of a traditional society, 15 or 16 features of a modern society, and they get transformed—stemming from the heritage of Max Weber, Karl Marx, and Talcott Parsons. We made up index typologies.

That did not do too well because it was so far removed from empirical reality that there were no constraints on generalization. We moved from functional particularism to specificity diffuseness, but no one in the world knew when that was taking place. Everything was mixed.

They then moved on to a kind of an acculturation theory. They saw the problem *of* social and cultural change as *a* movement of technology in organizations, and ideas from the developed to the less-developed countries. But this kind of pitchforking—item by item by item—with the new social systems, was not very satisfactory either. We are now, I think, trying to construct what I have given my version of in its rudimentary form; this is a decision theory of social arid cultural change, which gets us down to contact with the economists. They know all about, decisions; now we want to think about, decisions which affect the social and cultural constitution of a society, and not only the allocation of resources,

I think we have an area of real mutual overlap, and we got there because we tried to stay away from each other and found that we could not. Where that leaves the policy man., I do not know,

Mr. HARING: Mow, having gotten the decisions, you will soon find that you need the political scientist,

Mr. NASH: Well, I think *a* political scientist is a sociologist with a strange vocabulary, (Laughter.)

Chairman KING: On that note, gentlemen, we will adjourn.

Notes

1. Ward Hunt Goodenough, *Cooperation in Change; an Anthropological Approach to Community Development* (New York: Russell Sage Foundation, 1963).
2. Lucy Philip Mair, *New Nations* (Chicago: University of Chicago Press, 1963).
3. Daniel Wit, *Labor Law and Practice in Thailand* (BLS Report Mo, 267) (Washington, D.C.: Bureau of Labor Statistics, 1964).
4. Kusum Nair, *Blossoms in the Dust: The Human Factor in Indian Development* (New York: Frederick A. Praeger, Inc., 1962).

Session VI

Perspectives for Cooperative Research

Chairman HARING: One word on why this Conference has been a success, a judgment which I do not have to belabor at all. I have heard it informally, outside the Conference, all through the weekend. It is that, unlike many conferences, this one did not consist of the production of a series of scholarly papers all typed and neat about which the author knew everything and nobody else knew much. This has been, as we have said, a brainstorming session, and this is the secret of the whole thing, and a great credit to the committee that set. It up in this fashion. Everybody has said unanimously, "I've learned an awful lot."

Now, I want to introduce the speakers. We have first Mr. C. Arnold Anderson, who was an educational-specialist with the World Bank and has been, particularly concerned with Kenya. He has taught in Sweden. He is now Director of the Comparative Education Center at the University of Chicago and a member of the Sociology Department,

Mr. T. David Williams was educated in England and. Canada and the United States—at MIT. He has done work in Ghana and at Harvard and is now Professor of Economics and Education at Northwestern,

Mr. Norton S. Ginsburg is a Professor of Geography and Associate Dean of the College at the University of Chicago and did his work here at Chicago. He has also been considerably active in Southeast Asia, Malaysia, and Indonesia, as you know.

Mr. ANDERSON: I shall proceed to talk about education in the form of a series of dicta which would be, so to speak, the topic sentences for paragraphs, if I had written a paper—which I did not. Let me first indicate that I think we might consider schools, or formal education, as having principally five functions. One is, of course, to indoctrinate children and give them loyalties and objects of Identification and self-conceptions. The second is to prepare them to share respectively in the universals, specialities, and alternatives of their culture. Third, schools perpetuate and elaborate intellectual systems and particularly the educational system itself. Schools select and mold elites. Finally, and least important, schools prepare individuals ready to be trained for vocations.

I would like to make next a few comments on how education plays its part in development. I think it is a remarkable and often unnoticed fact that formal education of the kind with which we have been familiar for many generations in the West is remarkably easy to transfer to other societies and to get operating as a going system. Always, of course, there will be some new results and a lack of some old ones, but the broader sorts of influences that one might call education rather than schooling, which are important for development—economic or political—are not so easy to transfer. Therein lie many of the problems we have been, talking about.

Now, there is actually a very uncertain and ambiguous correlation between formal education and economic development. Most of the literature setting forth correlation coefficients and so on is a tissue of exaggerations and half-truths. One difficulty is that we fail to distinguish the long- from the short-run effects, for they are quite different.

Clearly, you cannot have technological development without skills in the population to operate, that technology, and this requires training. It does not follow, however, that a proliferation and extension of schooling of any kind will produce development. There is also the very uncertain problem of lead and lag between economic development and formal education. Such evidence as we now have indicates that, in the short run, it is economic development which leads and formal education which lags. This is the real proof contained in the new Harbison-Myers book,[1] contrary to the authors' own assertions.

I think it is also very important to keep in mind, though we know very little about this in detail, that the usefulness of school to a society, and the usefulness of the graduates of schools, depend upon how these individuals are taken hold of by other agencies or institutions in the society and how these other agencies motivate the products of schools to use what they presumably learned in the schools.

Looking at our own history, I think that we frequently do not realize that in our past the ways of life of the populace were the stuff of economic activity and of economic change. Changes in those activities that we now call economic development did not require the populace to rapidly acquire a whole new civilization, which is more or less the burden that is being put on the peoples of many countries around the world today.

It is risky to extrapolate Western experience for, among other reasons, the following: today education is more demanded because it has become a political object, regarded as good in itself. Second, the technology being developed today—being borrowed around the world—is much more complex than that of the past. Third, there is the fact that countries today want rapid economic development, a conception that was relatively-foreign to our ancestors. Fourth, that these countries, in many instances, must develop both their polity and their economy simultaneously, a task that very few Western societies faced.

I think then, that we have to conclude that the payoff in economic terms from a given amount of formal education will be less in today's developing countries than it was in our countries. Nevertheless, and this is not really *a* paradox, the incremental effect—or the distinctive effect—of education could be greater in the new countries than it was in our society.

I am always impressed, as I go back and reread it, with Walinsky's remarks. He points out repeatedly essentially the following: there was no important economic project in Burma which was held up, frustrated, or seriously compromised because of the lack of trained manpower.[2] I think this is a statement that we are going to find being made more and more about developing countries—which essentially is to elaborate a point that Manning Nash made at the end of his paper.

Now, some comment on the problem of balancing economic and other criteria of education. Obviously, nobody in his right mind would say that the main purpose or sole purpose of education is to produce economic development. We happen to be living in a period when people are obsessed with the manpower view of education. The payoff in conferences and discussions and. consultantships and so on for one specializing in education is to relate it to economic development, but this is clearly a partial and provincial view.

One of the things I think we too often fail to ask ourselves in looking at the manpower studies is: what are the so-called needs for manpower that these studies set forth? You can read planning documents by the score, with elaborate tables often down to the individual unit, of the number of different kinds of trained manpower needed. It is almost impossible, however, to find out the criteria of need that are used.

Simultaneously, you have the fact that these countries face staggering unemployment—as Arthur Lewis was pointing out—and yet, curiously, both things are set forth by international agencies this way: "This country has great unemployment of educated people; this country needs an. enormous increase in the number of educated people." That is ridiculous.

Now, there is always, in trying to assess the role of education in development, the investment, problem, and investment choices are marginal. It makes no sense to say that this country would be much better off if it would spend X billion dollars, or X million pounds, or francs, or whatever on schools. It has to make choices at the margins between schools and other agencies, and the problem of conserving resources that are truly scarce is a. formidable one.

Most of the people who are writing the pronouncements on manpower and education fail to face the problem, of what might be accomplished in development by shifting money away from education. Parenthetically, I would be very happy if every developing country would take 10 per cent, annually from now on of its education budget, and use it as s. subsidy for the advertising industry, as a prod to development. That, is a dictum.

I think we need to relate educational programming in an ecological framework to the ecological processes of development (political, economic, and social) which are going on. One of the most impressive things one finds in all of these countries is that there are large local differences in the readiness for education, the willingness to use it: if it is made available, the willingness to make a substantial financial contribution to it. The indexes of readiness *ail* vary enormously among the ecological areas or zones of the country, and there is a rather close correlation with the evidences of economic development when those are also put in ecological terms.

One could comment extensively on the formidable technical problem in international trade, of the international trade and skills. There has been almost nothing written on this and it is, I think, an important problem.

Now, with respect to some criteria for policy, one important dilemma we face is whether we are going to manage people's choices of jobs and schools in accordance with some manpower expert's judgment of what is good for people, or whether we are going to develop mechanisms so that the "spontaneous choices" that people make in education and vocations will be allowed to express themselves in the determination of educational policy.

I would say in very brief compass that much of the literature on educational planning which, has been written Is nonsense. The most formidable difficulty with the literature as it exists now is that nearly every statement is based upon the assumption that there are fixed coefficients of a demand for certain kinds of skills for certain kinds of activities in the economy. This, I think, cannot be defended; even as a non-economist, I think that such assumptions of fixed coefficients are fallacious,

There is also an over-simple idea of the correlation between the jobs that people perform and their schooling. I recommend that you look at the U.S. census, or the census of Israel, or the census of India, or any other country that has tabulated education against occupation. In no country is the correlation much more than about 0.5, and that's hardly gambler's odds,

There is always, *in* making plans, the formidable problem of balancing three criteria: efficiency, equity, and free choice. There are always compromises needed. On so-called democratic grounds, many countries will argue for equity in providing educational opportunity; but no developing country can afford to operate on the basis of equity because this would be a formula for dispersing its resources into a whole series of bottomless pits.

They must operate to a greater extent on the basis of efficient, allocation of resources for schooling in relation to the use that will be made of it. This means that they must also take account of the choices that individuals would like to make, but to see that those choices are linked in with other development processes.

I would also point out that most of the literature that, argues that education is the instrument of social mobility is fallacious, both with regard, to developing countries and to our own society. The correlation between education and vertical social mobility is very modest.

If you have been enamored of the Soviet claims for educational planning, I suggest you read more carefully the literature which is becoming available, which is making it very clear that the Russians have, for the most part, not in fact conducted educational planning, and they are now admitting it.

Now, some comments on the problem of balance and complementarities in the educational tasks between schools and other agencies. Obviously, human resource development is not synonymous with education, and obviously education is not synonymous with schools, but, to a very large extent, societies in policy-making do think mainly of schools.

Here is a country and it has these "needs" for economic development. So you then ask: how could you tell whether the school system of this country is or is not adapted to the needs or the characteristics of the country? The literature is filled with statements that the school system must be adapted to the needs of a changing and. developing society. How would you know if it were adapted? Is American education adapted to the needs of American society?

This is, I think, an essentially unanswerable question because it is stated in far too broad terms. One is led immediately into raising questions about the balance between general education and technical education, on which there is not time to comment. I do think there is beginning to emerge a consensus that the principal task of schools, through secondary education, is to prepare people to be ready for vocational education, and that, in most countries—until they are well developed—the setting up of specific technical schools is a misplaced use of resources.

One can state that alternatively: in general, technical training should be given, as nearly as possible, at the point of use. There is, of course, also in the literature—you read it yourselves—a great deal of talk about the importance of localizing curricula; that the countries will make more use of their education, and that their citizens will be better educated, if they study a localized curriculum instead of one that was originally brought to them by the British, or the French, or the Americans.

I suggest that you look at the school books your own children have used, and ask how much of what they are being taught is localized to the United States—or ever was. The great McGuffey's readers, which are supposed to have been the foundation for American society in recent generations, in very large part were made up of material which is not American; it is British, it is medieval, it is Greek, it is Roman, it is fairy tales.

The concept of a localized curriculum, except in certain obvious areas such as geography, is *a* concept with little meaning. Most of the discussion which goes on to the effect that, if we would just teach the little children in the right way, they would all like to be good little farmers, is nonsense. We never learned how to do it, so why should we expect Ghana to learn how to do it?

The more fundamental point is that curricula make very little contribution to motivation, except under unusual circumstances. Incidentally, the work that is coming out now on political socialization of the Russian youth indicates very clearly that the system did not work.

There is also a real dilemma—and this touches on many points we have, talked about—as to whether schools shall be used, to produce national consensus, or shall schools be permitted or encouraged to relate people to a somewhat smaller and warmer society of their *own* province, or tribe, or locality?

I think the idea that somehow you pick little Kikuyu children up in *a* bush, and you make Kenya citizens out of them in six or seven years—and possibly even citizens of the United Nations—may be asking the schools to do too much.

The general questions we have to ask on most specifications for using schools for development is the following: are not people overloading the schools? We have difficulty here in this respect, you know.

In Chicago there is *a* very large proportion of the schools that operate only with a policeman inside the building. Now, why can't we socialize our children? We have all the resources available, but apparently we cannot do it. How, then, should, one expect these countries to use schools (which are very formal, impersonal, and abstract mechanisms) to create a whole new human nature?

Another task we need to face is the building of adaptability into the educational system. I would argue that the particular content of schools or the particular structure of a country, is much less important than whether or not there is flexibility so that different parts of the society can do different things, or different schools can do different things, and so that individuals can manipulate the educational opportunities open to them.

I think, next, that we have to take a new look at the question of quality. It is true that many countries will insist upon quality because they think this is the only way they can get respectability in the eyes of the world. They want to have an education as good as their colonial masters had—and all of this sort of thing. If one separates out the political issue, the concept of quality is very dangerous for two reasons.

To give you an ad hoc illustration, the United States built the world's technologically most: advanced and economically most dynamic society with what has generally been regarded as the world's worst educational system among the developed countries: a system which had no standards and which, as yet, has no standards, which has never succeeded in producing a university degree that has any recognizable definition. Yet we manage to operate an amazing society.

The problem of quality is a red herring. I think one can illustrate this by indicating some of the reasons why elaborate examination systems, which are so much favored in many countries, prove to be dysfunctional. First of all, I doubt that the skills tested by academic examinations are very good predictors of the kinds of skills which will make men productive in any activity. Second, examinations tend to lead to the stereotyping of schools. Teachers teach what children are going to be examined on, and children will study only what they know they are going to be examined on.

Third, the use of examinations and the related worry about quality leads to the undue prolongation of schooling, to putting too much schooling into children for the current needs of the society.

Fourth, there is the concern for academic orderliness. I suppose there is a certain kind of selectivity of people who become academics. Academic orderliness tends to be antipathetic to flexibility. The net result of concern for standards, as one finds it, for instance, in Ghana or some other parts of the world, is to diminish the elasticity of the supply of skills, Yet what a developing country needs is a very elastic supply curve for all kinds of skills.

Fifth, a school system that is built around a rigid examination system produces too narrow an elite for the demands of a changing society.

There are three principal ways, it seems to me, in which schools serve to recruit elites. You have the kind of system we had in the United States, and I suppose in essence still have: that the schools give part of the training to part of the people in an extremely diversified set of elites. Second, you have a system like nineteenth-century England, where the schools mainly polish the people who are predestined in any event to become the leaders of the society. Finally, you have what now one finds in many places in Africa and elsewhere: that the schools beyond the elementary years are available to very few people, and you cannot get into the elite unless you go through those particular schools.

You get very different results, depending upon which of these particular recruitment patterns you have and I suspect you get very different impacts upon the development processes.

I think also, we gain—and this was implicit in much of the discussion in these days of the conference—by viewing elites as devices for linking the energies of the populace to the actions which produce development. Then the questions we have to ask are: which kinds of elites can do this for which kinds of activities, for which sub-populations, and so on. This, of course, touches on points Manning Nash raised.

How does the system of education affect the relations of elites to each other? I was very much, impressed in Kenya with the disgruntlement of the British technically trained people with, the monopoly on good jobs held by the British arts-degree graduates, This is one example and you can find, many others. Imagine what American society and education would be like if Harvard and Princeton and Yale had ever had the degree of dominance in determining educational policy that Oxford and Cambridge had in England. Our society would be at least different, and I suspect it would be one that we would less like to live in. The question of how schools affect the relations among different parts of the elite, or different sub-elites, is, therefore, important.

Finally, I am impressed with the fact that a very large part of the intellectuals in many new countries are being sterilized for policy-making, because the party or the civil service absorbs them; and the party and the civil service are one. There are few independent sources of decision-making or of opinion-making. In a sense, therefore, you have to discount a large part of the intellectual roster of many countries. It has been sterilized for decision-making. This is an aspect of the one-party system in some new countries that I think one does not always give attention to.

Then, there is the question: do elites have a chance to function so as to express the interests—in the good old hardboiled sense of the word "interests"—the interests that are the texture of development? Development is not an abstract set of equations. Development is activities, and. these activities are related to, expressed as, or exemplified in the hard economic interests that are the stuff of development, and the stuff of politics. The question, then, is: in what ways can the elites serve to express these interests, to articulate them, to phrase them in ways that contribute to or hold back development?

For example, a centralized press means that there can be no local elites who can use the printed word as a device for trying to tell the public, in all sorts of ways, what is expected of it if it is to contribute to, or participate in, development. One can illustrate this in many other ways. Let me describe the American town of the nineteenth century and early twentieth century—in a set of circumstances which was almost optimal for development. The spread of schooling was occurring in communities possessing an elaborate equipment of other cultural agencies—agencies that were needed as auxiliaries to schools.

For centuries Western communities generally possessed a representative of the learned clergy, who more or less effectively conveyed the powerful influences of Christianity upon aspirations and conduct. Often there were representatives of the legal and medical professions and growing numbers of teachers. There were literate businessmen and representatives of the crafts. At the end of the fifteenth century, even, practically all businessmen in London were literate. The local press was well established by the nineteenth century. There were substantial proportions of literate mothers. And always there was a thickening network of communications with the world of technology, business, and knowledge. In the United States, the presses began turning out books on the frontier as soon as settlement took place. There were many stimuli to rationality, to social consensus and to economic change. Extra-school training—apprenticeship, on-the-job experiences, and work in family enterprises—was a major part of the educational process. A large proportion of the literates acquired even that skill outside of the schools.

Now, this is the kind of community setting for development which one can find in very few parts of the world today. How many of those things can you leave out, and still get development with any kind of conceivable elaboration of mere formal education.

Mr. WILLIAMS: The relationship between what. I have to say and what Professor Anderson has said may remind some of you of the dictum of Sidney Smith, that a man should never read a book before reviewing it because it always prejudices you so.

I had, in. fact, jotted down a few things that. I wanted to say before I saw what Professor Anderson was going to say, although there is perhaps some relationship between them, I want to deal with a few topics in each case, to suggest the development of sub-categories which might enable us to distinguish between different types of problems. The topics start off with: the effective changes in the level and amount of education, the government as entrepreneur, forms of expression of work-protest—more or less as it relates to trade unions—and, possibly, some comments on the use of the symbolic investment.

First let me say a few words about the payoff to educational expansion. Let us look first at: the outputs of education.

There is the question of whether or not an undeveloped country should place its priority on high-level manpower or on a more widespread primary system. The distinction, of course, cannot be a complete one since an adequate selection of high-level manpower requires a fairly broad base of primary and secondary education, while widespread primary and secondary education, while widespread primary education requires an expansion of high-level education in teacher training and school administrators.

Newly independent countries with the most primitive levels of education are critically short of the number of administrators, bureaucrats, diplomats, schoolteachers, and so on, required for the most elementary forms of the new nation's business. Here it is evident that the amount of indigenous high-level manpower should be increased as quickly as possible, and should be given first priority within the educational system.

Some of the more advanced but still underdeveloped areas—Ghana, for example—can meet their own basic needs, and even lend experts to international agencies in other African countries. Their demand for high-level manpower is due to: one, a substantial expansion of government functions; two, the planned rapid expansion of the so-called modern sector of the economy; and three, a program of universal primary education.

In saying that these are distinct stages of development, I have used the question-begging phrase that "they can meet the basic functional requirements of independent states." I wonder whether, in this connection, political scientists can tell us anything about the minimal administrative requirements of effective independent states, and the approximate levels of competence required for various tasks. Once one is over that hump—wherever it comes—and in terms of meeting these minimal requirements, one should give more serious consideration to starting and improving primary education. Here, it seems to me, one might be able to distinguish between states, or regions of states, where there is already some demonstrated short-run growth potential, and those where it is a much more long-run speculative thing.

Let me give an example. In Ghana, there has, in the last 50 years, been a striking development of effective, small-scale entrepreneurship, and a desire for self-improvement which is manifested in the great degree of sacrifice the people are willing to undertake in order to gain an education. My impression is that in Guatemala the rural areas appear to be characterized by apathy and stagnation. I do not mean that there is no change, but not nearly the same kind of change.

It is at least possible that the payoff to elementary education will be much higher in the near future in the first than in the second case; that is, the payoff will be greatest where there has already been some sort of manifest economic change.

Given the will to entrepreneurship, basic literacy should, one sup-poses, greatly increase the effectiveness of the entrepreneurs; adding secondary to primary education may add very little to effective func-tional, skills. If this is so—and it raises some other problems I will, deal with in a moment—the economists and the anthropologists could do a lot to locate growth cones in the economy—those areas in which a significantly large group *of* people are sufficiently concerned about improving their welfare to manipulate their economic environment in as favorable a way as possible.

In Ghana the cocoa farmers migrated to better lands. They formed companies to purchase land because they got a better return this way than if they purchased individually. They commissioned the building of roads and buildings, and so on.

Now, most of these things are missed in aggregative analysis, the kind of stuff that economists usually do; and indeed, much of our knowledge about the remarkable achievements of the cocoa farmers In Ghana is due to many years of careful and imaginative work by one person. Miss Polly Hill. She discovered, for example, this business of building roads and bridges, much of which had simply gone unnoticed at the time. She found roads and bridges which were not even on the maps, and yet they were being used effectively for the extension of the local market.

It is, however, possible that if the cocoa farmers had received an educa-tion they would not have been better entrepreneurs, but not entrepreneurs at all. They might have been junior clerks or swelled the ranks of the urban unemployed, hanging around the cities hoping to get jobs.

This raises the question of the effects of education on aspiration—and why. Earlier, Professor Kreinin raised the point that education appears to induce an anti-manualist mentality.

Professor Anderson, as I recall, suggested that, anti-manual ism was typically associated with low wages for manual work, rather than with any particular lack of education. The evidence from West Africa shows clearly enough that there are, and have been, enormous disparities in the returns for different occupations, or perhaps more accurately, to occupations in different sections of the economy. There appear to be large numbers of middle-school leavers who want to be artisans; and in this connection a very interesting study was done by Phillip Foster of Chicago.

Mr. ANDERSON: One should also mention a whole series of papers that are about to appear from Nigeria by Archibald Callaway. You ought to watch for his name in the literature, because he has some fascinating stuff.

Mr. WILLIAMS: Yes, I have seen some of his work.

I was referring to these middle-school leavers who want to be artisans, but want to be artisans with the government, where they will get an apprenticeship—where they undergo an apprenticeship and then get a good job. Once in a good job a man is more or less set for life in these societies. Outside the good-job group, the passing years simply make it less likely that he will ever get the security he wants. What needs to be studied here, I think, is the pattern of returns to particular job complexes, and to other aspects of the growing power of the urban areas.

I suspect, but cannot at this stage prove, that people in Ghana respond very sensibly—by which I mean in the way we would respond—to the incentive pattern inherent in the present labor market structure in the urban-rural disparity.

Let me perhaps give you some specific examples. If a person goes to the town and wants to become a mechanic there, he gets a job if he is fortunate. Say he gets a job with Texaco. He works for several years at Texaco and he might get a formal Apprenticeship certificate as a result, or even if he does not get a formal Apprenticeship certificate, he will at least have the say-so of the manager at Texaco: "This man has performed faithful service for four years." The chances are that he will never again have any difficulty getting a good secure job.

If, however, there happened to be, as there almost always are, many more applicants for the job at Texaco than there were openings, he has two alternatives. He can either go and get a job in a small shop somewhere, a small garage or something like that, or he can hang around hoping eventually that his turn will come, and he will get the job at Texaco.

If he goes into the small shop, he is going to earn some money, but not very much, and he is going perhaps to build up some skills; but he is not going to acquire anything formal which is going to be particularly useful to him later on. Not only that, but, because of the way in which people find jobs—which is through the Labor Exchange—if he actually has a job in a small shop, he cannot even show up at the Labor Exchange.

Now, it may strike people who have not been in these areas that what he should do is to put his name down on a list at the Labor Exchange and then, when a job comes up, they will notify him of the job—at Texaco, say.

But, quite apart from the question of minor corruption and. this sort of thing, the fact is that people simply do have not addresses to which you can send a letter. I had the experience of trying to find somebody in the center of Accra. I knew the man's address and I went to the police station and asked them if they could tell me where the house was; I had a rough idea of where it was, but, even so, they could not help me. The only way I found it was by walking up and down the street until eventually I found somebody who knew the man; he took me to the house.

Therefore, if you want a job *at* Texaco or some place like this, you simply have to go to the Labor Exchange every day, otherwise you lose your chance. By taking a job in a small shop you are, of course, losing out on this option.

There is also the fact, which I will not draw too much on, of the enormous number of advantages to be derived from living in the city—and I am not thinking—just now about high-jinks in the city rather than the rural areas. Take a young chap who wants to make some sort of a mark. Let us say, as is possible in some of these areas—certainly in Ghana—he has some sort of athletic aspirations and he thinks he can make some sort of a name for himself as a member of a football team, or as a boxer or something of this sort—and there are lots of guys who want to do this and quite properly so, If he stays in his rural area, there is simply no chance whatsoever of his ever making his mark, He must go to the city to do it.

I think that one thing we ought to try to concentrate on, therefore—if we are interested in development—is to see how it. may be possible to restructure this pattern of incentives so that at least there is not a disincentive to people being employed in the cities.

It does, however, raise some difficult problems. Insistence on formal qualifications, which is part of the problem, at the moment for all jobs in the modern sector, does put some check on nepotism and patronage. A man may still hire his relatives, but at least his relatives must have some qualifications, unless, of course, the qualifications themselves can be bought—but that is another matter.

Now, if we are going to try to induce people, let us say, to work in a small shop rather than hang around the Labor Exchange waiting for an opening at Texaco, we have to find some way by which a person who has had experience in a small shop can move up to some higher level—into the good-job complex.

Questions which I think, need to be answered here are whether or not psychologists and sociologists, and possibly anthropologists, can develop adequate tests which will distinguish, in terms of competence and reliability, between different groups of experienced, though not qualified, applicants (that is, not qualified in the formal sense).

Another question: can the administrative experts and sociologists tell us anything about the effects on the present rigidly hierarchical administrative structure if people could, in fact, be promoted from outside the structure?

There are several other things I would like to say about education and its effects, but I want to move on and make a few other comments.

One person discussed the possibility that government should have a significant role as investor, and as economic innovator, because there are no entrepreneurs in a society. This is a familiar argument. It is contained, for example, in Ben Higgins' book on economic development.[3]

Now, do we mean, when we say that there are no entrepreneurs: A, that there are no people in the society with the complex motives and capabilities required for successful business activity? Or do we mean: B, that there are such people, but that the social-economic system denies them access to positions of power?

If we mean the former, there that, are just no people of this kind in the society, then government investment, will not help. It will merely mean that public money will he spent on very risky projects.

If we mean the second, that there are people but that in the existing system they are denied access to positions of power, then we have to decide: A, how we can locate the people with the appropriate talent; B, how we can give these people, rather than political hacks, access to business power; and C, how, after having given them this access, we can insulate them from constant political pressure.

Can the political scientists suggest institutional requirements or possibilities for the establishment of more or less autonomous investment agencies of public enterprises in the developing economy?

Russia, I think, is not a good example. In Russia, when the Bolsheviks came to power, there were already big enterprises; there already was an established scientific and engineering elite. There was a highly disciplined party with a respect for managerial competence, and even with all this, Stalin came close to wrecking it.

A related problem, related to this question of government investment and the government role in underdeveloped areas, concerns the requirements for effective large-scale organization. It is another thing frequently said—by Higgins among others—that, for many reasons apart from the entrepreneurial one, the government can and should play a much larger role in these areas than it should in the more developed areas.

How is one, however, in a large enterprise to develop the working rules and standardized objectives which will enable effective delegation of authority? You not only have lack of experience on the part of people in running large organizations, but you also have virtually no experience of what the standard patterns of behavior in a modern society are going to be like in these societies.

Let us take one question, industrial relations. If we are trying to work out some pattern—for example, the way in which industrial relations should operate in a large American firm—and we are doing this in order to delegate authority to a personnel manager to undertake certain decisions, we have the advantage of experience over a long period of time with the way workers operate in the American social environment in an industrial situation. There is an enormous number of people—scholars, businessmen, trade unionists, journalists, and so on—who have been writing about and examining these problems for a long period of time. There is, I think, a reasonably good and reliable set of expectations about the way in which people will behave (in our society).

If, however, you are trying to work out what should be the policy of a personnel manager in a large firm, in a new industrial complex in West Africa, you simply do not know what the appropriate patterns of incentives are, or how people are going to respond to certain situations.

It seems to me, therefore, that, while it would, in fact, be *a* relatively simple matter to nationalize General Motors, or I.C.I [Imperial Chemical Industries, Ltd.] in Britain; the effects of such nationalization would be just marginal. Output might go up 5 per cent or down 5 per cent—and I am not saying that this is not important—but it would be essentially a rather trivial kind of thing in terms of any overall output levels. You would simply tell people to behave in very much the same way they are behaving now.

It seems to me that it is immeasurably more difficult to develop the same kind of patterns in an underdeveloped area.

The third point I want to deal with relates to trade unions. Here I think we have to ask ourselves: how is worker protest expressed when there are no independent forms of worker organizations? The problem I am concerned with here is whether trade unions stimulate worker dissatisfaction or whether they channel it in a particular direction.

Sometimes, clearly, they stimulate it; but we must ask what happens generally over the long haul if you do not have an effective trade union organization. I have in mind here, for example, the Italian experience from 1900 to 1914. There was no encouragement for stable national unions. There were, nevertheless, local unions which had developed one way or the other. It seems quite possible that stable and effective national trade unions may have favored a much more orderly set of industrial relations than actually occurred. What one had was wave after wave of general strikes, in various cities and regions, which reflected a blend of frustration and, I suggest, *dis*organization—rather than organization.

Here I am curious as to whether sociologists and political scientists can tell us anything about the ignition points of dissatisfaction. When does dissatisfaction reach a point where, in the absence of some way to canalize it, it will express itself in a kind of Luddite machine-smashing and sporadic outbursts of violence?

I think we want to ask, too: to what extent is a politically controlled trade union able to direct the energies of workers toward goals which are consistent with the government's plans? Here we need to know a lot more about grass-level operations, although this may, for *a* variety of reasons be impossible to learn. The Ghana trade unions, for example, may be much more effective, from the workers' point of view, at local-level bargaining than are the. independent, but small, poor, fragmented Nigerian trade unions.

I think we need to explore here the question of whether or not workers will, or under what circumstances they will, voluntarily accept lower wages—lower in the sense that they are lower than they could get by acting in a certain way—if these lower wages are compensated for in other ways, for example, in job tenure, severance pay, adequate grievance procedures, and so on.

To what extent can politically oriented trade unions encourage productivity improvements? To what extent can they, within the framework of the national plan, negotiate trade-outs between higher wages, in which the government is giving up something on the one hand, and greater effort or improved efficiency on the other hand? This involves the institutional structure, the political balance of power, and the allocation of resources, and I think it is something about which political scientists, economists, and sociologists, all might have something useful to say.

I now come to my fourth point, and I will deal very briefly with this. In dealing with the question of che building of monuments, I think we could distinguish between different types of monuments. I will just briefly run through some distinctions.

The first I will call monuments for the masses. I have in mind the kind of thing that is represented by the Freedom Arch in Accra—the Freedom Arch is in a great big square where people can watch national demonstrations and this sort of thing.

I think this is something which does have, very probably, a payoff. That is, the people can come there, they can see it, and it means something to them; it stimulates them, it gives them a feeling, you know, that they are not working for nothing, and when the government calls upon them to make a sacrifice they can see that, and they say, "Well, that is one of the things we are making sacrifices for." It means something to them; whereas, if you said to them—let's say that the cost of the Freedom Arch, if you spent it some other way, might have made a difference in the rise of national income of one-fourth of 1 per cent a year—now, you can go and say to the workers, "Look, chaps, if you will really dig in we can raise your national income by one-fourth of 1 per cent per year more than we are raising it now." This does not mean anything to anybody, but the Freedom Arch does mean something. I think.

On the other hand, there is another type of this sort of expenditure—I am talking about Ghana, now-such as the Ghana airways. It seems to me that the main thrust of this type is to influence the leaders of other countries in Africa. It is part of the Ghanian drive for a leadership position in the Pan-African movement. I doubt that there is any economic payoff at all, and I do not think that the regime expects to have a payoff. It is something that is costing quite a lot, but it is directed toward a political objective quite apart from economic growth.

Related to this are certain types of expenditures which attempt to tighten the ties with certain other countries. For example, when I was in Ghana there were some beginnings of an attempt to develop a direct telecommunication system between Accra and Conakry in Guinea and Bamako. At one level it seemed rather crazy. I lived nine miles outside of Accra, and every time the rains came the telephone system broke down between where I lived and Accra. You might think they should, perhaps, be spending more time getting the telephones working over this nine-mile distance instead of worrying about whether they are going to establish a system over the 2,000 miles between there and Bamako,

Another type of monument-building is designed to improve the image for foreign investors. This might, have a payoff. I mean, sometimes building roads, maybe even building certain kinds of fancier towers, gives the notion that this is a thriving kind of country, where people would like to invest. This might have an. economic payoff.

Finally—although there was not too much of this in Ghana, you find it, I am told, in many other countries—is the type where there is a significant diversion of expenditures toward large buildings whose prime, if not sole, function is to provide comfort for the rulers. This clearly has no economic payoff.

Mr. GINSBURG: I am grateful to both Mr. Anderson and Mr. Williams for giving me an opportunity to say something I wanted to say anyway.

Mr. Anderson spoke of ecological zones as something we ought to be concerned with, and Mr. Williams spoke of high growth potentials. I am not sure what either one of these things are, but they suggest a direction in which I would like to see our discussion move.

Nobody has mentioned geography heretofore but me, and I will mention it again. Geographers are concerned with the world ecosystem and how it operates; and within that ecosystem are a number of freely and arbitrarily given units which themselves form lesser ecosystems. We call these units "states."

We accept them as given—not naively, but for convenience—with the understanding that if we knew enough about how they operate, we might be able to determine the extent to which their "giveness" is appropriate or inappropriate—as the case may be. Then, if we become concerned with policy-making, we can make recommendations with respect to the location of boundaries and the exclusion or inclusion of areas.

The ecosystem notion has at least two major dimensions—it is a duodimensional concept—and both of these are relevant to what we are interested in here.

The more traditional dimension is one that is more strictly ecological in the common-sense notion of the term. It concerns natural resources as they relate to a particular society; as they are perceived by people in that society, because people with different cultures view their resource endowments in quite different ways; and as they are defined, utilized, managed, and even created within particular cultures. The relationships between natural conditions and the ways in which men make use of them, and transform them if need be, or depart from them, are of major interest. We are also concerned—and this relates to some of our previous discussions—with the possibilities for change in resource utilization patterns, both spatial and otherwise.

Parenthetically, perhaps you do not realize how little we know about some of the things one ordinarily accepts as well understood, with regard to this particular subject. For example, we know virtually nothing about the soils of the tropics, and most of the underdeveloped world, however, defined, is tropical. We know almost nothing—and this was referred to earlier this morning—about the relationship of fertilizers to tropical soils. Our agronomic and engineering experts are not expert in these particular directions. Of all the major crops in the world—and this is not irrelevant, particularly to the Asian situation—we know least about paddy, Relatively little is known about rice as compared with wheat, corn, and almost any other major grain. In fact, the talk about transferring Japanese paddy cultivation to India is particularly naive and does not take into account the fact that the varieties of paddy which were bred by the Japanese, and which played an important role in Japanese agricultural expansion, were all short-growing varieties adapted to the short-season growing conditions in Northern Honshu and Hokkaido. This experience is of little value in South and Southeast Asia. But I digress.

The second dimension of the ecosystem notion is spatial. At the outset of my course on China, I describe China as a gigantic spatial system and the function of the course is to analyze it. Analyze it into what? Analyze it into sub-systems; that is, spatial sub-systems, which may be described as regions, I do not know whether or not Mr. Anderson would call these regions "ecological zones," but then I do not pretend to know what an "ecological zone" is.

Now, I realize that one can carry too far this notion of "systems analysis" which, along with the concept of "culture," has been one of the major frauds perpetrated on American social science; but it is a useful idea, nevertheless, just as culture is useful in proper context.

When we are talking about a spatial system, we are talking about an areal entity that has certain characteristics. It has size and shape and internal and external accessibility. It is characterized by the distribution of resources of all kinds; and by these I mean, not only those of natural origin, but those of cultural origin. It has specific distributions of population, and it has, above all, a transportation network, or better, a system of circulation, reference to which is found deeply embedded in the geographical literature. So, too, are found references to problems of centripetal and centrifugal forces in polities and economies, to the problem of fragmentation and the problem of developing measures of integration. Thus, geographers are accustomed to ask: how well integrated Is a given state? How well integrated is Thailand as compared with Indonesia? What does this comparison tell us, if anything, about the problems and potentials of these two *spatial* systems for economic development? Linked with these questions is the general proposition which I think most of us will accept: that all planning decisions require locational decisions. Thus, we return to the points made by Mr. Anderson and Mr. Williams in different context and terminology: that we ought to be able to identify those areas within a given spatial system that have the most promise for development.

Here there are numerous opportunities for interdisciplinary cooperation, particularly, it seems to me, with economists; but not only with them, since the opportunities spread all the way along the social science spectrum. For example, the nature of the political administrative hierarchy as distributed in space is something that should be of great Interest to the political scientist; but, alas, the literature does not bear this out.

One may also question the extent to which it is valuable and desirable in the education of the Inhabitants of the so-called underdeveloped areas to bring the people to an awareness of the world about them. Few of them are possessed of the kind of world view that we assume they ought to have if they are to direct their energies toward some kind of social and economic change.

We have experimented in the teaching of geography at lower levels with using the immediate environmental situation of a student to introduce him to some of these ideas; and we introduce him to the notion of scale as well. For example, let's take the general proposition that every town or settlement has a hinterland. This is good sound common sense to us, but it does not do any good at ail to present the student In, say, Kuala Lumpur with the example of London to begin with. It is even less effective to use London in the case of students in a *kampong* somewhere in northeastern Malaya.

It is much better to start them out with the *kampong* itself and enlarge the scale of view to the nearest town, go from the nearest town to whatever is the largest city in Malaya, thence to the largest city in Southeast Asia, and ultimately to London, thereby creating a kind of world view based on size-functional hierarchies.

Similarly, we can reverse scales and proceed from larger to smaller units. I have been a consultant to the Calcutta Metropolitan Planning Commission for several years. One of the major problems there has been to identify, within the Calcutta Metropolitan Area, those areas which will lend themselves to certain kinds of remedial action—if you like, "planning areas" within the metropolis. Though practical, this is a difficult problem which has major theoretical concomitants.

General Discussion

Mr. WHITEFORD: I would like to ask Professor Anderson what he thinks the function of expatriate industry is in a training sense? How much of a contribution can expatriate industries in these various developing countries make to the whole educational process?

Mr. ANDERSON: Let me start out by pointing out first something which is more familiar to *you* than it is to me, and that is that in a large part of the world, sometimes called "colonial world," the principal source of training for non-agricultural skills has been the public service: posts, telegraphs, roads, public works, agriculture, railroads, and so on. Then, as other industries have come in, different countries have followed different policies.

Some firms, for whatever reasons, have developed very good training programs and, perhaps because they were early in the field, were able to cash in on them. As the network of industries becomes more complicated, clearly there have to be devices developed so that a firm which invests heavily in training does not lose its employees quickly to other firms.

This is leading to experiments in different countries. I think Brazil has been an innovator in ways of pooling the costs of these, programs, through tax levies and rebates, so that firms will participate in providing effective training but will not suffer if there is mobility of employees.

It seems to me that there is no reason why a very-large part of the training for the skills below the university level cannot be provided by firms. I think there are enough experiments around the world that can be generalized. Now, this does involve, as a prerequisite, that you have a fiscal office or tax system, or whatever, in the country which can perform the necessary coordination work so that the incentives for the firms are real ones, and not just outright impositions; but it seems to me that a very large part of the training can be so done and is being done in many countries.

Mr. MORGAN: I would like to ask Professor Anderson to give his evidence that the political indoctrination of Russian youngsters has not been successful.

Mr. ANDERSON: There I fall back on my colleagues who have been doing research extensively on and in Russia. There is a paper by

Azrael of the Chicago staff in the forthcoming volume on education and political development shortly to be published by Princeton University Press (edited by James Coleman),[4] He has a very long and detailed analysis of materials which he collected in Russia, in which I think he has demonstrated what we suspect from other kinds of evidence: that the specific indoctrination above and beyond the kind of thing that comes from A, living in a closed society, and B, absorbing the general climate of opinion around you—the more specific, tangible, and copper-riveted indoctrination seems not to have been successful in the Soviet Union. The evidence for this is mounting.

Mr. MORGAN: You are blocking out the simple fact of ignorance. In other words, if I live in a world in which I hear nothing within a certain range—

Mr. ANDERSON: Yes, I am blocking that out. I used the word "indoctrination," not "control." Obviously, you can control access to information and this will affect people's attitudes, but I mean specific indoctrination seems not to have had much take.

Mr. MORGAN: You are not throwing the baby out with the bath? In other words, keep me ignorant of three-quarters of the facts, and of course, I won't—

Mr. ANDERSON: Well, if you keep people ignorant, then you have a random factor, so to speak, and it is perfectly clear that there have been random elements. You also have, insofar as the communications blockade breaks down, as it began to do, first, in the war as the armies met each other, and second in the postwar period—then you began to get spreading spirals of change going on. There clearly seems to have been more change in the areas accessible to contact.

Now, there are other factors. For instance, in the Georgian universities the students seem to be more recalcitrant—but they always have been. Leningrad students seem to be more recalcitrant, but Leningrad people in general pride themselves on being international. Some of this attitude or self-conception seems to have persisted right through the whole period since the revolution. So you get all sorts of crosscurrents plus the simple fact that, as pressures began to let up a little since the death of Stalin, you had such things as the museums beginning to let people see the fabulous collections of nineteenth-century French paintings. When these began to become available, this was one of the things that undermined the Soviet conception of what good painting was. Once you lift the lid there are all sorts of spontaneous processes; but sheer indoctrination seems to have been of limited effect.

Chairman HARING: We are coming to the end of this Conference. I know I speak for everyone when I say we are extremely grateful to the sponsors of the Conference. It has been a long but most fruitful session and we are very grateful to all of you. Thank you very much.

Notes

1.   Frederick Harris Harbison and C.A. Myers, *Education, Manpower and Economic Growth: Strategies of Human Resource Development* (New York: McGraw-Hill, 1964).
2.   Louis J. Walinsky, *Economic Development in Burma, 1951-1960* (New York: The Twentieth Century Fund, 1962).
3.   Benjamin Howard Higgins, *Economic Development: Principles, Problems and Policies* (New York: Norton, 1959).
4.   James Smoot Coleman (ed.), *Education and Political Development* (Princeton, N.J.: Princeton University Press, 1965.

Appendices

**Midwest Research Conference on Educational Research
and a Reappraisal of Economic Development**
October 30 - November 1, 1964

Friday
Registration
  9:30 a.m. to 5:30 p.m.

Conferees to
are invited
browse in the

Library of
International
Relations
660 N. Wabash

Luncheon
  12:30 p.m.

Honoring
W. Arthur Lewis
Professor of
Economics and
International Affairs
Woodrow Wilson
School of Public
and International Affairs
Princeton University

Rosery College
River Forest

Welcome to the Conference
Sister Thomasine

Dinner
  6:00 p.m.

Introductions
and
Informal Discussion

The Kungsholm
100 E. Ontario

First Session
  7:30 p.m. to
  9:30 p.m.

Unemployment in
Developing Areas

The Kungsholm

Conference Chairman: George I. Blanksten
Keynote address: W. Arthur Lewis

211

Saturday
   Second Session   Underdeveloped   Library of
   10:00 a.m. to   Countries in the   International
   12:00 noon   World Economy   Relations

Chairman: Leonard Binder
Discussion Leader: Karl de Schweinitz, Jr.
Discussant: Andrew H. Whiteford
Discussant: Raymond L. Randall

Luncheon   Informal Discussion   The Arts Club
   12:30 p.m.   109 E. Ontario

Third Session   The International   Library of
   2:30 p.m. to   Politics and Diplomacy International
   4:30 p.m.   of Development   Relations

Chairman: George I, Blanksten
Discussion Leader: Robert T. Holt
Discussant: A. A. Fatouros
Discussant: Mordechai E. Kreinin

Dinner
   6:00 p.m.   Informal Discussion   Chez Paul
                                         660 N. Rush

Fourth Session   Economic Growth in   Library of
   7:30p.m. to   Newly Settled Areas International
   9:30 p.m.   as Contrasted with   Relations
                     Old Settled Areas

Chairman: James B. Hendry
Discussion Leader: Theodore Morgan
Discussant: Scott D. Johnston
Discussant: Jack Baranson

Sunday   Cultural Change   Library of
   Fifth Session   in Development   International
   10:30 a.m. to   Relations
   12:30 p.m.

Chairman: Frank H. H. King
Discussion Leader: Manning Nash
Discussant: Daniel Wit
Discussant: Edward E. Werner

Luncheon	Informal Discussion	Normandy House
12:45 p.m.		744 N. Rush

Sixth Session	Persepectives for	Normandy House
1:30 p.m. to	Cooporative Research	
3:00 p.m.		

Chairman: Philip S. Haring
Discussion Leader: C. Arnold Anderson
Discussant: T. David Williams
Discussant: Norton S. Ginsburg

Biographical Notes on Participants

C. Arnold Anderson

Director, Comparative Education Center, and Professor of Education and of Sociology, University of Chicago; Education Specialist on World Bank mission to Kenya; Fulbright Professor at Uppsala, Sweden; co-editor with Mary Jean Bowman of Education and Economic Development.

Robert P. Armstrong

Instructor in Economics Department, Lake Forest College; in Liberia 1961-62 as Research Associate, Northwestern University Economic Survey of Liberia; travel in twelve countries in the Middle East and Far East to study practices, problems, and prospects concerning economic development, 1962-63; author of chapters in Economic Survey of Liberia, Northwestern University; associate author of Puerto Rican Shipping and the U.S. Maritime Laws: An Economic Appraisal, the Transportation Center, Northwestern University.

Jack Baranson

Research Associate, International Development Research Center, Indiana University; research staff member, Committee for Economic Development; Research Associate, Brookings Institution; participant in an economic development mission to Latin America; author of various studies and articles on industrialization and economic development in Latin America and other underdeveloped areas.

Leonard Binder

Associate Professor of Political Science, University of Chicago; research on comparative politics, particularly in developing nations and on Near Eastern and Middle Eastern politics and Islamic culture; author of Religion and Politics in Pakistan, Iran: Political Development in a Changing Society, and several articles; Biennial Midwest Research Conference on Underdeveloped Areas, Advisory Committee 1964, participant 1962,1964.

George I. Blanksten

Professor and Chairman, Department of Political Science, Northwestern University; Governing Board, Library of International Relations, since 1959; with U.S. Coordinator of Inter-American Affairs, 1942-44; Political Analyst, U.S. Department of State, 1944-46; research and field experience in Latin American countries, 1950-59; author of books and articles on Latin American culture and politics, including Argentina and Chile, U.S. Role in Latin America and Peron's Argentina; Biennial Midwest Research Conference on Underdeveloped Areas, Advisory Committee 1959, 1962, 1964, participant 1959, 1962, 1964.

Karl De Schweinitz
Professor of Economics, Northwestern University; in Japan 1963-64 to study economic development and political change; author of Industrialization and Democracy; Biennial Midwest Research Conference on Underdeveloped Areas, Advisory Committee 1962, participant 1962, 1964.

A.A. Fatouros
Assistant Professor, School of Law, Indiana University; Lecturer and Assistant Professor, Faculty of Law, University of Western Ontario, 1960-63; visiting Assistant Professor, Law School, University of Chicago, 1963-64; author of Government Guarantees to Foreign Investors and articles in legal and political science journals, and co-author with R.N. Kelson of Canada's Overseas Aid.

Wesley R. Fishel
Professor of Political Science, Michigan State University; consultant on governmental reorganization, South Vietnam, 1954-55; Chief of the M.S.U. Vietnam Advisory Group in Public Administration and Public Safety, 1956-58; Guggenheim Fellow in Vietnam. 1962; editor and co-author of Problems of Freedom: South Vietnam since Independence; Biennial Midwest Research Conference on Underdeveloped Areas, Advisory Committee 1964, participant 1959.

Norton Sydney Ginsburg
Professor of Geography, University of Chicago, and Associate Dean of The College; Governing Board, Library of International Relations since 1959; member, United Nations Technical Mission to Japan on Metropolitan Planning, 1961-62 ; Consultant to Calcutta Metropolitan Planning Organization,1962-63; author of Atlas of Economic Development, co-author of Malaya and The Pattern of Asia, and numerous other books and articles; Biennial Midwest Research Conference on

Underdeveloped Areas, Advisory Committee 1959,1962,1964, participant 1959, 1964.

Philip S. Haring
Associate Professor of Political Science, Knox College, Galesburg, Illinois; field: Political Theory, Comparative Government, Economic Theory; Governing Board, Library of International Relations 1958-63; Biennial Midwest Research Conference on Underdeveloped Areas, participant 1959, 1962, 1964.

Philip M. Hauser
Chairman of the Department of Sociology, and Director of the Population Research and Training Center, University of Chicago; Governing Board, Library of International Relations since 1955, Trustee 1959-1963, Chairman 1959-61; United States representative to the Population Commission of the United Nations; United Nations Statistical Advisor to the Governments of Burma and Thailand; General Rapporteur of UN/UNESCO Seminars on urbanization in Asia and Latin America; author of Population Perspectives, The Study of Population, and other books, contributor to leading sociological journals; Biennial Midwest Research Conference on Underdeveloped Areas, Advisory Committee 1959, 1962, 1964, participant 1959, 1962.

James B. Hendry
Director, Economic and Agricultural Development Institute, and Associate Professor, Department of Economics and Agricultural Economics, Michigan State University; Economist with Michigan State Viet Nam Advisory Group, 1957-59; member, Harvard University Pakistan Advisory Group, 1962-64; author of The Small World of Khanh Hau and The Work Force in Saigon.

H. Murray Herlihy
Professor and Chairman, Department of Economics, Lake Forest College; industrial and labor relations specialist; co-author of Issues in Railroad Retirement.

Robert T. Holt
Professor of Political Science, University of Minnesota; Research Assistant, Center of International Studies, Princeton University, 1951-52;

Research Assistant, ONR Project, Research in Cohesive and Disruptive Tendencies in Coalition Type Groups, University of Minnesota, 1952; author of various articles on psychological and political aspects of foreign affairs; co-author of Strategic Psychological Operations and American Foreign Policy; author of The Political Basis of Economic Growth: An Explanation in Comparative Political Analysis and others.

Bert F. Hoselitz
Professor of Economics and Director of the Research Center in Economic Development and Cultural Change, University of Chicago; expert in Industrial Economy with the United Nations Technical mission to El Salvador; specialist in Metropolitan Planning with Ford Foundation project with the Ministry of Health and Local Government of India; author and editor of many books including Theories of Economic Growth, Sociological Aspects of Economic Growth, A Reader's Guide to the Social Sciences (ed.), and numerous articles in professional journals; Biennial Midwest Research Conference on Underdeveloped Areas, Advisory Committee 1959, 1962, 1964, participant 1959, 1962.

Scott D. Johnston
Professor and Head of Department of Political Science, Hamline University; Director, Falk Foundation Program in Politics; Coordinator, four-college Far East Area Study Program; Faculty Representative, Washington Semester Program; research in North Africa and the Middle East; author of various articles.

Frank Henry Haviland King
Associate Professor in Economics and member of Committee for East Asian Studies, University of Kansas; Acting Director, Center for East Asian Studies; author of The Malayan Nation, The Monetary System of Hong Kong, and numerous articles and other books on money and finances in the Far East.

Mordechai E. Kreinin
Professor of Economics, Michigan State University; Editorial Collaborator, Journal of the American Statistical Association; Consultant to Council on Foreign Relations; author of Israel and Africa, a Study in Technical Cooperation and numerous articles in professional journals and collections.

W. Arthur Lewis

Professor of Economics and International Affairs, Princeton University; Professor of Political Economy, University of Manchester, 1948-58; member U.N. Group of Experts on Underdeveloped Countries, 1951; member Colonial Development Corporation, 1951-1953; consultant to U.N. Economic Commission for Asia and the Far East, 1952; Consultant to Gold Coast Government, 1953; consultant to Government of West Nigeria, 1955; Economic Advisor to Prime Minister of Ghana, 1957-58; Principal and Vice-Chancellor, University College in the West Indies, 1959-62; articles in technical, economic, and law journals; author of Industrial Development in the Caribbean, the Principles of Economic Planning, Theory of Economic Growth, co-author of U.N. Report, Measures for the Economic Development of Underdeveloped Countries, and other books and articles.

Marvin P. Miracle

Assistant Professor of Agricultural Economics, University of Wisconsin; Research Associate, Food Research Institute, Stanford University, 1961-62; research experience in Belgian Congo, British East Africa, Northern Rhodesia, and other developing areas, principally in Africa; author of articles in professional journals and collections on African agricultural problems.

Theodore Morgan

Professor of Economics, University of Wisconsin; Consultant, Council of Economic Advisors; Deputy-Governor, Central Bank of Ceylon, 1952-53; Chairman, Wisconsin-Ford Foundation Project, Gadjah Mada University, Jogjakarta, Indonesia, 1959-60; consultant to International Bank for Reconstruction and Development as member of Mission to Kenya, 1961-62; co-author of The Economic Development of Kenya and Readings in Economic Development, and author of other books and numerous articles; Biennial Midwest Research Conference on Underdeveloped Areas, participant 1959, 1964.

Manning Nash

Associate Professor of Anthropology, Graduate School of Business, University of Chicago; Editor, Economic Development and Cultural Change since 1958; research in Mexico and Burma; author of Machine Age Maya, and numerous articles; Biennial Midwest Research Conference on Underdeveloped Areas, participant 1959, 1964.

Raymond L. Randall

Acting Director, Institute of Public Administration and Associate Professor of Government, Indiana University; formerly Chief of Party, Indiana-Indonesian Contract, Djakarta, Indonesia; Ford Visiting Professor of Public Administration, University of the Philippines; Advisor to the Philippine Government on the Philippine Executive Academy; Executive Development Advisor to the Government of Thailand; author of brochures and articles on executive development for Nation's Business, and other publications.

Eloise ReQua

Director, Library of International Relations; organized World Trade Reference Library for International House, New Orleans 1946; co-author with Jane Statham of The Developing Nations 1965; Biennial Midwest Research Conference on Underdeveloped Areas, Advisory Committee ex officio 1959, 1962, 1964.

Hugh H. Schwartz

Acting Assistant Professor of Economics, the University of Kansas; Organization of American States research fellowship in Argentina, 1960-62; author of articles on Argentina.

Hendrick Serrie

Instructor in Anthropology, Beloit College; Project Associate, developing use of solar cookers in Oaxaca, Mexico, 1961-62; directed two films in Mexico, 1962-63; taught English at University of Aleppo, Syria, 1963-64.

Jane Statham

Library of International Relations, Associate Director; co-author with Eloise ReQua of The Developing Nations, 1965; Editor, World in Focus 1945-51; Editor, International Information Service since 1963; Biennial Midwest Research Conference on Underdeveloped Areas, Advisory Committee ex-officio 1959, 1962, 1964.

Sister Thomasine

Professor and Chairman of the Department of Economics, Rosary College; research in the Middle East, Central and South America; Executive Council, Catholic Economic Association 1957-58, 1964-66; author of various pamphlets and articles, including "A Reappraisal of the Economic Record of Venezuela, 1939-1959," in Journal of Inter-American Studies, Biennial Midwest Research Conference on Underdeveloped Areas, Advisory Committee 1964, participant 1959, 1962, 1964.

Charles Preston Warren
Instructor in Anthropology, University of Illinois, Chicago Undergraduate Division; Fulbright Award, Research Scholar, anthropological research in the Philippine Islands; author of The Batak of Palawan: A Culture in Transition and numerous articles arid papers; Biennial Midwest Research Conference on Underdeveloped Areas, participant 1962, 1964.

Edward E. Warner
Associate Professor of Commerce and Director, Center for Developing Nations, University of Wisconsin; Professor and Chairman, University of Wisconsin-Ford Foundation Project at Gadjah Mada University in Jogjakarta, Indonesia, 1960-63; author of numerous articles and monographs including Some Aspects of Promotional Activities in Newly Developing Countries and Advertising in Indonesia.

Andrew H. Whiteford
Professor of Anthropology and Director, Logan Museum of Anthropology, Beloit College; community research in Popayán, Colombia, 1949-152 and 1962; urban survey of Central Mexico, 1956; study of culture change in Málaga, Spain, 1961; editor of Teaching Anthropology and author of Two Cities of Latin America and numerous articles; Biennial Midwest Research Conference on Underdeveloped Areas, Advisory Committee 1964, participant 1959, 1964.

T. David Williams
Lecturer in Economics, Northwestern University; Research Associate, Center for Studies in Development and Education, Harvard University, 1962-64; Lecturer in Economics, University of Ghana, 1961-62.

Daniel Wit
Professor of Political Science, Northern Illinois University; Public Administration Advisor to Government of Thailand and Visiting Professor, Institute of Public Administration, Bangkok, 1956-58; Director of International Studies, Governmental Affairs Institute, Washington, D.

C., 1959-1961; Peace Corps Lecturer for Malaya and the Phillippines training programs, 1961; contract research on Thailand for U. S. Department of Labor, 1963-64; author of numerous monographs and articles.

Selected Bibliographical References on Economic Development

The following references have been selected as representative of the major contributions to recent literature on theories of economic growth and development. The two bibliographies listed—Hazlewood and ReQua—provide annotated guides to numerous other sources on economic, political, and sociological problems of development as well as on specific geographic areas.

Bauer, P. T., and B. S. Yamey. *The Economics of Underdeveloped Countries* (Cambridge Economic Handbooks). Digswell Place, England: James Nisbet and Company; Cambridge, England: Cambridge University Press, 1957.

Brookings Institution. *Development of the Emerging Countries: An Agenda for Research*. Washington, B.C.: The Institution, 1962.

Enke, Stephen. *Economics for Development*. Englewood Cliffs, N.J.: Prentice-Hall, 1963.

Gerschenkron, Alexander, *Economic Backwardness in Historical Perspective: A Book of Essays*. Cambridge, Mass.: The Belknap Press of Harvard University Press, 1962.

Ginsburg, Norton S. *Atlas of Economic Development* (University of Chicago, Department of Geography, Research Paper No. 68). Chicago: University of Chicago Press, 1961.

Harbison, Frederick H. *Education, Manpower, and Economic Growth: Strategies of Human Resource Development*. New York: McGraw-Hill, 1964.

Hazlewood, Arthur, comp, *The Economics of "Under-Developed" Areas: An Annotated Reading List of Books, Articles, and Official Publications*. (2d enl. ed.) London: Oxford University Press for the Institute of Colonial Studies, 1962.

Higgins, Benjamin. *Economic; Development: Principles, Problems, and Policies*. New York: W. W. Norton, 1959.

Hirschman, Albert O. The Strategy of Economic Development (Yale Studies in Economics: 10), New Haven, Conn.: Yale University Press, 1959.

Hoselitz, Bert F., ed, *The Progress of Underdeveloped Areas*. Chicago: University of Chicago Press, 1952.

Leibenstein, Harvey. Economic Backwardness and Economic Growth: Studies in the Theory of Economic Development. New York: John Wiley & Sons; London: Chapman & Hall, 1957.

Levin, Jonathan V. *The Export Economies: Their Pattern of Development in Historical Perspective* (Harvard Law School, International Program in Taxation). Cambridge, Mass.: Harvard University Press, 1960.

Lewis, W. Arthur. *The Theory of Economic Growth.* Homewood, 111.: Richard D. Irwin, 1955.

McClelland. David C. *The Achieving Society.* Princeton, N.J.: D. Van Nostrand, 1961.

Meier, Gerald M. *International Trade and Development.* New York and Evanston: Harper and Row, 1963.

Millikan, Max F., and Donald L. M. Blackmer, eds. The Emerging Nations: Their Growth and United *States Policy.* Boston and Toronto: Little, Brown, for the Center for International Studies, Massachusetts Institute of Technology, 1961.

Myrdal, Gunnar. *Economic Theory and Under-Developed Regions.* London: Gerald Duckworth, 1957.

Nurske, Ragnar. *Problems of Capital Formation in Underdeveloped Countries.* New York: Oxford University Press, 1953.

ReQua, Eloise G., and Jane Statham. *The Developing Nations: A Guide to Information Sources Concerning Their Economic, Political, Technical and Social Problems.* Detroit, Mich.: Gale Research Company, 1965.

Rostow, W. W., ed. *The Economics of Take-Off into Sustained Growth; Proceedings of a Conference Held by the International Economic Association.* New York: St. Martin's Press, Inc., 1963.

——*The Stages of Economic Growth: A Non-Communist Manifesto.* Cambridge, England: Cambridge University Press, 1963.

Singer, Hans W. *International Development: Growth and Change.* New York: McGraw-Hill.

United Nations. Department of Economic Affairs. *Measures for the Economic Development of Under-Developed Countries: Report by a Group of Experts Appointed by the Secretary-General of the United Nations.* (United Nations document E/1986, St/ECA/10.) New York: United Nations, 1951. (Sales No.: 1951.II.B. 2.)

United Nations. Department of Economic and Social Affairs. *Processes and Problems of Industrialization in Under-Developed Countries.* (United Nations document E/2670, St/ECA/29.) New York: United Nations, 1955. (Sales No.: 1955 .II .B . 1.)

——————— *A Study of Industrial Growth.* (United Nations document ST/ECA/74.) New York: United Nations, 1963. (Sales No.: 63.II. B.2.)

United Nations Conference on the Application of Science and Technology for the Benefit of the Less Developed Areas, Geneva, February 1963. *Science and Technology for Development,* 8 vols. (United Nations document E/Conf. 39/1, Vols. I-VIII.) New York: United Nations, 1963. (Sales Nos.: 63.1.21-28.)

United Nations Conference on Trade and Development, Geneva, March 23-June 16, 1964. *Proceedings,* 8 vols.

(United Nations document E/Conf.46/141 Vols. I-VIII.), New York: United Nations, 1964. (Sales Nos.: 64.11. B.11-18.)

For Product Safety Concerns and Information please contact our EU
representative GPSR@taylorandfrancis.com
Taylor & Francis Verlag GmbH, Kaufingerstraße 24, 80331 München, Germany